U.S. PRIVATE-
PRIVACY

Law and Practice for Information Privacy Professionals

Peter P. Swire, CIPP/US

Kenesa Ahmad, CIPP/US

An IAPP Publication

Cover design: Noelle Grattan, -ing designs, llc.

Copy editor: Sarah Weaver

Compositor: Ed Stevens, www.EdStevensDesign.com

Indexer: Jan Bednarczuk, Jandex Indexing

ISBN 978-0-9795901-8-4
Library of Congress Control Number: 2012938597

About the IAPP

The International Association of Privacy Professionals (IAPP) is the largest and most comprehensive global information privacy community and resource, helping practitioners develop and advance their careers and organizations manage and protect their data.

The IAPP is a not-for-profit association founded in 2000 with a mission to define, support and improve the privacy profession globally through networking, education and certification. We are committed to providing a forum for privacy professionals to share best practices, track trends, advance privacy management issues, standardize the designations for privacy professionals, and provide education and guidance on opportunities in the field of information privacy.

The IAPP is responsible for developing and launching the first broad-based credentialing program in information privacy, the Certified Information Privacy Professional (CIPP). The CIPP remains the leading privacy certification for professionals who serve the data protection, information auditing, information security, legal compliance and/or risk management needs of their organizations. Today, many thousands of professionals worldwide hold a CIPP certification.

In addition, the IAPP offers a full suite of educational and professional development services and holds annual conferences that are recognized internationally as the leading forums for the discussion and debate of issues related to privacy policy and practice.

Contents

CHAPTER THREE

Global Information Management from a U.S. Perspective

CHAPTER FOUR

Medical Privacy: HIPAA and GINA

CHAPTER FIVE

Financial Privacy

CHAPTER SIX

Education Records

CHAPTER SEVEN

Telecommunications and Marketing

CHAPTER EIGHT

Privacy Statutes About Online Activities

CHAPTER NINE

Information Security and Data Breach Notification Laws

CHAPTER TEN

Privacy Issues in Investigations and Litigation

CHAPTER ELEVEN

Workplace Privacy

Figure List

Preface

At privacy conferences over the years, I have sometimes heard that "the United States doesn't have a privacy law." Such a speaker is likely contrasting the U.S. approach to privacy to that in the countries in the European Union, who each follow the EU Data Protection Directive of 1995, and thus have one broadly inclusive law to cover privacy and data protection issues.

Although the U.S. doesn't have one comprehensive privacy law, this book shows that the U.S. does have a great amount of law (and good practice) governing the privacy of personal information held by the private sector. It discusses privacy law in industry sectors such as healthcare, financial institutions, education and marketing. There is a federal law for the privacy of children online, but the privacy of adults is governed more by the promises that companies make in their privacy policies. State laws are prominent in some areas, including workplace privacy and data breaches. In short, U.S. law has been created in the instances where the law and political system have found it necessary. Instead of one over-arching privacy law, we have many separate decisions about whether and when to place limits on the use of personal information.

The importance of privacy protections has risen with the multitudinous privacy issues posed by new technology. President Obama summarized the modern importance of privacy protection in a U.S. government report issued early in 2012:

> "The consumer data privacy framework in the United States is, in fact, strong. This framework rests on fundamental privacy values, flexible and adaptable common law protections and consumer protection statutes, Federal Trade Commission enforcement, and policy development that involves a broad array of stakeholders. This framework has encouraged not only social and economic innovations based on the Internet but also vibrant discussions of how to protect privacy in a networked society involving civil society, industry, academia, and the government."

It is an exciting and valuable task to participate in those "vibrant discussions," and I hope this book will help many of you do so.

In writing this book on U.S. privacy law for the private sector, I first want to thank my co-author, Kenesa Ahmad, who is finishing her work with me at the Future of Privacy Forum to begin as an associate in the global privacy practice of Promontory Financial Group. Steven Beale and others at the Future of Privacy Forum helped with research. Marla Berry was our chief contact at the International Association of Privacy Professionals. And there are so many others who have contributed to the writing of this book.

More broadly, I want to thank three people who helped me learn privacy in the mid-1990s, when I was trying to figure out this emerging field. Barbara Wellbery was then working in the U.S. Department of Commerce, focusing attention on the need for the U.S. and the EU to avoid a trade war around personal information. Barbara later led the daily work on the Safe Harbor negotiations, and without her I doubt they would have succeeded. Sadly, Barbara passed away far too soon, a decade ago now. On a happier note, Paul Schwartz and Joel Reidenberg were U.S. legal academics who already knew a great deal about privacy when I was taking my baby steps in the field. They were both generous of their time and expertise with me. And they both have continued to do world-class work on privacy issues since. My thanks to you both, and to the many other generous people who engage to address how information should be cared for in the information age.

Peter Swire, CIPP/US
Washington, D.C.
July, 2012

I would like to express my deepest appreciation to my mentor, Peter Swire, for his unfailing patience, encouragement and generosity, without which I would not be afforded this opportunity. Thank you Jules Polonetsky, for your guidance and insight during my time at the Future of Privacy Forum. I would also like to thank my parents, brothers, sister-in-law and nieces for their love and support throughout this process.

Kenesa Ahmad, CIPP/US
Washington, D.C.
July, 2012

Acknowledgments

The IAPP is proud to present *U.S. Private-sector Privacy: Law and Practice for Information Privacy Professionals*, the textbook that supports the Certified Information Privacy Professional/ United States (CIPP/US) program.

The very first CIPP exam was offered in October 2004. Much has changed in the field of information privacy since then, and we express gratitude to the many privacy professionals who have so willingly contributed their time and knowledge to the ongoing development of the CIPP/US program. In particular, I would like to acknowledge those who made this book possible.

We are thankful for the members of our U.S. Certification Advisory Board, who have shared their expertise in privacy and provided guidance on our CIPP/US program. Past and present members are:

Deborah Adleman, CIPP/US
Director, Ernst & Young

Jonathan Fox, CIPP/US
Director of Data Privacy, McAfee, Inc.

Fabian Gonzalez, CIPP/US, CIPP/IT
Director, Risk Consulting, KPMG

Robert Gratchner, CIPP/US
Vice President, Privacy, AudienceScience

Rebecca Herold, CIPP/US, CIPP/IT
Owner & Principal, "The Privacy Professor"®, Rebecca Herold & Associates, LLC

Heather Jahnke, CIPP/US
Manager, Privacy Office, Blue Cross Blue Shield of LA

John Kropf, CIPP/US, CIPP/G
Deputy Counsel for Privacy and Information Governance, Reed Elsevier

Kristen J. Mathews, CIPP/US
Partner and Chair of the Privacy & Data Security Practice Group, Proskauer Rose LLP

Terry McQuay, CIPP/US, CIPP/C, CIPP/E, CIPP/G
President, NYMITY Inc.

In 2007, Peter Swire coauthored with Sol Bermann the IAPP's very first certification textbook, *Information Privacy: The Official Reference for the Certified Information Privacy Professional.* We were honored that Peter, once again, agreed to write a textbook for us and we thank him and Kenesa Ahmad for the countless hours spent researching and writing *U.S. Private-sector Privacy: Law and Practice for Information Privacy Professionals.*

The development of this book was supported by Steven Beale, Colin Morrow and Brian Burke, who provided additional research and writing. I would like to recognize Colin's contributions to sections on GINA, VPPA, the Cable TV Privacy Act, e-Discovery, state breach legislation and updates to privacy concerns within human resources. I am indebted to Steven, Colin and Brian for their important contributions to this book.

Thank you to Peggy Eisenhauer, Heather Jahnke, John Kropf and Terry McQuay, who provided thoughtful and detailed reviews of the draft manuscript. I would also like to acknowledge Sarah Weaver, who provided the careful copyediting of the text, and Ed Stevens for providing layout and design. This group has ensured that the book you now hold in your hands is of the highest quality.

Hewlett-Packard and Microsoft were the founding grantors of the initial CIPP program. This program would not exist without their generous support. My gratitude to the IAPP's original CIPP Advisory Board, who articulated the initial requirements for the CIPP, and finally, I would like to acknowledge the contributors to our first CIPP textbook, *Information Privacy*—Dennis Becktell, Matt Beirlein, Margaret Betzel, Katy Delaney, Josh Deinsen, Peggy Eisenhauer, Jim Jordan, Barbara Lawler and Shannon Rogers.

I am grateful to everyone who has participated in the CIPP/US program, including current CIPP/US holders and those of you who now pursue your CIPP/US designation. The field of information privacy has grown much in the last few years, and we are honored that you have chosen to improve the profession through your involvement in the IAPP.

Richard Soule, CIPP/E
Certification Director
International Association of Privacy Professionals

Introduction

It is with great pleasure that I bring to you our newest information privacy reference guide. *U.S. Private-sector Privacy: Law and Practice for Information Privacy Professionals* is the culmination of the collective expertise and deep information privacy knowledge of Professor Peter Swire, CIPP/US; information privacy attorney Kenesa Ahmad, CIPP/US; and the IAPP Certification Advisory Board. This text encompasses all of the major U.S. privacy laws and regulations as well as the corporate compliance obligations every U.S.-based privacy practitioner should know.

Since our flagship reference guide, *Information Privacy*, was launched in 2007, much in the privacy landscape has changed. Lawmakers have passed comprehensive legislation affecting multiple industry sectors—particularly health and finance. The Health Information Technology for Economic and Clinical Health Act of 2009 expands security and privacy obligations with regard to electronic health records and covered entities; the Genetic Information Nondiscrimination Act of 2008 prevents the use of genetic information in health insurance and employment; and, in response to the last decade's financial crisis, the Dodd-Frank Wall Street Reform and Consumer Protection Act attempts to promote financial transparency and additional consumer protection.

All of these significant acts of legislation are covered here and will be essential nuggets of knowledge for aspiring privacy professionals and seasoned privacy experts alike.

In conjunction with *Foundations of Information Privacy and Data Protection: A Survey of Global Concepts, Laws and Practices*, this text helps form the backbone of study for those planning to take the Certified Information Privacy Professional/U.S. exam. It's becoming clear that more and more businesses across industry sectors need the talents of privacy professionals.

If you're an established professional looking for an updated reference guide, this text is for you. And if you aspire to certification and a career in privacy, this book is an important step toward achieving that goal. I applaud your efforts.

J. Trevor Hughes, CIPP
President and CEO
International Association of Privacy Professionals

CHAPTER ONE

U.S. Legal Framework

This chapter introduces basic concepts and terms used by privacy professionals in the United States. Much of the material in this chapter will be familiar to lawyers. Privacy compliance in most organizations today, however, involves substantial participation by nonlawyers, including people whose primary background ranges from marketing, information technology and human resources to public relations and other areas. For all readers, the goal of this chapter is to provide a helpful introduction to the terminology used by privacy professionals.

1. Branches of the Government

The U.S. Constitution establishes the framework of the legal system, creating three branches of government. The three branches—legislative, executive and judicial—are designed to provide a separation of powers with a system of checks and balances among the branches. These three branches are also found at the state (and often the local) levels. The legislative branch is made up of elected representatives who write and pass laws. The executive branch's duties are to enforce and administer the law. The judicial branch interprets the meaning of a law and how it is applied, and may examine such things as a law's constitutionality and the intent behind its creation.

Table 1-1. Three Branches of U.S. Government

	Legislative Branch	Executive Branch	Judicial Branch
Purpose	Makes laws	Enforces laws	Interprets laws
Who	Congress (House and Senate)	President, vice president, cabinet, federal agencies (such as FTC)	Federal courts
Checks and Balances	Congress confirms presidential appointees, can override vetoes	President appoints federal judges, can veto laws passed by Congress	Determines whether the laws are constitutional

The U.S. Congress, consisting of the Senate and the House of Representatives, is the legislative branch. Aside from passing laws, Congress can override presidential vetoes and the Senate confirms presidential appointees. When enacting legislation, Congress may also delegate the power to promulgate regulations to federal agencies. For example, Congress has enacted several laws that give the U.S. Federal Trade Commission (FTC) the authority to issue regulations to implement the laws.

The executive branch consists of the president, vice president, the president's cabinet and other federal agencies that report to the president. The agencies implement the laws through rule making and enforce the laws through civil and criminal procedures. In addition, the president has veto power over laws passed by Congress and the power to appoint federal judges.

The judicial branch encompasses the federal court system. The lowest courts in the federal system are the district courts, which serve as federal trial courts. Cases decided by a district court can be appealed to a federal appellate court, also referred to as a circuit court. The federal circuit courts are not trial courts but serve as the appeals courts for federal cases. The appeals courts are divided into 12 regional circuits and each district court is assigned to a circuit; appeals from a district court are considered by the appeals court for that circuit. In addition, there are special courts such as the U.S. Court of Federal Claims and the U.S. Tax Court.

At the top of the federal court system is the U.S. Supreme Court, which hears appeals from the circuit courts and decides questions of federal law, including interpreting the U.S. Constitution. In certain circumstances, the U.S. Supreme Court may also hear appeals from the highest state courts. In rare instances, the U.S. Supreme Court also has the ability to function as a trial court.

As mentioned above, when given the authority by Congress, federal agencies may promulgate and enforce rules pursuant to law. In this sense, agencies may wield power that is characteristic of all three branches of government. This means that agencies may operate under statutes that give them legislative power to issue rules, executive power to investigate and enforce violations of rules and statutes, and the judicial power to settle particular disputes.

2. Sources of Law in the United States

The numerous sources of law in the United States include federal and state constitutions, legislation, case law (such as concerning contracts and torts), and regulations issued by agencies.

2.1 Constitutions

The supreme law in the United States is the U.S. Constitution, drafted originally by the Constitutional Convention in 1787. The U.S. Constitution does not contain the word *privacy*. Some parts of the Constitution directly affect privacy, such as the Fourth Amendment limits on government searches. In addition, the Supreme Court has held that a person has a right to privacy over personal issues such as contraception and abortion, arising from more general protections of due process of law.[1]

State constitutions are also sources of law and may create stronger rights than are provided in the U.S. Constitution. For example, the California state constitution expressly recognizes a right to privacy.

2.2 Legislation

Both the federal Congress and the state legislatures have enacted a variety of privacy and security laws. These regulate many different matters, including certain applications of information (such as use of information for marketing or preemployment screening), certain industries (such as financial institutions or healthcare providers), certain data elements (such as Social Security numbers or driver's license information) or specific harms (such as identity theft or children's online privacy).

In the United States, law-making power is shared between the national and state governments. The U.S. Constitution states that the Constitution, and laws passed pursuant to it, is "the supreme law of the land." Where federal law does not prevent it, the states have power to make law. Under the Tenth Amendment to the Constitution, "[t]he powers not delegated to the United States by the Constitution, nor prohibited by it to the States, are reserved to the States respectively, or to the people." In understanding the effect of federal and state laws, it's important to consider whether a federal law "preempts," or overrides, any state laws on the subject. In many instances, such as for the HIPAA (Health Insurance Portability and Accountability Act) medical privacy rule, states may pass privacy or other laws with stricter requirements than federal law. In other instances, such as the limits on commercial e-mails in the CAN-SPAM (Controlling the Assault of Non-Solicited Pornography and Marketing) Act, federal law preempts state law, and the states are not permitted to pass stricter provisions.

Aside from this governmental ability to make and enforce laws and regulations, the U.S. legal system relies on legal precedent based on court decisions, the doctrines implicit in those decisions and their customs and uses. Two key areas of the common law are contracts and torts, discussed in Sections 2.6 and 2.7.

2.3 Regulations and Rules

Some laws require regulatory agencies (such as the FTC or the Federal Communications Commission [FCC]) to issue regulations and rules. These place specific compliance expectations on the marketplace. For example, in 2003 the U.S. Congress passed the CAN-SPAM Act, which requires the senders of commercial e-mail messages to offer an "opt-out" option to recipients of these messages. CAN-SPAM provides the FTC and the FCC with the authority to issue regulations that set forth exactly how the opt-out mechanism must be offered and managed.

2.4 Case Law

Case law refers to the final decisions made by judges in court cases. When similar issues arise in the future, judges look to past decisions as precedents and decide the new case in a manner that is consistent with past decisions. The following of past precedent is known as *stare decisis* (a Latin term meaning "to let the decision stand"). As time passes, precedents often change to reflect technological and societal changes in values and laws.

Common law refers to legal principles that have developed over time in judicial decisions (case law), often drawing on social customs and expectations. Common law contrasts with law created by statute. For privacy, the common law has long upheld special privilege rules such as doctor-patient or attorney-client confidentiality, even in the absence of statutes protecting that confidentiality.

2.5 Consent Decree

A consent decree is a judgment entered by consent of the parties whereby the defendant agrees to stop alleged illegal activity, typically without admitting guilt or wrongdoing.[2] This legal document is approved by a judge and formalizes an agreement reached between a federal or state agency and an adverse party. The consent decree describes the actions the defendant will take, and the decree itself may be subject to a public comment period. Once approved, the consent decree has the effect of a court decision.

In the privacy enforcement sphere, for example, the FTC has entered into numerous consent decrees with companies as a result of alleged violations of privacy laws, such as COPPA (the Children's Online Privacy Protection Act).[3] These consent decrees generally require violators to pay money to the government and agree not to violate the relevant law in the future.

Aside from promulgating rules and enforcing them, agencies provide guidance in the form of opinions. Agency opinions do not necessarily carry the weight of law, but do give specific guidance to interested parties trying to interpret agency rules and regulations.[4]

2.6 Contract Law

A contract is a legally binding agreement enforceable in a court of law. For example, a privacy-related contract between a company in Europe and its data processor in the United States might include a provision requiring the U.S. company to abide by the U.S.–EU's Safe Harbor framework.[5] The contract might also include provisions on issues such as data usage, data security, breach notification, jurisdiction and damages.

However, not every agreement is a legally binding contract. There are certain fundamental requirements for forming a binding contract:[6]

- An **offer** is the proposed language to enter into a bargain. An offer must be communicated to another person and remain open until it is accepted, rejected, retracted or has expired. Some terms of an offer, like price, quantity and description, must be specific and definite. Note: A counteroffer ends the original offer.
- **Acceptance** is the assent or agreement by the person to whom the offer was made that the offer is accepted. This acceptance must comply with the terms of the offer and must be communicated to the person who proposed the deal.
- **Consideration** is the bargained-for exchange. It is the legal benefit received by one person and the legal detriment imposed on the other person. Consideration usually takes the form of money, property or services. Note: An agreement without consideration is not a contract.

A privacy notice may be a contract if a consumer provides data to a company based on the company's promise to use the data in accordance with the terms of the notice.

2.7 Tort Law

Torts are civil wrongs recognized by law as the grounds for lawsuits. These wrongs result in an injury or harm that constitutes the basis for a claim by the injured party. Primary goals of tort law are to provide relief for damages incurred and deter others from committing the same wrongs.

There are three general tort categories:

1. **Intentional torts.** These are wrongs that the defendant knew or should have known would occur through their actions or inactions; for example, intentionally hitting a person or stealing personal information.
2. **Negligent torts.** These occur when the defendant's actions were unreasonably unsafe; for example, causing a car accident by not obeying traffic rules or not having appropriate security controls.
3. **Strict liability torts.** These are wrongs that do not depend on the degree of carelessness by the defendant, but are established when a particular action causes damage.[7] Product liability torts fall into this category since they concern potential liability for making and selling defective products, without the need for the plaintiff to show negligence by the defendant.

Historically, the concept of a personal privacy tort has been a part of U.S. jurisprudence since the late 1890s.[8] Privacy torts continue today for actions such as intrusion on seclusion, public revelation of private facts, interfering with a person's right to publicity and casting a person in a false light. These traditional privacy torts, however, are often subject to the defense that the speaker is exercising free speech rights under the First Amendment. In addition, courts in recent years have considered a range of other privacy-related torts, such as allegations that a company was negligent for failing to provide adequate safeguards for personal information, and thus caused harm due to disclosure of the data. The lack of adequate safeguards thus may expose a company to damages under tort law.

3. Key Definitions

Here are a few important legal terms and definitions that will help you understand the framework of U.S. privacy law.

- **Person:** Any entity with legal rights, including an individual (a "natural person") or a corporation (a "legal person").
- **Jurisdiction:** The authority of a court to hear a particular case. A court must have jurisdiction over both the type of dispute ("subject matter jurisdiction") and the parties ("personal jurisdiction"). Government agencies have jurisdictional limits also.

- **Preemption:** A superior government's ability to have its laws supersede those of an inferior government. For example, the U.S. federal government has mandated that state governments cannot regulate e-mail marketing. The federal CAN-SPAM Act preempts state laws that might impose greater obligations on senders of commercial electronic messages.
- **Private right of action:** The ability of an individual harmed by a violation of a law to file a lawsuit against the violator.

It is also useful to review the concepts of notice, choice and access in the context of U.S. privacy law.

3.1 Notice

Notice is a description of an organization's information management practices. Notices have two purposes: (1) consumer education and (2) corporate accountability. The typical notice tells the individual what information is collected, how the information is used and disclosed, how to exercise any choices about uses or disclosures, and whether the individual can access or update the information. However, it is important to note that many U.S. privacy laws have additional notice requirements. In addition, for most industries, the promises made in a company's privacy notice are legally enforceable by the Federal Trade Commission and states.

Privacy notices may also be called privacy statements or even privacy policies, although the term *privacy policy* is often used to refer to the internal standards used within the organization, whereas *notice* refers to an external communication, issued to consumers, customers or users.

3.2 Choice

Choice is the ability to specify whether personal information will be collected and/or how it will be used or disclosed. Choice can be express or implied.

The term *opt in* means an affirmative indication of choice based on an express act of the person giving the consent. For example, a person opts in if he or she says yes when asked, "May we share your information?" Failure to answer would result in the information not being shared.

The term *opt out* means a choice can be implied by the failure of the person to object to the use or disclosure. For example, if a company says "unless you tell us not to, we may share your information," the person has the ability to opt out of the sharing by saying no. Failure to answer would result in the information being shared.

Choice is not always appropriate, but if it is offered, it should be meaningful—that is, it should be based on a real understanding of the implication of the decision.

3.3 Access

Access is the ability to view personal information held by an organization. This may be supplemented by allowing updates or corrections to the information. U.S. laws often provide for access and correction when the information is used for any type of substantive decision making, such as for credit reports.

4. Regulatory Authorities

At the federal level, a number of agencies engage in regulatory activities concerning privacy in the private sector. The FTC has general authority to enforce against "unfair and deceptive trade practices," notably including the power to bring "deception" enforcement actions where a company has broken a privacy promise.[9] In certain areas, such as marketing communications and children's privacy, the FTC has specific regulatory authority.

Other federal agencies have regulatory authority over particular sectors. These include the federal banking regulatory agencies (such as the Consumer Financial Protection Bureau, Federal Reserve, and Office of the Comptroller of the Currency), the FCC, the Department of Transportation, and the Department of Health and Human Services, through its Office for Civil Rights. The Department of Commerce does not have regulatory authority for privacy, but often plays a leading role in privacy policy for the executive branch.

At the state level, state attorneys general bring a variety of privacy-related enforcement actions, often pursuant to state laws prohibiting unfair and deceptive practices.[10] Each state attorney general serves as the chief legal advisor to the state government and as the state's chief law enforcement officer. Many states have successfully pursued such actions, including Washington and Minnesota.[11]

5. Self-regulation

As discussed in Chapter 2, self-regulatory regimes play a significant role in governing privacy practices in various industries. Examples include the Network Advertising Initiative, the Direct Marketing Association and the Children's Advertising Review Unit. Some trade associations also issue rules or codes of conduct for members. In some regulatory settings, government-created rules expect companies to sign up for self-regulatory oversight. One example is the Safe Harbor for companies that transfer personal information from the EU to the United States.

6. Understanding Laws

To understand any law, statute or regulation, it is important to ask six key questions:

1. Who is covered by this law?
2. What types of information (and what uses of information) are covered?
3. What exactly is required or prohibited?
4. Who enforces the law?
5. What happens if I don't comply?
6. Why does this law exist?

The first two questions relate to the scope of the law. Even if you are not subject to the law, it may still be useful to understand it. For example, the law may suggest good practices that you want to emulate. It may provide an indication of legal trends. It may also provide a proven way to achieve a particular result, such as protecting individuals in a given situation.

Assuming you are subject to the law, question three tells you what you need to know to comply with the law. Questions four and five help you assess the risks associated with noncompliance or less than perfect compliance. In most cases, companies do what it takes to be materially compliant with applicable laws. However, there may be a situation where the costs of compliance outweigh the risks of noncompliance for a particular period of time. For example, if a system that is not appropriately compliant with a new law is going to be replaced in a few months, a company may decide that the risks of noncompliance outweigh the costs and risks of trying to accelerate the system transition.

The final question helps you understand the motivation behind the law. Most companies try to comply with both the letter and the spirit of the law, and knowing why the law was written helps you understand the spirit of the legislation. Knowing why a law was written can also help you improve other processes and thus achieve desired results. It may also help you anticipate regulatory trends.

As an example, we will consider the security breach notification law in California, which was the first such law enacted and covers the largest population.[12]

- **Who is covered?** This law regulates entities that do business in California and that own or license computerized data, including personal information. It applies to natural persons, legal persons and government agencies.

  If you do business only in Montana or New York, you are not subject to this law (although you may wish to be careful about what counts as "doing business"). Even if you conduct business in California, you are not subject to this law if you don't have computerized data.

- **What is covered?** This law regulates computerized personal information of California residents. "Personal information" is an individual's name in combination with any one or more of (1) Social Security number, (2) California identification card number, (3) driver's license number or (4) financial account number or credit or debit card number in combination with any required security code, access code or password that would permit access to an individual's financial account, when either the name or the data elements are not encrypted.

  If your databases contain only names and addresses, or if your database contains only encrypted information, you are not subject to this law.

- **What is required or prohibited?** This law requires you to disclose any breach of system security to any resident of California whose unencrypted personal information was or is reasonably believed to have been acquired by an unauthorized person. A "breach of the security of the system" means unauthorized acquisition of computerized data that compromises the security, confidentiality or integrity of personal information maintained by the person. The disclosure must be made "in as expedient manner as possible."

There is an exception for the good faith acquisition of personal information by an employee or agent of the business, provided the personal information is not used or subject to further unauthorized disclosure. You may also delay providing notice, if law enforcement requests such a delay.

- **Who enforces?** The California attorney general enforces the law, and there is a private right of action.
- **What happens if I don't comply?** The California attorney general or any citizen can file a civil lawsuit against you, seeking damages and forcing you to comply.
- **Why does this law exist?** SB 1386 was enacted because there is a fear that security breaches of computerized databases cause identity theft—and individuals should be notified about the breach so that they can take steps to protect themselves. If you have a security breach that puts people at real risk of identity theft, you should consider notifying them even if you are not subject to this law.

7. Conclusion

This chapter has introduced legal concepts and terminology about basic topics, including the structure of the U.S. government and legal system. Privacy compliance requires knowing the applicable legal rules, as well as fulfilling each organization's policies and goals. The next chapter examines the structure in the United States of enforcement actions for alleged privacy violations.

Endnotes

1 Many of these cases have their foundation in protecting private sexual conduct. Cases include *Griswold v. Connecticut* (1965), voiding a state statute preventing the use of contraceptives; *Roe v. Wade* (1973), overturning state law that barred abortion; and *Lawrence v. Texas* (2003), striking down antisodomy laws.

2 *Black's Law Dictionary*, 9th ed., 2009, s.v. "consent decree."

3 "Ohio Art Consent Decree," April 2004, www.ftc.gov/os/2002/04/ohioartconsent.htm; "FTC Protecting Children's Privacy Online," Federal Trade Commission press release, April 22, 2002, www.ftc.gov/opa/2002/04/coppaanniv.htm.

4 Federal Trade Commission, "Advisory Opinions," www.ftc.gov/ftc/opinions.shtm.

5 "Welcome to the U.S.-EU & U.S.-Swiss Safe Harbor Frameworks," Export Portal, U.S. Dept. of Commerce, http://export.gov/safeharbor/.

6 Sherrie Bennett, "Contract Basics," Lawyers.com, http://contracts.lawyers.com/contracts/Contract-Basics.html.

7 "Tort," Cornell University Law School, Legal Information Institute, www.law.cornell.edu/wex/Tort.

8 "The Privacy Torts," Privacilla, www.privacilla.org/business/privacytorts.html.

9 15 U.S.C. § 45 (2011), "[U]nfair or deceptive acts or practices in or affecting commerce, are hereby declared unlawful. . . . The [FTC] is hereby empowered and directed to prevent persons, partnerships, or corporations, except [certain institutions] . . . from using unfair methods of competition in or affecting commerce and unfair or deceptive acts or practices in or affecting commerce." For a listing of recent enforcement actions see http://business.ftc.gov/legal-resources/29/35.

10 "Enforcement Activity," Privacy Exchange, www.privacyexchange.org/legal/enforcement.html.

11 Office of the Attorney General, State of Washington, "Washington e-Commerce Company May Owe You Money," www.atg.wa.gov/ecommercesettlement.aspx; ConsumerAffairs.com, "Minnesota Settles Consumer Fraud Suit with MemberWorks," www.consumeraffairs.com/online/memwrks_mn_ag.html.

12 http://info.sen.ca.gov/pub/01-02/bill/sen/sb_1351-1400/sb_1386_bill_20020926_chaptered.html.

CHAPTER TWO

Federal and State Regulators and Enforcement of Privacy

This chapter discusses the enforcement of privacy law by federal and state regulators. Enforcement through civil and criminal litigation in the courts is covered, as well as agency enforcement actions, self-regulation and other forms of accountability.

This chapter focuses particular attention on the Federal Trade Commission (FTC). The FTC is an independent agency governed by a chairman and four other commissioners. Their decisions are not under the president's control. With exceptions for certain industries, the FTC has authority to enforce against "unfair and deceptive trade practices." Along with this general authority, the FTC has specific statutory responsibility for issues such as children's privacy online and commercial e-mail marketing. Among federal agencies, the FTC has played a prominent role in the development of U.S. privacy standards, including public workshops on privacy issues and reports on privacy policy and enforcement.

This leading role for the FTC exists in a context where numerous other federal agencies are involved in privacy enforcement, as well as more general privacy oversight and policy development. This chapter outlines the roles for these agencies, many of which are discussed in more detail in later chapters. It then examines FTC enforcement in more detail before turning to privacy enforcement in the states, concluding with discussion of enforcement in self-regulatory systems and across borders.

1. Types of Litigation and Enforcement

For non-lawyers, it is useful to define the main categories of legal action: civil litigation, criminal litigation and administrative enforcement.

Civil litigation occurs in the courts, when one person (the plaintiff) sues another person (the defendant) to redress a wrong. The plaintiff often seeks a monetary judgment from the defendant. The plaintiff may also seek an injunction, which is a court order mandating the defendant to stop engaging in certain behaviors. Important categories of civil litigation include contracts and torts. For instance, a plaintiff might sue for a breach of a contract that promised confidential treatment of personal information. In a tort action, a plaintiff might sue for an invasion of privacy where the defendant surreptitiously took pictures in a changing room and broadcast the pictures to the public. Some privacy laws create private rights of action, enabling an individual plaintiff to sue based on violations of the statute. The Fair Credit Reporting Act, for instance, has a private right of action, allowing a person to sue a company if his consumer reports have been used inappropriately.

Criminal litigation involves lawsuits brought by the government for violations of criminal laws. This contrasts with civil litigation, which generally involves an effort by a private party to correct specific harms. Criminal prosecution can lead to imprisonment and criminal fines. In the federal government, criminal laws are prosecuted by the Department of Justice. States typically place criminal prosecutorial power in the hands of the state attorney general and local officials, such as a district attorney.

Administrative enforcement actions are carried out pursuant to the statutes that create and empower an agency, such as the FTC. In the federal government, the basic rules for agency enforcement actions occur under the Administrative Procedure Act (APA).[1] The APA sets forth basic rules for adjudication within an agency, where court-like hearings may take place before an administrative law judge. Federal agency adjudications can generally be appealed to federal court. In addition, a federal agency may sue a party in federal court, with the agency as the plaintiff in a civil action. How the FTC typically conducts privacy enforcement actions, notably by the use of consent decrees, is discussed in more detail in Section 4.

2. Federal Privacy Enforcement and Policy Outside of the FTC

Depending on the statutes or regulations violated, agencies other than the FTC may be responsible for privacy enforcement. For example, the following agencies are discussed in the chapters noted:

- Medical privacy—the Office for Civil Rights in the Department of Health and Human Services (HHS), for the Health Insurance Portability and Accountability Act (HIPAA), Chapter 4
- Financial privacy—the Consumer Financial Protection Bureau for financial consumer protection issues generally; federal financial regulators such as the Federal Reserve and the Office of Comptroller of the Currency, for institutions under their jurisdiction under the Gramm-Leach-Bliley Act (GLBA), Chapter 5
- Education privacy—Department of Education for the Family Educational Rights and Privacy Act, Chapter 6
- Telemarketing and marketing privacy—the Federal Communications Commission (together with the FTC), under the Telephone Consumer Protection Act and other statutes, Chapter 7

- Workplace privacy—agencies including the Equal Employment Opportunity Commission, for the Americans with Disabilities Act and other antidiscrimination statutes, Chapter 11

In addition, other federal agencies are involved in privacy oversight, enforcement and policy. Privacy professionals should thus be alert to the possibility that federal agencies other than the FTC will be relevant to their organizations' activities.

- The Department of Commerce plays a leading role in federal privacy policy development and administers the Safe Harbor agreement between the U.S. and the EU.
- The State Department has been increasingly active over time on privacy, especially by negotiating internationally on privacy issues with other countries and in multinational groups such as the United Nations or the Organisation for Economic Co-operation and Development (OECD).
- The Department of Transportation is the agency responsible for transportation companies under its jurisdiction and for enforcing violations of the Safe Harbor agreement between the U.S. and the EU.
- The U.S. Office of Management and Budget is the lead agency for interpreting the Privacy Act of 1974, which applies to federal agencies and private sector contractors to those agencies. The OMB also issues guidance to agencies and contractors on privacy and information security issues, such as data breach disclosure and privacy impact assessments.
- The Internal Revenue Service is subject to privacy rules concerning tax records, including disclosures of such records in the private sector. Other parts of the Department of Treasury are also involved with financial records issues, including compliance with money-laundering rules at the Financial Crimes Enforcement Network.
- The Department of Homeland Security faces numerous privacy issues, such as the E-Verify program for new employees, rules for air traveler records (Transportation Security Administration), as well as immigration and other border issues (Immigration and Customs Enforcement).

As new technologies emerge, additional agencies become involved in privacy. For instance, the development of the smart grid is making privacy an important issue for the electric utility system, thus involving the Department of Energy. The increased use of Unmanned Aerial Vehicles, or drones, and the surveillance implications have raised privacy issues for the Federal Aviation Administration. In short, almost every agency in the federal government is or may soon become involved with privacy in some manner within that agency's jurisdiction.

The Department of Justice is the sole federal agency to bring criminal enforcement actions, which can result in imprisonment or criminal fines. Some statutes, such as HIPAA, provide for both civil and criminal enforcement. In such cases, procedures exist for the roles of both HHS and the Department of Justice.[2]

3. FTC Jurisdiction

The FTC was founded in 1914 for the purpose of enforcing antitrust laws, and its general consumer protection mission was established by a statutory change in 1938.[3] The FTC navigates both roles today, and privacy and computer security issues have become an important part of its work. The FTC is an independent agency, which means that it is governed by the decisions of its chairman and four other commissioners, instead of falling under the direct control of the president.

Section 5 of the FTC Act is perhaps the single most important piece of U.S. privacy law. Section 5 notably says that "unfair or deceptive acts or practices in or affecting commerce, are hereby declared unlawful," although it does not mention privacy or information security.[4] The application of Section 5 to privacy and information security, however, is clearly established today. The FTC has enforced privacy violations for decades, beginning with the Fair Credit Reporting Act of 1970. During the 1990s, the FTC began bringing privacy enforcement cases under its powers to address unfair and deceptive practices. Congress added privacy-related responsibilities to the FTC over time, such as those under the Children's Online Privacy Protection Act (COPPA) of 1998 and the Controlling the Assault of Non-Solicited Pornography and Marketing (CAN-SPAM) Act of 2003. Among other authoritative powers, Section 6 of the FTC Act vests the commission with the authority to conduct investigations and to require businesses to submit investigatory reports under oath.[5]

Section 5 of the FTC Act applies to unfair and deceptive practices "in commerce," and does not apply to nonprofit organizations. The commission's powers also do not extend to certain industries, including banks and other federally regulated financial institutions as well as common carriers, such as the transportation and communications industries.[6]

In addition to the authority granted under Section 5, the FTC retains separate and specific authority over privacy and security issues under other federal statutes. Until the creation of the Consumer Financial Protection Bureau (CFPB), the FTC issued rules and guidance for the Fair Credit Reporting Act, as amended by the Fair and Accurate Credit Transactions Act of 2003, and for the Gramm-Leach-Bliley Act of 1999. Now, the CFPB has authority to issue rules for those areas and shares enforcement authority with the FTC for financial institutions that are not covered by a separate financial regulator.

The FTC is also the rule-making and enforcement agency for COPPA. With the FCC, it shares rule-making and enforcement power under the Telemarketing Sales Rule and the CAN-SPAM Act. The FTC also shares rule-making and enforcement power with HHS for data breaches related to medical records, under the Health Information Technology for Economic and Clinical Health (HITECH) Act of 2009. These laws are discussed in more detail later in this chapter.

The FTC has general authority to issue regulations to implement protections against unfair and deceptive acts and practices.[7] Such regulations, however, are not promulgated under the usual procedures of the Administrative Procedure Act. Instead, any such regulation must comply with the more complex and lengthy procedures under the Magnuson-Moss Warranty Federal Trade Commission Improvement Act of 1975.[8] As of the date of writing, the FTC had not put forth any privacy or information security regulation under its Magnuson-Moss authority. The FTC has supported congressional proposals to provide the FTC with APA rule-making authority; such proposals have not been successful to date, in part due to opposition from companies that are against increased regulation.

4. FTC Enforcement Process and Consent Decrees

The typical FTC enforcement action begins with a claim that a company has committed an unfair or deceptive practice or has violated a specific consumer protection laws. The enforcement action can be brought to the FTC's attention in numerous ways, such as press reports covering questionable practices or complaints from consumer groups or competitors. If the violation is minor, the FTC may work with the company to resolve the problem without launching a formal investigation. If the violation is more significant or there is a pattern of noncompliance, the FTC may proceed to full enforcement.

The FTC has broad investigatory authority, including subpoenas of witnesses, civil investigative demands and requirements for businesses to submit written reports under oath.[9] Following an investigation, the commission may initiate an enforcement action if it has reason to believe a law is being or has been violated.[10] The commission issues a complaint, and an administrative trial can proceed before an administrative law judge (ALJ). The decision of the ALJ can be appealed to the five commissioners. That decision, in turn, can be appealed to federal district court.

An order by the commission becomes final 60 days after it is served on the company. Although the FTC lacks the authority to assess civil penalties, if an FTC ruling is ignored, the FTC can seek civil penalties in federal court of up to $16,000 per violation and can seek compensation for those harmed by the unfair or deceptive practices.[11] Each violation of such an order is treated as a separate offense and each day the violator fails to comply with the order is considered a separate offense. The court can also order redress for consumers harmed by the act or practice. Additional penalties can be assessed if a company does not respond to a complaint or order. The court can also mandate an injunction against a violator.[12]

In practice, FTC privacy enforcement actions have been settled through consent decrees and accompanying consent orders. In a consent decree, the respondent does not admit fault, but promises to change its practices. Consent decrees are posted publicly on the FTC's website, and the details of these decrees provide guidance about what practices the FTC considers inappropriate. Once an individual or company has agreed to a consent decree, any violation of that decree can lead, following an FTC investigation, to enforcement in the federal district court, including civil penalties, as discussed above. The federal court can also grant injunctions and other forms of relief. The FTC's Enforcement Division, within the Bureau of Consumer Protection, monitors and litigates violations of consent decrees, in cooperation with the Department of Justice.

Consent decree terms vary depending on the violation. Usually, the consent decree states what affirmative actions the respondent needs to take and which practices the respondent must refrain from engaging in. Consent decrees often require the respondent to maintain proof of compliance with the decree and to inform all related individuals of the consent decree obligations. The respondent is also usually required to provide the FTC with confirmation of its compliance with the decree and must inform the FTC if company changes will affect the respondent's ability to adhere to its terms. Respondents may also face civil penalties. Increasingly, in privacy cases, companies are subject to periodic outside audits or reviews of their practices, or they may be required to adopt and implement a comprehensive privacy program. Over time, consent decrees have become more specific in nature.

Both the company and the FTC have incentives to negotiate a consent decree rather than proceed with a full adjudication process. The company avoids a prolonged trial, as well as negative, ongoing publicity. It also avoids the details of its business practices being exposed to the public. The FTC (1) achieves a consent decree that incorporates good privacy and security practices, (2) avoids the expense and delay of a trial, and (3) gains an enforcement advantage, due to the fact that monetary fines are much easier to assess in federal court if a company violates a consent decree.

5. Privacy Policies and Notices, Early FTC Enforcement Actions and Deceptive Trade Practices

Long before the FTC began to use consent decrees in privacy cases, its Bureau of Consumer Protection negotiated such decrees for other consumer protection issues under Section 5 of the FTC Act. Review of nonprivacy decrees can be instructive for lawyers or others who seek to understand the FTC's approach to and priorities for consumer protection consent decrees.

As commercial activity on the Internet became significant in the mid-1990s, the FTC, along with the Commerce Department, began convening public workshops and conducting other activities to highlight the importance of privacy protection on websites.[13] Importantly, organizations began to post clearly stated privacy notices on their websites. These privacy notices helped inform consumers about how their personal information was being collected and used. The privacy notices were also important for enforcement purposes. If a company promised a certain level of privacy or security on a company website or elsewhere, and the company did not fulfill its promise, then the FTC considered that breach of promise a "deceptive" practice under Section 5 of the FTC Act.[14]

Although there is no omnibus federal law requiring companies to have public privacy notices, certain sector-specific statutes such as HIPAA, Gramm-Leach-Bliley, and COPPA do impose notice requirements. Also, as discussed in Chapter 8, California requires companies and organizations doing in-state business to post privacy policies on their websites.

Even in the absence of a legal requirement, the vast majority of commercial websites posted privacy notices, according to an FTC survey conducted in 2000.[15] By then, privacy notices had become a standard feature of legitimate commercial websites. In addition, the absence of a privacy notice is easily visible—any consumer advocate or regulator visiting the site can tell whether a notice is posted. In practice today, most commercial websites are expected to post a privacy notice.

As companies began to post privacy notices, the FTC started to investigate whether they adhered their own policies. If a company did not, the FTC would bring an enforcement action for deceptive trade practices.

5.1 In the Matter of GeoCities, Inc.

The first FTC Internet privacy enforcement action was *In the Matter of GeoCities, Inc.*[16] GeoCities operated a website that provided an online community through which users could maintain personal home pages. To register and become a member of GeoCities, users were required to fill out an online form that requested certain personal information, with which GeoCities created an extensive information database. GeoCities promised on its website that the collected information would not be sold or distributed without user consent.

The FTC brought an enforcement action against GeoCities for two separate unfair and deceptive practices. First, the FTC alleged that GeoCities misrepresented how it would use information collected from its users by reselling the information to third parties, which violated its privacy notice. Second, GeoCities collected and maintained children's personal information without parental consent. GeoCities settled the action and the FTC issued a consent order, which required GeoCities to post and adhere to a conspicuous online privacy notice that disclosed to users how it would collect and use personal information. GeoCities was also required to obtain parental or guardian consent before collecting information from children 12 years of age or under.

5.2 In the Matter of Eli Lilly & Co.

In 2004 the FTC brought an enforcement against Eli Lilly & Co., a pharmaceutical manufacturer that maintained a website where users would provide personal information for messages and updates reminding them to take their medication.[17] The website included a privacy notice that made promises about the security and privacy of the information provided. When Eli Lilly decided to end the program, it sent subscribers an e-mail announcement, inadvertently addressed to and revealing the e-mail addresses of all subscribers. The FTC enforcement action against Eli Lilly resulted in settlement terms, which required Eli Lilly to adhere to representations about how it collects, uses and protects user information. It also required, for the first time in an online privacy and security case, that Eli Lilly develop and maintain an information privacy and security program. Before this case, the FTC had only required companies to stop current unfair and deceptive practices. After the settlement, it became clear that the scope of settlement terms had expanded to include implementation and evaluation of security programs.

5.3 In the Matter of Microsoft Corp.

In 2002, the FTC brought an enforcement action against Microsoft Corp. concerning Microsoft's security representations about information collected through its "Passport" website service.[18] Microsoft Passport was an online service that allowed customers to use single sign-in to access multiple web services. Microsoft made claims about the high level of security used to protect users' personal and financial information, as well as Passport's parental controls for its children's services. The FTC alleged that these representations of high-level online security were misleading because the security of the personal information was within the control, not of Microsoft, but Microsoft's vendors and business partners. The FTC also asserted that the Passport service collected and shared more information than disclosed in its privacy notice, and claimed that the access controls for the children's website were inadequate.

Microsoft settled the action with the FTC. Under the settlement terms, Microsoft was prohibited from making future misrepresentations about the security and privacy of its products, and was required to adopt and implement a comprehensive information security program. As part of the program, Microsoft was required to undergo a biannual third-party audit to ensure compliance with its program terms.

6. Enforcement Actions and Unfair Trade Practices

As discussed above, early privacy and security enforcement actions focused on deceptive practices. By 2004, the FTC began to enforce "unfair" practices as well. The scope of the term *unfairness* was clarified in a 1980 policy statement[19] and in 1994 amendments to the FTC Act.[20]

For a practice to be considered "unfair," the injury caused must be (1) substantial, (2) without offsetting benefits and (3) one that consumers cannot reasonably avoid. Each step involves a detailed, fact-specific analysis that must undergo careful consideration by the commission.[21]

6.1 In the Matter of Gateway Learning Corp.

The 2004 Gateway Learning case was the first instance of the FTC basing an enforcement action on a company's material change to its personal information-handling practices, and the first privacy case based on unfairness.[22]

Gateway Learning Corporation marketed and sold popular educational aids under the "Hooked on Phonics" product line. Its website privacy notice stated that Gateway Learning would not sell, rent or loan any personal information without explicit customer consent. The notice also stated that Gateway Learning would provide consumers with an opportunity to opt out of having their information shared if this practice changed. However, Gateway Learning started renting personal customer information to third-party marketers and advertisers without providing the opt-out. It subsequently revised its website privacy notice to allow for disclosures to third-party advertisers and continued to rent consumer information without providing notice to customers about the change in policy.

The consent decree stated that the retroactive application of material changes to the company's data sharing policy was an unfair trade practice. The settlement prohibited Gateway from sharing any personal information collected from users under its initial privacy notice unless it obtained an affirmative opt-in from users. It also required Gateway to relinquish the money earned from renting consumer information.

6.2 In the Matter of BJ's Wholesale Club, Inc.

In a 2005 enforcement action, the FTC alleged that BJ's Wholesale Club did not engage in reasonable security practices to protect the personal and financial information of its consumers.[23]

The complaint stated that BJ's failed to encrypt the information and failed to secure wireless networks to prevent unauthorized access, among other security lapses. The security flaws caused substantial injury to consumers and resulted in almost eight hundred cases of customer identity theft. In the settlement, the consent decree required BJ's to implement a comprehensive information security program, including regular audits.

In the Matter of BJ's Wholesale Club was the first time the FTC alleged only unfair, and not deceptive, acts for the basis of a privacy or information security case. The FTC established its view that failing to implement basic security controls to protect consumer information alone constitutes an enforceable unfair trade practice, without any need for the FTC to allege deception. Thus, even in the absence of the heightened security requirements under sector-specific statutes, such as HIPAA, COPPA and GLBA, companies now faced potential enforcement action based on the FTC's Section 5 unfairness authority.

More recent enforcement actions indicate the FTC's willingness to impose stringent information-handling practices. In addition to the consent decrees with Google and Facebook discussed below, in 2010 Twitter entered a consent decree promising to protect privacy and security, and to implement a comprehensive security program subject to outside audit.[24]

6.3 In the Matter of Google Inc.

In 2011, the FTC announced a settlement with Google Inc. over charges that it engaged in deceptive trade practices and violated its own privacy policies with the launch of its Google Buzz social networking service.[25] The FTC complaint stated that Google Buzz was a social networking service integrated with Google's e-mail service, Gmail. When this service launched, consumers were automatically enrolled in Buzz services without having to provide consent. Buzz also exposed personal information harvested from Gmail to the public without making this clear to users. These actions conflicted with Google's privacy notice on its website. The FTC alleged that automatic enrollment without prior notice and explicit consent was a deceptive trade practice. Further, the FTC asserted that Google was in violation of the U.S.–EU Safe Harbor Framework, which provides a method for U.S. companies to transfer personal data from the EU to the United States in compliance with EU data protection requirements.

The Google settlement is noteworthy for two reasons. First, this consent decree was the first in which a company agreed to implement a "comprehensive privacy program." At the time of writing in 2012, it is not clear what exact elements a "comprehensive" program should contain. However, the term *comprehensive* seems to signal that the FTC believes privacy should be thoroughly integrated with product development and implementation. To enforce the comprehensive privacy program, Google agreed to undergo independent third-party privacy audits on a biannual basis.

Second, the Google consent decree was the first substantial U.S.–EU Safe Harbor enforcement by the FTC. The complaint stated that Google had represented it would use personal information only for the purposes for which it was initially collected or consented to by users. Along with violating Section 5 of the FTC Act, the complaint stated that Google failed to live up to its promise to comply with the notice and choice principles of Safe Harbor.

6.4 In the Matter of Facebook Inc.

In 2011, the social networking service Facebook Inc. settled an FTC enforcement action on charges that it engaged in deceptive practices.[26] The FTC's eight-count complaint alleged, among other claims, that Facebook deceived consumers by repeatedly making changes to services so that information designated as private was made public. This was in violation of promises Facebook made in its privacy notice. The settlement required Facebook to provide users with clear notice and obtain user consent before making retroactive changes to material privacy terms, and barred Facebook from making any further deceptive privacy claims. Facebook was also required to establish and maintain a comprehensive privacy program. Further, Facebook must obtain biannual independent third-party audits of its privacy program for the next 20 years. The case further indicates broader government efforts to hold companies accountable for information-handling practices.

7. Federal 2012 Privacy Reports and the Future of Federal Enforcement

In early 2012 the Obama administration issued a report titled "Consumer Data Privacy in a Networked World: A Framework for Protecting Privacy and Promoting Innovation in the Global Digital Economy" (hereafter referred to as "White House Report").[27] The FTC also issued a report striking many of the same themes, titled "Protecting Consumer Privacy in an Era of Rapid Change: Recommendations for Businesses and Policymakers" ("FTC Report").[28] Together, the two reports appear to illustrate the important evolution from earlier methods of privacy enforcement to current approaches.

The FTC primary method of enforcement used under Chairman Robert Pitofsky in the late 1990s is sometimes referred to as the "notice and choice approach." During that period, emphasis was placed on having companies provide privacy notices on their websites, and offering choice to consumers about whether information would be shared with third parties. Enforcement actions were based on deception and the failure to comply with a privacy promise rather than specific, tangible harm to consumers.[29]

In the mid-2000s, Chairmen Timothy Muris and Deborah Platt Majoris adopted the "harm-based model" approach to enforcement. As discussed in connection with the Gateway and BJ's Warehouse cases, this approach placed new emphasis on addressing substantial injury, as required under the FTC's unfairness authority.

Under Chairman Jon Leibowitz, appointed in 2009, the FTC began to include the requirement of a comprehensive privacy program in consent decrees. This more comprehensive approach to privacy enforcement is reflected in the 2012 White House and FTC reports.

The White House Report contains a preface signed by President Obama and defines the "Consumer Privacy Bill of Rights" based on traditional fair information practices. The report states that these rights should apply to commercial uses of personal data:

1. **Individual control.** Consumers have a right to exercise control over what personal data companies collect from them and how they use it.
2. **Transparency.** Consumers have a right to easily understandable and accessible information about privacy and security practices.
3. **Respect for context.** Consumers have a right to expect that companies will collect, use, and disclose personal data in ways that are consistent with the context in which consumers provide the data.
4. **Security.** Consumers have a right to secure and responsible handling of personal data.
5. **Access and accuracy.** Consumers have a right to access and correct personal data in usable formats, in a manner that is appropriate to the sensitivity of the data and the risk of adverse consequences to consumers if the data is inaccurate.
6. **Focused collection.** Consumers have a right to reasonable limits on the personal data that companies collect and retain.
7. **Accountability.** Consumers have a right to have personal data handled by companies with appropriate measures in place to assure they adhere to the Consumer Privacy Bill of Rights.

The report recommends that these rights be included in federal legislation, with use of multistakeholder processes to develop enforceable codes of conduct until legislation is passed. The report emphasizes the importance of achieving international interoperability, including with trans-border cooperation on privacy enforcement. It also emphasizes the role and expertise of the FTC for privacy enforcement.

The FTC Report, issued shortly after the White House Report, states many of the same themes. In its summary, the FTC emphasizes three areas:

1. **Privacy by Design.** Companies should promote consumer privacy throughout their organizations and at every stage in the development of their products and services. Companies should incorporate substantive privacy protections into their practices, such as data security, reasonable collection limits, sound retention and disposal practices, and data accuracy.
2. **Simplified consumer choice.** Companies should simplify consumer choice. Companies do not need to provide choice before collecting and using consumer data for practices that are consistent with the context of the transaction or the company's relationship with the consumer, or are required or specifically authorized by law. For practices requiring choice, companies should offer the choice at a time and in a context in which the consumer is making a decision about his or her data. Companies should obtain affirmative express consent before (1) using consumer data in a materially different manner than claimed when the data was collected or (2) collecting sensitive data for certain purposes.

3. **Transparency.** Privacy notices should be clearer, shorter and more standardized to enable better comprehension and comparison of privacy practices. Companies should provide reasonable access to the consumer data they maintain; the extent of access should be proportionate to the sensitivity of the data and the nature of its use. All stakeholders should expand their efforts to educate consumers about commercial data privacy practices.

The FTC also announced five priority areas for attention:

1. **Do Not Track.** The FTC has encouraged industry to create a mechanism for consumers to signal if they do not wish to be tracked for online behavioral advertising purposes.
2. **Mobile.** The FTC encourages greater self-regulation in the swiftly evolving area of location and other mobile-related services.
3. **Data brokers.** The FTC supports targeted legislation to provide consumers with access to information held about them by data brokers who are not already covered by the Fair Credit Reporting Act.
4. **Large platform providers.** The FTC is examining special issues raised by very large online companies that may do what the FTC calls "comprehensive" tracking.
5. **Promoting enforceable self-regulatory codes.** The FTC will work with the multistakeholder processes that are being facilitated by the Department of Commerce.

Taken together, the White House Report and FTC Report indicate a significantly more comprehensive approach to privacy protection and enforcement than the FTC's earlier approaches to enforcement.

8. State Enforcement

Each state has a law roughly similar to Section 5 of the FTC Act. These laws are commonly known as Unfair and Deceptive Acts and Practices, or UDAP statutes. In addition to covering unfair and deceptive practices, some statutes allow enforcement against "unconscionable" practices, a contract law term for a range of harsh seller practices.[30] UDAP laws are enforced by state attorneys general, who serve as the chief legal officer of each state.

Some federal statutes, such as CAN-SPAM, also allow state attorneys general to bring enforcement actions along with the relevant federal agency. Several states allow private rights of action under their state UDAP laws, so individuals can bring suit against violators.[31]

State enforcement of information security lapses has been especially prominent, driven by data breach notifications. Since California enacted the first breach notification law in 2002, almost every state has passed a similar breach notification law. Many of these laws, as discussed in Chapter 9, require organizations to furnish the state attorney general with reports about breaches when they occur. These laws also impose enforcement responsibility on state attorney generals if the breach notification reveals the implementation of inadequate security controls.

States have many other specialized statutes protecting privacy. These exist for the medical, financial, workplace and other sectors, as discussed in their relevant chapters of this book.[32] As with federal law, new issues arise with changing technology. State public utilities commissions, for instance, have started to set rules for personal information collected in connection with the smart grid.[33]

Apart from statutes, state common law is an additional source of privacy enforcement. Plaintiffs can sue under the privacy torts, which traditionally have been categorized as intrusion upon seclusion, appropriation of name or likeness, publicity given to private life and publicity placing a person in false light.[34] Plaintiffs may also sue under a contract theory in certain situations, such when a physician, financial institution or other entity holding sensitive information breaches a promise of confidentiality and causes harm.

The National Association of Attorneys General Consumer Protection Project helps coordinate the work of state attorneys general. The project "works to improve the enforcement of state and federal consumer protection laws by State Attorneys General, as well as supports multistate consumer protection enforcement efforts."[35] The project also "promotes information exchange among the states with respect to investigations, litigation, consumer education, and both federal and state legislation."

9. Self-regulation and Enforcement

The term *self-regulation* refers to a variety of approaches to privacy protection. Self-regulation, similar to government regulation, can occur through the three traditional separation of powers components: legislation, enforcement and adjudication.[36] Legislation refers to the question of who should define appropriate rules for protecting privacy. Enforcement refers to the question of who should initiate enforcement actions. Adjudication refers to the question of who should decide whether a company has violated the privacy rules, and with what penalties.

For enforcement under Section 5 of the FTC Act or state UDAP laws, self-regulation only occurs at the legislation stage. A company writes its own privacy policy, or an industry group drafts a code of conduct that companies agree to follow. Under Section 5, the FTC can then decide whether to bring an enforcement action, and adjudication can occur in front of an administrative law judge, with appeal to federal court. Referring to this approach as "self-regulation" is somewhat confusing, because a government agency is involved at the enforcement and adjudication stage.

Other self-regulatory systems engage in all three roles without the involvement of a government agency. For example, the Payment Card Institute Data Security Standard (PCI DSS) provides an enforceable security standard for payment card data. The rules were drafted by the Payment Card Industry Security Standards Council, which built on previous rules written by the various credit card companies. Except for small companies, compliance with the standard requires hiring a third party to conduct security assessments and detect violations. Failure to comply can lead to exclusion from Visa, MasterCard or other major payment card systems, as well as penalties of $5,000 to $100,000 per month.[37]

Third-party privacy seal and certification programs play an important role in providing assurances that companies are complying with self-regulatory programs. Services offered by TRUSTe, the Better Business Bureau and others provide methods for third parties to oversee compliance. Companies may demonstrate compliance and thus improve consumer confidence by displaying a trust mark in the form of a seal, logo or certification showing that the company is part of a certification program. It can serve as a way to comply with legal requirements. For instance, the U.S.–EU Safe Harbor Framework requires participating companies to name a compliance third party. COPPA authorizes the FTC to confirm that certification programs are in compliance with the law. Companies are deemed to meet compliance requirements through their participation in that certification program.

One prominent self-regulatory effort involves the Digital Advertising Alliance(DAA), a coalition of media and advertising organizations. The DAA helped develop an icon program, intended to inform consumers about how they can exercise choice with respect to online behavioral advertising.[38] The future of this self-regulatory program is closely linked to ongoing policy debates about whether and how a Do Not Track program will be instituted.

Self-regulation is controversial. Privacy advocates and supporters of the European approach to data protection often express concern that industries are not strict enough when creating, adhering to and enforcing privacy rules or codes of conduct. European regulators, for instance, say that privacy is a fundamental human right, and data protection authorities should be involved in defining and protecting that right. Supporters of self-regulation tend to emphasize the fact that industry has greater expertise about how their systems operate and therefore should lead the creation, establishment and enforcement of those rules.

Based on the 2012 White House and FTC reports, there is increased attention on new self-regulatory efforts. The White House Report stressed the importance of engaging in a "multi-stakeholder process," with the Department of Commerce facilitating these efforts. This process has important similarities to earlier self-regulatory efforts, in terms of industry experts working together to craft enforceable rules. One important difference, however, is that consumer groups and other stakeholders are explicitly included in the process, instead of industry alone defining the rules.

10. Cross-border Enforcement Issues

As the volume of cross-border data transfers increases, privacy enforcement increasingly involves companies and government agencies in more than one jurisdiction. Key issues include cooperation between enforcement agencies, conflicts between privacy laws and laws seeking to compel disclosure, as well as cross-border enforcement.

10.1 Cooperation Between Enforcement Agencies

One trend in cross-border enforcement is for enforcement agencies in different countries to engage in closer cooperation. In 2007, the OECD adopted the Recommendation on Cross-Border Co-operation in the Enforcement of Laws Protecting Privacy.[39] The recommendation focuses on the need to address common privacy issues on a global scale, rather than focusing on country-by-country differences in law or enforcement power. The recommendation calls for member countries to:

- Discuss the practical aspects of privacy law enforcement cooperation
- Share best practices in addressing cross-border challenges
- Work to develop shared enforcement priorities
- Support joint enforcement initiatives and awareness campaigns[40]

In response to the recommendation, the FTC, along with enforcement authorities from around the world, established the Global Privacy Enforcement Network (GPEN) in 2010. The GPEN aims to promote cross-border information sharing as well as investigation and enforcement cooperation among privacy authorities around the world.

Another cross-border enforcement cooperation effort is the Asia-Pacific Economic Cooperation (APEC). The APEC Cross-border Privacy Enforcement Arrangement (CPEA) aims to establish a framework for participating members to share information and evidence in cross-border investigations and enforcement actions in the Asia-Pacific region.[41] The CPEA also will facilitate cooperation and communication between APEC and non-APEC members. The FTC is a CPEA participant.

10.2 Conflicts Between Privacy and Disclosure Laws

Conflicts can arise when the privacy laws in one country prohibit disclosure of information, but laws in a different country compel disclosure. For instance, the United States generally permits a greater range of discovery in litigation than European courts, with a party to the litigation in the U.S. potentially facing fines or contempt of court if it does not produce records. By contrast, the EU Data Protection Directive and the laws of EU member states may prohibit disclosure of the same records. Although U.S. courts have found ways to resolve such disputes, concerns persist.[42]

In early 2012, the International Chamber of Commerce released a policy statement entitled "Cross-border Law Enforcement Access to Company Data—Current Issues Under Data Protection and Privacy Law."[43] The statement highlights problems that may arise when law enforcement compliance requirements conflict with data protection and privacy commitments. It provides analysis of these issues as well as recommendations for law enforcement bodies that face these challenges.

10.3 U.S. Actions That May Lead to Enforcement Abroad

There is uncertainty about the extent to which the EU and other jurisdictions will bring enforcement actions against companies that operate only in the United States. Companies with assets and employees in the EU, who also operate in the EU, are subject to the EU data protection laws. The 1998 Data Protection Directive is somewhat ambiguous in its language addressing whether and when a company operating outside of the EU is subject to enforcement there.[44] Companies wishing to transfer personal data from the EU to the U.S. have various, lawful options. For instance, these companies—and other multinational corporate entities with a presence in Europe—may draft binding corporate rules (BCR), subject to review and authorization by member states.[45] Other options include participation in the U.S.–EU Safe

Harbor program and using contracts for data export that have been approved by a data protection authority. Each of these options allows companies to comply with "adequate" data protection and the limits on trans-border data flows under Articles 25 and 26 of the Data Protection Directive.

In early 2012, the EU Council introduced a draft Data Protection Regulation with provisions that would replace the Data Protection Directive. Article 3 of the draft regulation has language suggesting that EU law applies to online sellers who operate only in the United States. Article 3 says: "The Regulation applies . . . where processing activities are related to (a) the offering of goods or services to such data subjects in the Union; or (b) the monitoring of their behavior."[46] This broad language is modified by the next part of Article 3: "This Regulation applies to the processing of personal data by a controller not established in the Union, but in a place where the national law of a Member State applies by virtue of public international law." The extraterritorial applicability of any new EU-wide data protection rules to sellers who operate only in the United States is likely to be a source of ongoing discussion. As a practical matter, companies with any EU presence will find that enforcement occurs locally.

11. Conclusion

Over the years, the FTC's enforcement has evolved from focusing on deceptive practices to a more comprehensive approach—moving beyond the mere punishment of violators to requiring the implementation of best practices in privacy.

The chapter has also highlighted, however, the large number of other agencies and actors that are now involved in U.S. privacy enforcement. These enforcement efforts come from other federal agencies, the states, self-regulatory regimes, and from organizations and countries outside of the United States. A privacy professional must be aware of both domestic enforcement authorities and potential enforcement authorities in other countries.

Endnotes

1 www.archives.gov/federal-register/laws/administrative-procedure/.

2 42 U.S.C. 1320d–6(a).

3 J. Howard Beales III, "The FTC's Use of Unfairness Authority: Its Rise, Fall, and Resurrection," www.ftc.gov/speeches/beales/unfair0603.shtm.

4 15 U.S.C. § 45(a)(1).

5 15 U.S.C. §§ 46(a)-(b).

6 15 U.S.C. § 45.

7 15 U.S.C. § 57A.

8 15 U.S.C. § 45.

9 15 U.S.C. § 46, 49, 57b-1.

10 Federal Trade Commission, "A Brief Overview of the Federal Trade Commission's Investigative and Law Enforcement Authority," www.ftc.gov/ogc/brfovrvw.shtm.

11 16 C.F.R. § 1.98(d); 15 U.S.C. § 45(m)(1)(A)16 CFR § 1.98(d), 15 U.S.C. § 45.

12 15 U.S.C. § 53.

13 Peter P. Swire, "Trustwrap: The Importance of Legal Rules for E-commerce and Internet Privacy," *Hastings L.J.* 54 (2003): 847 (discussing the history).

14 "Gateway Learning Settles FTC Privacy Charges," FTC press release, July 7, 2004, www.ftc.gov/opa/2004/07/gateway.htm.

15 Federal Trade Commission, *Privacy Online: Fair Information Practices in the Electronic Marketplace, A Report to Congress* (2000), www.ftc.gov/reports/privacy2000/privacy2000.pdf.

16 Decision and Order, *In the Matter of GeoCities, Inc.*, FTC File No. 982-3015 (Feb. 12, 1999), www.ftc.gov/os/1999/02/9823015.do.htm.

17 Decision and Order, *In the Matter of Eli Lilly & Co.*, FTC File No. 012-3214 (May 10, 2002), www.ftc.gov/os/2002/05/elilillydo.htm.

18 Decision and Order, *In the Matter of Microsoft Corp.*, FTC File No. 012-3240 (Dec. 24, 2002), www.ftc.gov/os/2002/12/microsoftdecision.pdf.

19 The Unfairness Policy Statement was published in International Harvester Co., 104 F.T.C. 949, 1070 (1984).

20 15 U.S.C. § 45(n).

21 Beales, "The FTC's Use of Unfairness Authority."

22 Decision and Order, *In the Matter of Gateway Learning Corp.*, FTC File No. 042-3047 (Sept. 17, 2004), www.ftc.gov/os/caselist/0423047/040917do0423047.pdf.

23 Agreement Containing Consent Order, *In the Matter of BJ's Wholesale Club, Inc.*, FTC File No. 042-3160 (Sept. 23, 2005), www.ftc.gov/os/caselist/0423160/092305do0423160.pdf.

24 Decision and Order, *In the Matter of Twitter, Inc.*, FTC File No. 092-3093 (Mar. 2, 2011), www.ftc.gov/os/caselist/0923093/100624twitteragree.pdf.

25 Decision and Order, *In the Matter of Google Inc.*, FTC File No. 102-3136, (Mar. 30, 2011), www.ftc.gov/os/caselist/1023136/110330googlebuzzagreeorder.pdf.

26 Decision and Order, *In the Matter of Facebook, Inc.*, FTC File No. 092-3184 (Nov. 29, 2011), http://ftc.gov/os/caselist/0923184/111129facebookagree.pdf.

27 www.whitehouse.gov/sites/default/files/privacy-final.pdf.

28 http://ftc.gov/os/2012/03/120326privacyreport.pdf.

29 *In re Cliffdale Assoc.*, 103 F.T.C. 110 (1984).

30 HI § 480-2, www.capitol.hawaii.gov/hrscurrent/vol11_ch0476-0490/hrs0480/hrs_0480-0002.htm. A detailed definition of "unconscionable" is contained in 13 Ohio Revised Code § 1345.03.

31 California Business and Professions Code § 17200-17210, www.leginfo.ca.gov/cgi-bin/displaycode?section=bpc&group=17001-18000&file=17200-17210.

32 Robert Ellis Smith, *Compilation of State and Federal Privacy Laws* (Providence: Privacy Journal, 2012).

33 For example, Decision and Order, *Adopting Rules to Protect the Privacy and Security of the Electricity Usage Data* (July 29, 2011), http://docs.cpuc.ca.gov/WORD_PDF/FINAL_DECISION/140369.pdf and 4CCR 723-3 (updated January 14, 2012), www.dora.state.co.us/puc/rules/723-3.pdf.

34 Restatement (Second) of Torts, § 652A-E.

35 Consumer Protection, www.naag.org/consumer_protection.php.

36 Peter P. Swire, "Markets, Self-Regulation, and Government Enforcement in the Protection of Personal Information," in U.S. Department of Commerce, *Privacy and Self-Regulation in the Information Age* (1997), http://ssrn.com/abstract=11472.

37 PCI Compliance Guide, *PCI FAQs and Myths*, www.pcicomplianceguide.org/pcifaqs.php#11.

38 www.aboutads.info/.

39 www.oecd.org/dataoecd/43/28/38770483.pdf.

40 Global Privacy Enforcement Network, www.privacyenforcement.net/.

41 www.apec.org/Groups/Committee-on-Trade-and-Investment/Electronic-Commerce-Steering-Group/Cross-border-Privacy-Enforcement-Arrangement.aspx.

42 *Volkswagen, A.G. v. Valdez*, 909 S.W. 2d 900 (Tex. 1995) (avoiding conflict with German data protection law).

43 www.iccwbo.org/uploadedFiles/Law_enforcement_access_to_company_data_final_20March12.pdf.

44 Peter P. Swire, "Elephants and Mice Revisited: Law and Choice of Law on the Internet," *U. Penn. L. Rev. 1975* 153 (2005); Peter P. Swire, "Of Elephants, Mice, and Privacy: International Choice of Law and the Internet," *The International Lawyer* 32 (1998): 991, http://ssrn.com/abstract=121277.

45 European Commission on BCRs, http://ec.europa.eu/justice/policies/privacy/binding_rules/index_en.htm.

46 http://eur-lex.europa.eu/LexUriServ/LexUriServ.do?uri=COM:2012:0011:FIN:EN:PDF.

CHAPTER THREE

Global Information Management from a U.S. Perspective

The first two chapters discussed the U.S. legal framework and legal privacy concepts. This chapter will focus on privacy management policies. Privacy and information management in most organizations require a combination of skills, including legal skills but also often expertise in marketing, sales, human resources, public and government relations and information technology. In large organizations, privacy professionals may be part of a team that draws on a mix of these skill sets.

This chapter begins by examining some major benefits and risks of using personal information (PI) in the private sector. Next, it discusses best practices for developing an information management program that addresses privacy and other information management concerns, including security. A related task is to perform a data inventory of an organization's data storage and transfers, and to achieve benefits and mitigate risks based on the results of that inventory.

The chapter then turns to management issues connected to the prominent fair information practices of notice, choice and access, and concludes with a discussion of contract and vendor management.

This material should be read in the context of more detailed discussions of legal rules in the other chapters of this book. The important information management issues associated with data breach and incident response are examined in Chapter 9. Considerable discussion of information security issues is provided in Chapter 4 of *Foundations of Information Privacy and Data Protection: A Survey of Global Concepts, Laws and Practices*.

1. The Role of the Privacy Professional

Privacy professionals need to appreciate both the benefits and the risks of using personal information. PI is essential to most businesses—every organization with employees or even volunteers manages PI. Organizations may collect consumer PI for many purposes, both directly from prospective and existing customers and indirectly through enhanced data available from public and private sources. Organizations may disclose information to service providers, affiliates, business partners and government agencies for a wide range of purposes. At the same time, as discussed in this book and Chapter 1 of *Foundations of Information Privacy and Data Protection*, many risks can arise from the collection, use and disclosure of PI.

Perceptions of acceptable privacy practices vary, creating challenges for privacy professionals. Decades of opinion surveys show that substantial parts of the population fit within three groups: the "privacy concerned" (people with a strong desire to protect privacy), the "privacy unconcerned" (people with low worries about privacy) and the "privacy pragmatists" (people whose concern about privacy varies with context and who are willing to give up some privacy in exchange for benefits).[1] Perceptions about privacy risks not only vary within the population, they also shift over time. Sometimes the shift is toward greater privacy protection. For example, Social Security numbers used to be visible through the envelope window of millions of Social Security and Supplemental Security Income checks mailed by the U.S. Treasury. With rising fears of identity theft, that practice was abolished in 2000.[2] Sometimes the shift is toward less privacy protection. For example, people post intimate details of their lives on widely adopted social networks.

Established standards exist for information security, such as installing firewalls or using industry-standard encryption for communications. For many privacy issues, there is less consensus about good practice. Laws vary across jurisdictions and industry sectors, and views about good practice often differ, both within an organization and in the general public. One role for privacy professionals is to alert their organizations to these often divergent perspectives.

Privacy professionals also help their organizations manage a range of risks that can arise from processing personal information, and do so in a manner consistent with meeting the organization's growth, profitability and other goals. Privacy professionals can help the organization to identify areas where compliance is difficult in practice, and design policies to close gaps between stated policies and actual operations.

2. Risks of Using PI Improperly

Four types of risks must always be considered and balanced.

1. **Legal risks.** The organization must comply with applicable laws—state, federal and international—regarding its use of information or potentially face litigation or regulatory sanctions such as lengthy consent decrees. The company must also comply with its contractual commitments, privacy promises and some industry standards, such as the Payment Card Institute Data Security Standard.
2. **Reputational risks.** Organizations can face legal enforcement and reputational harm if they announce privacy policies but do not carry them out. An organization should seek to protect its reputation as a trusted institution with respected brands.
3. **Operational risks.** Organizations must also ensure that the privacy program is administratively efficient and cost-effective. If a privacy program is too heavy-handed, it may interfere with relationships and inhibit use of PI in ways that would benefit the organization and your customers, such as for personalization or risk management.

4. **Investment risks.** The organization must be able to receive an appropriate return on its investments in information, information technology and information processing programs, in light of evolving privacy regulations, enforcement and expectations.

3. Developing an Information Management Program

Over time, PI management has become vital to a large range of organizations. It is now increasingly common for companies to develop an information management program, to seek a holistic approach to the risks and benefits of processing PI. The program, in turn, helps create policies and practices for important parts of the organization's activities. Common activities for such policies include maintaining preference lists for direct marketing, developing appropriate security for human resources data, executing proper contracts to authorize international data flows and publishing online privacy notices when data is collected.

In creating the information management program, privacy leaders help their organizations develop privacy policy in an organized way, meeting policy goals as well as preserving business flexibility. Privacy professionals seek to understand and anticipate future changes both in the regulatory environment and in their companies' business needs. To achieve these objectives, companies should take four distinct steps.

3.1 Four Basic Steps for Information Management

Figure 3-1 summarizes the four steps—discover, build, communicate and evolve—followed by a closer look at each phase.

Figure 3-1. Steps for Information Management

1 **Discover**
- Issue identification and self-assessment
- Determination of best practices

2 **Build**
- Procedure development and verification
- Full implementation

3 **Communicate**
- Documentation
- Education

4 **Evolve**
- Affirmation and monitoring
- Adaptation

3.1.1 Phase 1: Discover

Before drafting or updating a privacy policy, consider the company's environment, information goals and corporate culture. What laws regulate the company's collection or use of information? Does the company wish to be aggressive in its use of information? Does the company instead plan to be more cautious in its use of PI, to reduce legal and reputational risks or perhaps to achieve a competitive advantage as a privacy-sensitive leader? How do the company's information policy objectives mesh with those of its competitors, customers and business partners? The answers to these questions can help an organization define its information policy goals. These goals serve as the foundation upon which the company's policies are built.

In addition to the many state, federal and international laws that regulate the collection, use and/or disclosure of personal information, many industry groups have promulgated self-regulatory guidelines. Some of these standards are mandatory for members of the specific industry group, as discussed in Chapter 2.

Useful privacy guidance for an organization depends on an accurate understanding of the company's actual data practices, as well as its intended data use. The successful privacy professional forges honest and open relationships with individuals across departments and at different levels in the organization's hierarchy. The participation of a range of departments, including legal compliance, customer service, marketing, IT, human resources and sales, is often beneficial in the creation of an information plan. The team should have the knowledge base and influence in the organization to determine and articulate the company's current practices and future goals.

Figure 3-2. Sample Organization Chart for Privacy and Data Protection Activities

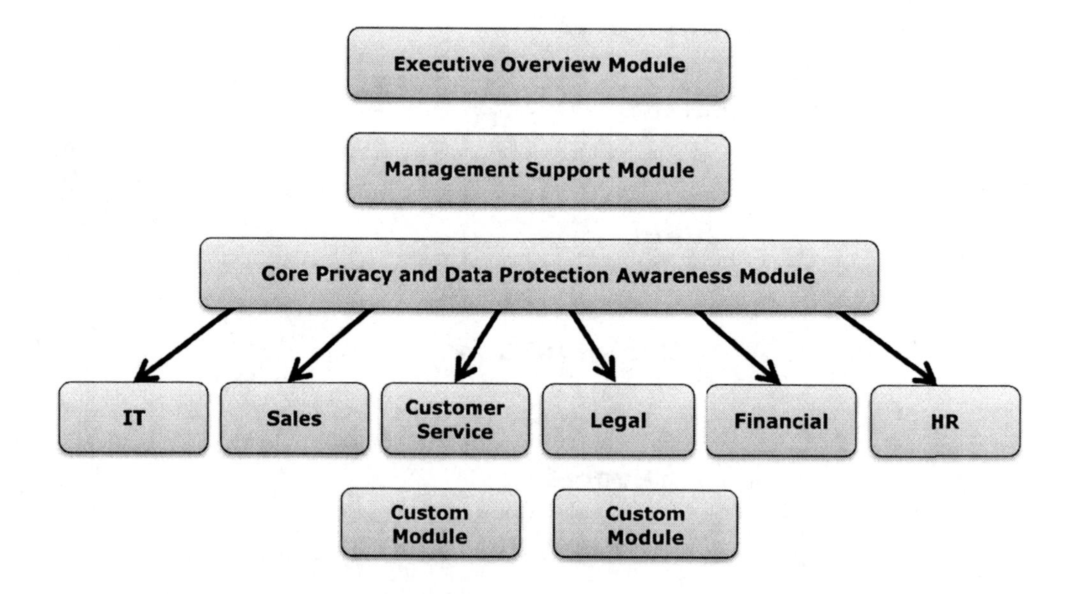

3.1.2 Phase 2: Build

Armed with an accurate assessment of the organization's practices and goals, the privacy professional can help determine how best to meet those goals, by both facilitating and restricting flows of PI where appropriate. Successful building of the information management program requires close coordination between those writing the policies (whose expertise may include legal compliance and protection of reputation) and those who actually operate consistent with the policies.

3.1.3 Phase 3: Communicate

Along with developing and implementing the information management program, the organization must assure effective communication to internal and external audiences. Internal audiences must be trained on policies and procedures, with individual accountability for compliance. Specific policies and more general goals should be communicated clearly to the organization's decision makers and consumer-facing employees, so they can shape appropriate messages to relevant audiences.

Transparency is also critical. A written privacy notice must accurately reflect the company's practices. As discussed further below, companies over time have increasingly used a layered privacy notice approach—placing a summary form that highlights key terms of the policy on top of a longer, more detailed statement of privacy and security practices.

3.1.4 Phase 4: Evolve

Information uses constantly evolve in response to changing technology, laws, market conditions and other factors. Once an information management program is established, there must be a process for review and update.

4. Data Sharing and Transfer

This section examines practices and controls for managing PI in the often complex flows among U.S. business enterprises, both within the United States and across geographic boundaries, and addresses data inventory, data classification, documenting data flows and determining data accountability.

4.1 Data Inventory

It is important for organizations to undertake an inventory of the PI that it collects, stores, uses or discloses—whether within the organization or to outside entities. This inventory should include both customer and employee data records. It should document data location and flow as well as evaluate how, when and with whom the organization shares such information—and the means for data transfer used.

This sort of inventory is legally required for some institutions, such as those covered by the Gramm-Leach-Bliley Act (GLBA) Safeguards Rule, discussed in Chapter 5. The benefits of the inventory apply more generally, by identifying risks that could affect reputation or legal compliance. If a problem subsequently occurs, penalties are likely to be less severe if the company has an established system of recording and organizing this inventory. The inventory should be reviewed and updated on a regular basis.

4.2 Data Classification

After completing an inventory, the next step is to classify data according to its level of sensitivity. The data classification level defines the clearance of individuals who can access or handle that data, as well as the baseline level of protection that is appropriate for that data.

More sensitive data generally requires greater protection than other information, and may be segregated from less sensitive data, such as through access controls that enable only authorized individuals to retrieve the data, or even kept in an entirely separate system. By contrast, if all data is held in the same system, then temporary or lower-level employees might gain access to sensitive data. Holding all data in one system can increase the consequences from a single breach.

Most organizations handle different types of PI, such as personnel and customer records, along with other information the organizations treats as sensitive, such as trade secrets and business plans. In the United States, classification is often important for compliance purposes because of sector-specific privacy and security laws. As discussed throughout this book, different rules apply to financial services information, medical information and numerous other categories. An effective data classification system helps an organization address compliance audits for a particular type of data, respond to legal discovery requests without producing more information than necessary, and use storage resources in a cost-effective manner.

4.3 Documenting Data Flows

Once data has been inventoried and classified, its data flows should be examined and documented. An organization chart can be useful to help map and document the systems, applications and processes handling data. Documenting data flows helps identify areas for compliance attention.

4.4 Determining Data Accountability

Privacy professionals often have significant responsibility within an organization to assure compliance with privacy laws and policies. Here are some helpful questions for privacy professionals when doing due diligence and for an organization to consider as it addresses privacy risks:

- ***Where, how and for what length of time is the data stored?***
  Data breach laws have focused increasing attention on where and how an organization stores PI. The organization needs policies to address potential risks of data lost from laptops as well as centralized computer centers.
- ***How sensitive is the information?***
  As discussed above, data should be classified according to its level of sensitivity. Though the data management cycle includes many participants—from the data owner to the

privacy professional, the information security professional, the vendor (if applicable), the auditor (if applicable) and the end user—ultimately, the data owner is responsible for assigning the appropriate sensitivity level, or classification, to the information based on company policy. Common categories include confidential, proprietary (e.g., property of the organization), sensitive, restricted (e.g., available to select few) and public (e.g., generally available).

- ***Should the information be encrypted?***
  Under many breach notification laws, no notice is required if the lost PI is encrypted or protected by some other effective technical protection. Such laws have encouraged greater use of encryption for stored data, and security good practices have included a wider use of encryption over time.[3] On the other hand, encryption can be difficult to implement correctly and may reduce function in some applications. IT professionals should be consulted about how to take advantage of encryption while achieving other organization goals.
- ***Will the information be transferred to or from other countries, and if so, how will it be transferred?***
  Because different countries have significantly different privacy laws, an organization should familiarize itself with the privacy requirements of both origination and destination countries for trans-border data flows.
- ***Who determines the rules that apply to the information?***
  U.S. privacy professionals have increasingly used some terms that are included in the EU Data Protection Directive—for example, a "controller" is an entity who "determines the purposes and means of the processing of personal data" and a "processor" is an entity that "processes personal data on behalf of the controller."[4] Privacy professionals should assess which organization determines the rules that apply to the processing of data. If an organization stores data on behalf of another, the organization should expect to be required to meet the privacy policy guarantees of the other entity (the controller) in the use and storage of such data. Most likely, a storing company (or processor) will be required to sign a contract to this effect.
- ***How is the information to be processed, and how will these processes be maintained?***
  The processes through which personal information is processed also must be defined. Steps should be taken to train staff members involved in the processes, and computers on which the information will be processed should be secured appropriately to minimize the risk of any data leak or breach. Physical transfer of the data also should be secured.
- ***Is the use of such data dependent upon other systems?***
  If the use of personal data depends on the working condition of other systems, such as specialized computer programs, the condition of those systems must also be evaluated and updated if necessary. A system that is outdated may call for developing a new method or program for using the relevant data.

5. Privacy Policies and Disclosure

Privacy policies are central to information management programs. They inform relevant employees about how PI must be handled, and in some cases are made public in the form of a privacy notice for the purpose of transparency. As discussed in the previous chapter on enforcement, they also are important as legal documents. If an organization violates a promise made in a privacy policy that is also communicated in the privacy notice, then the FTC or state attorney general may bring an enforcement action for a deceptive practice.

Statements on a company website are often called either "privacy notices" or "privacy policies." This book uses the term ***privacy policy*** *when referring to the internal organization statement of policies, designed to communicate to those inside the organization what practices to follow, and* ***privacy notice*** *for external communications. In practice, however, "privacy policy" is often used to refer to statements made for both external and internal audiences.*

5.1 One or Multiple Privacy Policies

An organization must determine whether to have one privacy policy that applies globally to all of its activities, or multiple policies. One policy makes sense if an organization has a consistent set of values and practices for all its operations. Multiple policies may make sense for a company that has well-defined divisions of lines of business, especially if each division uses customer data in very different ways, does not typically share PI with other divisions and is perceived in the marketplace as a different business.

Sometimes separate corporations decide to use a common privacy policy. For financial holding companies, the same corporate name may be used by multiple subsidiaries and affiliates, and a single privacy policy can avoid confusion about how PI will be handled. More specifically, mutual funds and their advisors are separate corporations, but may decide to adopt a joint privacy policy and a joint form of notice.[5] All of the mutual funds in a corporate "family" may use joint notices.

Conversely, using multiple policies can create complications. One division's privacy policy may be more stringent in a particular way than another division's, preventing sharing of customer information between two parts of the same company. Where multiple policies are used, it makes sense to align policies as closely as possible so as not to hinder cooperation between divisions.

5.2 Policy Review and Approval

An organization should not finalize a privacy policy without legal consultation followed by executive approval. If the policy is not strict enough, then consumers, regulators and the press may criticize the company for its failure to protect privacy. If a policy is too strict, then open-ended statements or overly ambitious security promises can result in legal penalties or reputational problems if the promises are not met.

If a privacy policy is revised, the organization should announce the change first to employees, then to both current and former customers in the form of a notice. In a 2012 report, the FTC stated that companies should obtain express affirmative consent (opt-in) before making material retroactive changes to privacy representations. The FTC stated that a "material" change "at a minimum includes sharing consumer information with third parties after committing at the time of collection not to share the data would constitute a material change."[6]

5.3 Communication of Privacy Policy Through a Notice

The content of privacy notices is based on fair information practices such as the OECD Guidelines and Asia-Pacific Economic Cooperation (APEC) Principles. It is generally easy to see the privacy notices of competitors, other organizations or your own organization by going to the relevant websites.

Communication to consumers and other external stakeholders may use multiple methods:

1. **Make the notice accessible in places of business.** Clearly post the organization's privacy notice at the location of business in areas of high customer traffic and in legible form. Organization staff also should have ready access to copies of the up-to-date company privacy policy in case a customer wishes to obtain a copy for review.
2. **Make the notice accessible online.** The websites of most organizations, even those primarily involved in offline commerce, today contain the privacy notice. It is standard to have a link from the company's front page.
3. **Provide updates and revisions.** For financial institutions, GLBA requires that customers receive the privacy notice annually, with clear notice of the customer's right with respect to opt-outs. For institutions without this sort of required updating, provide good notice when the privacy policy is revised, with express customer consent for material changes and a clear opportunity to opt out for smaller changes.
4. **Ensure that the appropriate personnel are knowledgeable about the policy.** Organization staff who interact with PI should receive training in the organization's privacy policy. HIPAA creates specific training requirements for all employees of covered entities.[7] Especially for employees working with sensitive data, organizations should provide regular training and keep records of which employees have been trained.

As one type of appropriate training, customer service representatives (CSRs), such as in customer call centers, should receive a summary statement or script that describes the privacy notice and can be used to answer customer questions. CSRs should have a full copy of the privacy notice in their standard reference material and should retain the ability to send or direct customers to a copy of the privacy notice that they can review in detail. They should know how to escalate privacy issues or incidents once observed.

5.4 Policy Version Control

An organization's privacy policy will need to be updated as information collection, use and transfer needs evolve. As such changes occur, a new version of the privacy policy must be drafted to replace the older version. Replacement of the policy must occur systematically across all areas of posting (physical and electronic) to reduce the risk that representations made under different versions of the policy will be implemented. Privacy policies should reflect the policy revision date along with a version number, if used.

For compliance purposes, it is useful to save and store older versions of the privacy policy and its associated notice. These earlier versions may be useful internally, such as to show what representations have been made in connection with which customer transactions. The earlier versions may also be useful in the event of an enforcement action, to reduce the risk that the company will be held to an incorrect set of representations.

6. Managing User Preferences and Access Requests

In following their privacy policies, organizations can face management challenges on topics including how to manage user (data subject) preferences and respond to requests for access and correction. Legal rules may set basic requirements for what must be done, but privacy professionals must often choose options within those requirements, and ensure that implementation occurs correctly. The discussion here illustrates major areas where user preferences are handled through opt-in, opt-out or no option, and then examines management issues for handling user preferences and customer access and redress requests.

6.1 Opt-in, Opt-out and No Option

Privacy professionals should become aware of situations that call for different approaches to user preferences, notably an opt-in (also called "affirmative" or "express" consent), an opt-out or no option for the consumer.

Some U.S. privacy laws require **affirmative consumer consent,** or **opt-in**, before data is used or collected. For instance, COPPA requires express consent from a parent before a child's PI is collected. HIPAA requires opt-in consent before personal health information is disclosed to third parties, subject to important exceptions. The Fair Credit Reporting Act requires opt-in before a consumer's credit report may be provided to an employer, lender, or other authorized recipient. As discussed above, the FTC believes that opt-in consent should occur before PI collected under one privacy notice is processed under a materially changed privacy notice.

Some industry segments commonly employ opt-in, such as for e-mail marketers who send a confirmation e-mail requiring a response from the subscriber before the subscriber receives actual marketing e-mails. This e-mail approach is sometimes called "double opt-in" or "confirmed opt-in," because a consumer first indicates interest in the mailing list and then confirms that interest in response to the follow-up e-mail. In addition, the EU takes a general position that opt-in consent is the appropriate way for marketing to occur, and this position was underscored in the draft Data Protection Regulation issued in early 2012.

On the other extreme, **no consumer choice**, or **no option**, is expected in a range of situations. The 2010 preliminary FTC staff report, *Protecting Consumer Privacy in an Era of Rapid Change*, called these situations "commonly accepted practices." For example, a consumer who orders a product online expects her PI to be shared with the shipping company, the credit card processor and others who are engaged in fulfilling the transactions. The consumer does not expect to have to sign an opt-in or be offered an opt-out option for the shipping company to learn the address. In addition to product fulfillment, other examples provided by the FTC include "internal operations such as improving services offered, fraud prevention, legal compliance and first-party marketing" by the seller to the customer.[8] The FTC received public comments that the term "commonly accepted practices" would not work well for companies providing innovative services. The final report, in 2012, addressed the same issue by saying: "Companies do not need to provide choice before collecting and using consumers' data for practices that are consistent with the context of the transaction, consistent with the company's relationship with the consumer, or as required or specifically authorized by law."[9]

It is common practice for companies to offer an opt-out, sometimes referred to as consumer choice, before customer information is sold or shared with third parties. This privacy notice creates an enforceable promise. If an individual sells the information for individuals who have opted out, the FTC or state enforcers may bring suit under the unfair and deceptive trade practices laws.

Some U.S. statutes require that a company provide at least an opt-out. For example, GLBA requires an opt-out before transferring the PI of a customer of a financial institution to an unaffiliated third party for its own use. The Video Privacy Protection Act requires an opt-out before covered movie and other rental data is provided to a third party. The CAN-SPAM Act requires e-mail marketers to provide an opt-out. The Do Not Call rules provide the opportunity to opt out of telemarketing phone calls, both in general or on a company-by-company basis.

Opt-outs are required for companies who subscribe to any of a number of self-regulatory systems. For instance, the Direct Marketing Association has long operated an opt-out system for consumers who do not wish to receive commercial mail sent to their homes.[10] The Network Advertising Initiative[11] and Digital Advertising Alliance[12] operate opt-out systems in connection with online advertising.

6.2 Managing User Preferences

Effective management of user preferences can become quite challenging, especially for organizations that interact with their customers with multiple channels and for multiple products. The following are some of these challenges.

1. The **scope** of an opt-out or other user preference can vary. As mentioned above, financial institutions must provide an opt-out by law prior to sharing personal information with third parties, but sharing with affiliates can be done without offering such an opt-out. An organization must decide how broadly an opt-out or other user preference will apply. Some opt-out rules are by channel, such as specific limits on phone calls or commercial e-mails.
2. The **mechanism** for providing an opt-out or other user preference can also vary. A good rule of thumb is that the channel for marketing should be the channel for exercising a user preference. This rule is written into law for the CAN-SPAM Act, where an e-mail solicitation must be exercisable by the consumer through an online mechanism; it is not acceptable under the law to require the customer to mail or call in their opt-out. Similarly, if communication with a customer is done via a website, good

practice is to enable user preferences to be expressed through a web channel, and not to insist on mailing or a phone call.

3. **Linking** of a user's interactions can be a management challenge when customers interact with an organization through multiple channels, including in person, by phone (phone number), by e-mail (e-mail address) or by web. Good practice is for the organization to implement the opt-out or other user preference across channels and platforms. Under GLBA a bank receiving an opt-out request from a customer must comply across all communications regardless of the media used to communicate the request.
4. The **time period** for implementing user preferences is sometimes provided by law. For instance, the CAN-SPAM Act and Telemarketing Sales Rules mandate specific time periods for processing customer preferences.
5. **Third-party vendors** often process PI on behalf of the company that has the customer relationship. In such instances, the user preferences expressed to the first organization should be honored by the vendor.

6.3 Customer Access and Redress

Some U.S. laws provide consumers with clear rights to access the PI held about them. For instance, individuals have the right to access their credit reports under the Fair Credit Reporting Act, and rectify incorrect data. Patients can access their medical records under HIPAA, with records that the patient believes are incorrect noted as such in the patient files. Where customer access is not required under a specific statute, access is included in statements of fair information practices such as the OECD Guidelines and the APEC Principles, and in the U.S.–EU Safe Harbor agreement and the EU Data Protection Directive. The 2012 White House and FTC reports also place increased emphasis on a general consumer right to access with respect to data held in the commercial sector.

A good baseline to determine when access requests should be granted is the APEC Principles, which provide guidance on the proper scope of access requests and appropriate exceptions to providing access:[13]

Individuals should be able to:

a) obtain from the personal information controller confirmation of whether or not the personal information controller holds personal information about them;

b) have communicated to them, after having provided sufficient proof of their identity, personal information about them;

i. within a reasonable time;

ii. at a charge, if any, that is not excessive;

iii. in a reasonable manner; and,

iv. in a form that is generally understandable;

c) challenge the accuracy of information relating to them and, if possible and as appropriate, have the information rectified, completed, amended or deleted.

Such access and opportunity for correction should be provided except where:

i. the burden or expense of doing so would be unreasonable or disproportionate to the risks to the individual's privacy;

ii. the information should not be disclosed due to legal, security or commercial proprietary reasons; or,

iii. the information privacy of persons other than the individual would be violated.

If a request under (a) or (b) or a challenge under (c) is denied, the individual should be provided with reasons why and be able to challenge such denial.

7. Contract and Vendor Management

Many U.S. organizations elect to outsource information processing to an outside vendor or plan to sell the collected information to a third party. Specific precautions must be taken if a company plans to share personal data with a third-party data processor.

7.1 Vendor Contracts

Companies are responsible for the actions of vendors they contract with to collect, analyze, catalog or otherwise provide data management services on the company's behalf. The claims in a privacy policy also apply to third parties when they are working with an organization's data. To ensure the responsibility and security of data once it is in the hands of a contractor or vendor, precautions to consider incorporating in written contracts include:

1. **Confidentiality provision.** Contractors and vendors involved in personal information collection for an organization—or with whom an organization shares data—should be required to sign a contract containing a confidentiality provision before engaging in business that uses the information.
2. **No further use of shared information.** The contract with the vendor managing personal information on the organization's behalf should specify that the data be used only for the purposes contracted.
3. **Use of subcontractors.** If the vendor intends to use subcontractors in the collection or use of personal information, the contractor organization should require that all subcontractors follow the privacy and security protection terms in the vendor's contract (which, in turn, should be consistent with the organization's own privacy protection terms). Vendor contracts should also address whether the data can flow across borders to ensure that the organization's policy on this issue is not violated.
4. **Requirement to notify and to disclose breach.** An organization should require prompt notification in the event of a data breach or breach of contract. Details of the breach should be disclosed promptly and in detail.
5. **Information security provisions.** Contracts may include provisions concerning specific security controls; encryption of data in transit, on media and on portable

devices; network security; access controls; segregation of data; employee background checks; audit rights and so on.

7.2 Vendor Due Diligence

A procuring organization may have specific standards and processes for vendor selection. A prospective vendor should be evaluated against these standards. Standards for selecting vendors may include:

1. **Reputation.** A vendor's reputation with other companies can be a valuable gauge of the vendor's appropriate collection and use of personal data. Requesting and contacting references can help determine a vendor's reputation.
2. **Financial condition and insurance.** The vendor's finances should be reviewed to ensure the vendor has sufficient resources in the case of a security breach and subsequent litigation. A current and sufficient insurance policy can also protect the procuring organization in the event of breach.
3. **Information security controls.** A service provider should have sufficient security controls in place to ensure the data is not lost or stolen. Further discussion of these controls is contained in *Foundations of Information Privacy and Data Protection*.
4. **Point of transfer.** The point of transfer between the procuring organization and the vendor is a potential security vulnerability. Mechanisms of secure transfer should be developed and maintained.
5. **Disposal of information.** Appropriate destruction of data and/or information in any format or media is a key component of information management—for both the contracting organization and its vendors. As discussed in Chapter 5, the Disposal Rule under the Fair and Accurate Credit Transactions Act of 2003 sets forth required disposal protections for financial institutions. The Disposal Rule requirements provide a good baseline for disposal of PI more generally.
6. **Employee training and user awareness.** The vendor should have an established system to train its employees about its responsibilities in managing personal or sensitive information.
7. **Vendor incident response.** Because of the potentially significant costs associated with a data breach, the vendor should clearly explain in advance its provisions for responding to any such breach.

8. Conclusion

Effective information management addresses legal and reputation risks while using information appropriately to meet the organization's goals. Protection of privacy requires far more than writing policies that comply with applicable law; actual implementation must occur within the fast-paced and demanding setting of modern business. By designing and implementing a good information management program, privacy professionals can play a vital role in helping their company achieve both business success and good privacy practices.

Endnotes

1 Ponnurangam Kumaraguru and Lorrie Faith Cranor, "Privacy Indexes: A Survey of Westin's Studies" (Carnegie Mellon University, Institute for Software Research International, 2005), www.casos.cs.cmu.edu/publications/papers/CMU-ISRI-05-138.pdf.

2 U.S. Treasury Department, *Treasury Announces Steps to Increase Privacy Protections* (2000), www.treasury.gov/press-center/press-releases/Pages/ls859.aspx.

3 Peter Swire, *From Real-Time Intercepts to Stored Records: Why Encryption Drives the Government to Seek Access to the Cloud* (2012), http://ssrn.com/abstract=2038871.

4 EU Data Protection Directive 95/46/EC, Article 1.

5 Robert G. Bagnall, *Investment Company Regulation and Compliance Conference: Privacy*, SJ095 ALI-ABA 209 (2004).

6 Federal Trade Commission, *Protecting Consumer Privacy in an Era of Rapid Change: Recommendations for Businesses and Policymakers* (2012), http://ftc.gov/os/2012/03/120326privacyreport.pdf.

7 45 C.F.R. § 164.530(b)(1).

8 Federal Trade Commission, Preliminary FTC Staff Report, *Protecting Consumer Privacy in an Era of Rapid Change, A Proposed Framework for Businesses and Policymakers* (2010), vi, www.ftc.gov/os/2010/12/101201privacyreport.pdf.

9 Federal Trade Commission, *Protecting Consumer Privacy* (2012), iv.

10 www.dmachoice.org/dma/static/about_dma.jsp.

11 www.networkadvertising.org/managing/opt_out.asp.

12 www.aboutads.info/choices/.

13 *APEC Privacy Framework*, www.apec.org/Groups/Committee-on-Trade-and-Investment/~/media/Files/Groups/ECSG/05_ecsg_privacyframewk.ashx.

CHAPTER FOUR

Medical Privacy:

HIPAA and GINA

Special privacy protections for healthcare date back thousands of years. The modern Hippocratic oath states, "I will respect the privacy of my patients, for their problems are not disclosed to me that the world may know."[1] There are several reasons why relatively strict privacy laws exist for healthcare. First, at the most basic level, medical information is related to the inner workings of one's body or mind. One's individual sense of self may be violated if others have unfettered access to this information. Second, most doctors believe that patients will be more open about their medical conditions if they have assurance that embarrassing medical facts will not be revealed. Third, medical privacy protections can protect employees from the risk of unequal treatment by employers. For instance, a person who uses birth control, has had an abortion, contracted a sexually transmitted disease or had psychiatric treatment could potentially be fired if a prejudiced employer gained access to this information. Health insurers and employers may also have incentives to avoid employing or insuring workers who suffer from expensive medical conditions or who may be at higher risk for such conditions based on their genetic background.

Despite the existence of strict laws protecting medical information within the healthcare industry, modern medical and insurance practices often use patient medical information quite intensively. For example, information about medical procedures is frequently used to assure accurate payment for those services. Doctors in one location may wish to access records about a patient's medical treatment in other cities in order to treat the patient appropriately. Researchers also use medical information, sometimes de-identified, in trying to find new patterns as they seek to develop cures for illnesses and promote public health. Records of many patients' outcomes may be used to evaluate healthcare providers on the overall quality of care.

This chapter explains the basic privacy and security provisions of the Health Insurance Portability and Accountability Act of 1996 (HIPAA), as updated by the Health Information Technology for Economic and Clinical Health Act of 2009 (HITECH). State healthcare privacy laws are not discussed here, but it is important to know that HIPAA does not preempt stricter state privacy laws. The chapter then discusses the Genetic Information Nondiscrimination Act of 2008 (GINA).

One source of potential confusion is that an individual's health-related information in the United States is legally protected in some settings but not others. HIPAA applies to "covered entities," notably including healthcare providers and insurers as well as "business associates" who receive data from covered entities. By contrast, health information in the hands of other entities is not protected by HIPAA. Suppose, for instance, that an individual buys a book about a rare form of cancer. That book purchase, along with other book purchases, is covered by the bookstore's privacy policy, but is not covered by HIPAA. Similarly, the records of a website that provides detailed information about this form of cancer may show that the same user has come back repeatedly with questions about the disease. The website, however, is not a medical provider or health insurer, and is outside the scope of HIPAA. Because U.S. privacy law varies by sector, the privacy professional should examine carefully whether personal information, including health-related information, is covered by HIPAA or some other sector-specific law.

1. The Health Insurance Portability and Accountability Act of 1996

The initial reason for HIPAA was not to protect privacy and security. Instead, Congress was seeking to meet other goals, including to improve the efficiency of healthcare delivery. To improve efficiency, HIPAA required entities receiving federal healthcare payments such as Medicare and Medicaid to shift reimbursement requests to electronic formats. At the same time, Congress realized that the shift from paper to electronic reimbursements posed a threat to privacy and security. Accordingly, HIPAA required the Department of Health and Human Services (HHS) to promulgate regulations to protect the privacy and security of healthcare information.

Protected health information (PHI) *is defined as any individually identifiable health information that is transmitted or maintained in any form or medium; is held by a covered entity or its business associate; identifies the individual or offers a reasonable basis for identification; is created or received by a covered entity or an employer; and relates to a past, present or future physical or mental condition, provision of health care or payment for health care to that individual.*

Electronic protected health information (ePHI) *is any PHI that is transmitted or maintained in electronic media (such as computer hard drives, magnetic tapes or disks, or digital memory cards, all of which are considered electronic storage media). Paper records, paper-to-paper fax transmissions, and voice communications (e.g., telephone) are not considered transmissions via electronic media.*

This statutory link to electronic reimbursements helps clarify which healthcare information is covered under HIPAA. Entities that are directly covered under HIPAA ("covered entities") include:[2]

- Healthcare providers (e.g., a doctor's office or hospital) that conduct certain transactions in electronic form
- Health plans (e.g., health insurers)

- Healthcare clearinghouses (e.g., third-party organizations that host, handle or process medical information)[3]

It is important to understand that HIPAA applies to these covered entities, but not to other healthcare providers and services. For instance, some doctors accept only cash or credit cards, and do not bill for insurance. They are not covered by HIPAA. More broadly, individuals reveal medical information in a wide variety of settings, ranging from conversations with friends and colleagues, to purchasing books about healthcare, to surfing on healthcare websites and even posting medical information online. These sorts of healthcare information are outside the scope of HIPAA.

Before the HITECH update, ***business associates*** *were not subject to HIPAA but became subject to privacy and security protections under the written contracts that they signed with covered entities. Under HITECH, however, HIPAA privacy and security rules are codified and apply directly to business associates.*[4]

Beyond covered entities, HIPAA creates important obligations for "business associates" (see the box). Under the Privacy Rule, a business associate is any person or organization, other than a member of a covered entity's workforce, that performs services and activities for, or on behalf of, a covered entity, if such services or activities involve the use or disclosure of PHI.[5] Business associates may provide services and activities such as claims processing, data analysis, utilization review and billing as well as legal, actuarial, accounting, consulting, data aggregation, management, administrative, accreditation and/or financial services.

When a covered entity engages another entity to provide the activities and services described above, the Privacy Rule requires that the covered entity enter into a business associate contract with that other entity. This contract must include provisions that pass the privacy and security standard down to the contracting entity. The business associate contract must be in writing, although it may be signed electronically as long as such signatures are valid as "written signatures" under the applicable state's contract laws.

1.1 The HIPAA Privacy Rule

In August 2000, HHS promulgated the regulations on standard electronic formats for healthcare transactions, known as the "Transactions Rule." This was followed in December 2000 by rules to protect the privacy of personal health information, known as the "Privacy Rule."[6] The initial HIPAA Privacy Rule was revised somewhat in 2002. In February 2003, HHS promulgated the final "Security Rule." The definition of "covered entity" is the same for all three rules.

1.1.1 The Privacy Rule and the Fair Information Privacy Practices

Compared with other U.S. privacy laws, HIPAA provides perhaps the most detailed implementation of the Fair Information Privacy Practices, including requirements concerning privacy notices, authorizations for use and disclosure of PHI, limits on use and disclosure to the minimum necessary, individual access and accounting rights, security safeguards, and accountability through administrative requirements and enforcement. There are also a number of important exceptions to the HIPAA rules. The following are some of the key privacy protections.

Privacy notices. The Privacy Rule generally requires a covered entity to provide a detailed privacy notice at the date of first service delivery. There are some defined exceptions to the notice requirements. For example, a privacy notice does not have to be provided when the healthcare provider has an "indirect treatment relationship" with the patient or in the case of medical emergencies. The rule is quite specific about elements that must be included in the notice, including detailed statements about individuals' rights with respect to their PHI.

Authorizations for uses and disclosures. Consistent with the statutory goal of improving efficiency in the healthcare system, HIPAA itself authorizes the use and disclosure of PHI for essential healthcare purposes: treatment, payment and operations (collectively, TPO), as well as for certain other established compliance purposes. Other uses or disclosures of PHI require the individual's opt-in authorization. An authorization is an independent document that specifically identifies the information to be used or disclosed, the purposes of the use or disclosure, the person or entity to which a disclosure may be made, and other information. A covered entity may not require an individual to sign an authorization as a condition of receiving treatment or participating in a health plan. Additional, strict rules apply for authorizations to use or disclose psychotherapy notes.

Specific rules define when the opt-in is required for marketing purposes. For instance, face-to-face communications by a covered entity to an individual are not considered "marketing."

"Minimum necessary" use or disclosure. Other than for treatment, covered entities must make reasonable efforts to limit the use and disclosure of PHI to the "minimum necessary" in order to accomplish the intended purpose. As discussed more fully below, covered entities may disclose PHI to a business associate (such as a billing company, third-party administrator, attorney or consultant) only if the covered entity has a contract ensuring that the business associate will be bound by all of the obligations applicable to the covered entity, including the minimum necessary standards.

Access and accountings of disclosures. Under the Privacy Rule, individuals have the right to access and copy their own PHI from a covered entity or a business associate. The right applies to PHI kept in a "designated record set," which is a fairly broad definition including a patient's medical records and billing records, or other records used by the covered entity to make decisions about individuals. Only fairly narrow exceptions exist to this right of access. Additionally, individuals have a right to receive an accounting of certain disclosures of their PHI that have been made. A reasonable charge may be assessed to cover the costs of providing access.

Individuals also have the right to amend PHI possessed by a covered entity. If the covered entity denies the request to amend the PHI, the individual may file a statement that must then be included in any future use or disclosure of the information.

Safeguards. The Privacy Rule requires that covered entities implement administrative, physical and technical safeguards to protect the confidentiality and integrity of all PHI. The HIPAA Security Rule requires both covered entities and business associates to implement administrative, physical and technical safeguards only for electronic PHI (ePHI). Similar to the Privacy Rule, the HIPAA Security Rule aims to prevent unauthorized use or disclosure of PHI. However, the Security Rule also aims to maintain the integrity and availability of ePHI. Accordingly, the Security Rule addresses data backup and disaster recovery, among other related issues. These are discussed further below.

Accountability. To foster compliance, covered entities are subject to a set of administrative requirements. Covered entities must designate a privacy official who is responsible for the development and implementation of privacy protections. Personnel must be trained, and complaint and other procedures must be in place.

Accountability is furthered by a range of enforcement agencies. The primary enforcer for the Privacy Rule in HHS is the Office for Civil Rights (OCR), which processes individual complaints and can assess civil monetary penalties of up to $1.5 million per year per type of violation. The OCR has assessed substantial penalties under HIPAA in recent years. For example, Cignet Health of Maryland was fined $4.3 million for violations related to the company's denial of access to patient records in 41 instances between 2008 and 2009.[7] Soon after that, OCR entered into a resolution agreement, including a $1 million settlement, with Massachusetts General Hospital for the loss of 192 billing records for HIV and AIDs patients.[8] The OCR has started to audit up to 150 covered entities per year to ensure HIPAA compliance.[9]

The U.S. Department of Justice has criminal enforcement authority, with prison sentences of up to 10 years. For the many companies within its jurisdiction, the FTC can bring enforcement actions for unfair and deceptive practices, even for entities covered by HIPAA. State attorneys general can also bring enforcement for unfair and deceptive practices, or pursuant to any applicable state medical privacy law.

1.1.2 Limits and Exceptions on the Privacy Rule

In issuing the Privacy Rule, HHS stressed the dual goals of protecting PHI while also improving the efficiency of the healthcare system. As mentioned above, the rule does not require authorizations for the major categories of treatment, payment and healthcare operations. Other limits on the scope of the rule include de-identified information and medical research.

De-identification. The Privacy Rule does not apply to information that has been "de-identified"—information that does not actually identify an individual and where there is no reasonable basis to believe that the information can be used to identify an individual. The Privacy Rule provides two methods for de-identifying data: (1) remove all of at least 17 data elements listed in the rule, such as name, phone number and address; or (2) have an expert certify that the risk of re-identifying the individuals is very small.

Research. The Privacy Rule has detailed provisions for how PHI is used for medical research purposes. Research can occur with the consent of the individual, or without consent if an authorized entity such as an institutional review board approves the research as consistent with the Privacy Rule and general rules covering research on human subjects. Research is permitted on de-identified information, and rules are more flexible if only a limited data set is released to researchers.

Other exceptions. The Privacy Rule contains a number of other exceptions under which PHI may be used without consent. These include information used for public health activities; to report victims of abuse, neglect or domestic violence; in judicial and administrative proceedings; for certain law enforcement activities; and for certain specialized governmental functions. A covered entity is required to release PHI to the individual to whom it pertains or to the person's representative (see "Access and Accountings of Disclosures," discussed above), and to the secretary of HHS to investigate compliance with the privacy rules.

1.2 The HIPAA Security Rule

The HIPAA Security Rule was finalized in February 2003. It establishes minimum security requirements for PHI that a covered entity receives, creates, maintains or transmits in electronic form (ePHI).[10] The Security Rule is designed to require covered entities to implement "reasonable" security measures in a technology-neutral manner. The goal is for all covered entities to implement "policies and procedures to prevent, detect, contain, and correct security violations."

The Security Rule is comprised of "standards" and "implementation specifications," which encompass administrative, technical and physical safeguards. Some of the implementation specifications are required, while others are considered "addressable." This means that the covered entity must assess whether it is an appropriate safeguard for the entity to adopt. If not, the covered entity must document why it is not reasonable, and, if appropriate, adopt an alternative measure.

The HIPAA Security Rule requires covered entities and business associates to:

1. Ensure the confidentiality, integrity and availability of all ePHI the covered entity creates, receives, maintains or transmits
2. Protect against any reasonably anticipated threats or hazards to the security or integrity of the ePHI
3. Protect against any reasonably anticipated uses or disclosures of such information that are not permitted or required under the Privacy Rule
4. Ensure compliance with the Security Rule by its workforce

As noted above, the Security Rule strives for a reasonable level of security. Accordingly, the rule permits a covered entity to "use any security measures that allow the covered entity to reasonably and appropriately implement the standards and implementation specifications." As it develops its security program, each covered entity must consider the following factors:

1. The size, complexity and capabilities of the covered entity
2. The covered entity's technical infrastructure, hardware and software security capabilities
3. The costs of security measures
4. The probability and criticality of potential risks to electronic protected health information

The HIPAA Security Rule also requires that:

1. Each covered entity must identify an individual who is responsible for the implementation and oversight of the Security Rule compliance program. (This may be the same person who oversees the Privacy Rule compliance program, if the organization is simple enough for these duties to be consolidated.)
2. Each covered entity must conduct initial and ongoing risk assessments. In particular, the covered entity must "conduct an accurate and thorough assessment of the potential risks and vulnerabilities to the confidentiality, integrity, and availability of electronic protected health information held by the covered entity." This assessment should identify potential risks and vulnerabilities, each of which must be addressed.
3. Each covered entity must implement a security awareness and training program for its workforce. Additionally, individual workers must be disciplined if they fail to comply with the policies and procedures.

2. The Health Information Technology for Economic and Clinical Health Act

HITECH was enacted as part of the American Recovery and Reinvestment Act of 2009 to promote the adoption and meaningful use of health information technology. HITECH codified and funded the Office of the National Coordinator for Health Information Technology and provided $19 billion in incentives for healthcare providers to adopt electronic health records and develop a national electronic health information exchange. HITECH also strengthened HIPAA to address the privacy impacts of the expanded use of electronic health records.[11]

2.1 Notice of Breach

In the event of a breach of unsecured information, a covered entity must conduct a risk assessment to determine the risk of harm. If there is a significant risk of harm (financial, reputational or other) from a breach, a covered entity must notify individuals within 60 days of discovery.[12] If a "business associate" discovers a breach it must notify the covered entity.[13] If the breach affects more than 500 people the covered entity must notify HHS immediately, and if the breach affects 500 or more in the same jurisdiction, it must notify the media.[14] All breaches requiring notice must be reported to

HHS at least annually. A breach applies only to "unsecured" information, and a covered entity can avoid liability if it utilizes encryption software to secure information.[15]

2.2 Increased Penalties

HHS has issued an interim final rule pursuant to HITECH that allows for penalties of up to $1.5 million for the most willful violations and extends criminal liability to individuals who misuse PHI. The enforcement rules provide for penalties even if the covered entity did not know of the violation.[16]

2.3 Limited Data

Patients who directly pay their provider for medical care may limit their PHI from being disclosed to a health plan. Furthermore, all disclosures should attempt to comply with the definition of a limited data set, and if this is not feasible then data disclosed must be the minimum amount necessary.[17]

2.4 Electronic Health Records (EHR)

The $19 billion in funding in HITECH has created important incentives for health providers to use EHRs more extensively. Providers who make "meaningful use" of EHRs can qualify for these funds.[18] In local markets, more practice groups are linking their EHRs with local hospitals. For broader geographic regions, there has been increased sharing of medical information toward the HHS goal of having a National Health Information Network.[19] Sharing of PHI is generally permitted under HIPAA to the extent necessary for treatment, payment or healthcare operations. Compliance issues become more important if information shared through EHRs is used for other purposes or with other entities, and such sharing can lawfully be done only with patient consent or under some other provision of HIPAA. Compliance also can become considerably more complex where the laws of different states apply to the same EHR system.

HITECH itself, along with providing funding for greater use of EHRs, made certain changes to HIPAA's legal treatment of EHRs. Covered entities must provide individuals with a copy of their EHR on request and must account for all non-oral disclosures made within three years on the request.[20] Additionally, covered entities may not sell EHRs without the consent of the patient and covered entities cannot receive payment for certain marketing plans.[21]

3. Genetic Information Nondiscrimination Act of 2008

GINA created new national limits on the use of genetic information in health insurance and employment.[22] In considering GINA, Congress found that genetic testing, before symptoms appeared, would allow individuals to take steps to reduce the likelihood of ultimately developing a disease or disorder. At the same time, such testing could create the risk of misusing that information for health insurance or employment.[23] Concerns about misuse were supported by historical examples of genetic discrimination, such as sterilization programs aimed at those with disorders that were perceived to be genetic, programs aimed at mandating sickle cell testing for African Americans, and pre-employment genetic screening of federal employees.[24] Generally, GINA prohibits health insurance companies from discriminating on the basis of genetic predispositions in the absence of manifest symptoms or from requesting that applicants receive genetic testing, and prohibits employers from using genetic information in making employment decisions.[25]

GINA amended a variety of existing pieces of legislation including, among others, the Employee Retirement Income Security Act (ERISA), the Social Security Act and the Civil Rights Act. The amendments to ERISA prohibit group health plan providers from adjusting premiums or other contribution schemes on the basis of genetic information, absent a manifestation of a disease or disorder.[26] GINA also amended ERISA to prohibit group health plan providers from requesting or requiring genetic testing in connection with the offering of group health plans, although an exception is carved out for requests for voluntary testing in connection with research.[27] For the research exception to apply, providers must notify the HHS secretary and make clear that compliance is voluntary, that noncompliance will have no effect on enrollment or contributions, and that no genetic information will be used for underwriting purposes.[28] The amendments to ERISA also allow for governmental enforcement.[29] A statutory penalty is set at $100 for each day of noncompliance (inclusive of the beginning date and date of rectification) with respect to each plan participant or beneficiary, although minimum penalties can rise to $15,000 in certain circumstances.[30] Some liability, however, may be avoided under this section if the grounds for liability could not have been discovered by exercising reasonable diligence.[31]

Similar provisions revise the Public Health Service Act and apply to participants in the individual market to prohibit adjustments to premiums or other contribution schemes on the basis of genetic information absent the manifestation of disease or disorder.[32] These revisions prohibit insurers from using a genetic predisposition to find an excludable preexisting condition.[33] Once again, the revisions allow for governmental enforcement against violators. Amendments to the Social Security Act extend similar provisions to the providers of Medicare supplemental insurance policies.[34] GINA also directs the secretary of HHS to revise HIPAA regulations such that genetic information is considered health information,[35] and the disclosure of such information may not be disclosed by covered entities, pursuant to HIPAA.[36]

Aside from health care insurance, GINA also takes aim at the possibility of employment discrimination based on genetic information in the absence of the manifestation of a disease or disorder.[37] Additionally, the employment-related sections of GINA prohibit discrimination against individuals because they have a family member who has manifested a disease.[38] These sections of GINA revised the Civil Rights Act and apply coextensively with that act.[39] Along with expressly prohibiting discrimination on the basis of genetic information, these portions of GINA prohibit employers from requiring, requesting or purchasing such genetic information about employees or family members unless an express exception applies.[40] Exceptions are provided for instances where (1) such a request is inadvertent, (2) the request is part of an employer-offered wellness program that the employee voluntarily participates in with written authorization, (3) the request is made to comply with the Family and Medical Leave Act of 1993, (4) an employer purchases commercially and publicly available materials that include the information, (5) the information is used for legally required genetic monitoring for toxin exposure in the workplace if the employee voluntarily participates with written authorization or (6) the employer conducts DNA analysis for law enforcement purposes and requests the information for quality-control purposes (i.e., to identify contamination).[41] These parts of GINA not only apply to employers, but also prohibit unions and training programs from excluding or expelling individuals on the basis of such information.[42]

GINA does recognize that employers or unions may have legitimate reasons for possessing such information (e.g., as part of a toxin exposure monitoring program or company-sponsored wellness program).[43] Accordingly, if an employer possesses such information, it must be kept on separate forms in separate medical files, and such files must be treated as confidential employee medical records.[44]

GINA itself does not provide for a private right of action, but—depending on the violation—private rights of action may be available under the federal laws that it revises, as well as under similar state laws.[45] Looking forward, GINA mandates the empanelment of a commission six years after its enactment (2014) to review the developments in the science of genetics and make recommendations as to whether to establish a disparate impact cause of action under GINA.[46]

4. Conclusion

U.S. law about medical and genetic privacy reflects the view that such personal information is particularly sensitive. This chapter has described the comprehensive HIPAA privacy and security rules, as updated by the HITECH Act, as well as GINA's comprehensive rules prohibiting discrimination based on genetic personal information. That said, there are also compelling reasons to use these categories of personal information. HIPAA notably enables use and disclosure of protected health information for treatment, payment and healthcare operations, as well as for medical research. Similarly, there is great interest in the promise of genetic research. Privacy professionals who work with health data need to be aware not only that strong protections are required, but also that such data is often used as permitted by the regulations.

Endnotes

1 Peter Tyson, "The Hippocratic Oath: Modern Version," WGBH Educational Foundation, 2001, www.pbs.org/wgbh/nova/body/hippocratic-oath-today.html.

2 "Are You a Covered Entity?" Centers for Medicare & Medicaid Services, www.cms.gov/Regulations-and-Guidance/HIPAA-Administrative-Simplification/HIPAAGenInfo/AreYouaCoveredEntity.html.

3 A healthcare clearinghouse means a public or private entity, including a billing service, repricing company, community health management information system or community health information system, and "value-added" networks and switches, that does either of the following functions:

- Processes or facilitates the processing of health information received from another entity in a nonstandard format or containing nonstandard data content into standard data elements or a standard transaction.

- Receives a standard transaction from another entity and processes or facilitates the processing of health information into nonstandard format or nonstandard data content for the receiving entity.

4 42 U.S.C. § 17921(2), www.hhs.gov/ocr/privacy/hipaa/understanding/coveredentities/hitechact.pdf; 45 C.F.R. § 160.103, www.hhs.gov/ocr/privacy/hipaa/understanding/coveredentities/businessassociates.html.

5 Please note that, in order to be a "business associate" under HIPAA, the person or organization must process PHI. Entities that do not process PHI (or whose access to PHI is truly incidental) are not business associates. Covered entities can themselves be business associates of other covered entities.

6 This HIPAA statute, Transaction Rule, Privacy Rule (with all the amendments), Security Rule, and published guidance can be found online at www.hhs.gov/ocr/privacy/.

7 "HHS Imposes a $4.3 Million Civil Money Penalty for HIPAA Privacy Rule Violations," www.hhs.gov/ocr/privacy/hipaa/news/cignetnews.html.

8 "Massachusetts General Hospital Settles Potential HIPAA Violations," www.hhs.gov/ocr/privacy/hipaa/enforcement/examples/massgeneralra.html.

9 "HIPAA Privacy & Security Audit Program," www.hhs.gov/ocr/privacy/hipaa/enforcement/audit/index.html.

10 HHS has indicated that it is considering extending the Security Rule to nonelectronic PHI, so that the provisions mirror the scope of protection offered by the Privacy Rule. (Note that the financial services counterpart, the Gramm-Leach-Bliley Act, does not limit applicability of its Safeguards Rule to electronic data. For health insurers subject to HIPAA and GLBA, the security program must encompass paper as well as electronic records.)

11 42 U.S.C. § 17921, www.hhs.gov/ocr/privacy/hipaa/understanding/coveredentities/hitechact.pdf.

12 42 U.S.C. § 17932, www.law.cornell.edu/uscode/html/uscode42/usc_sec_42_00017932----000-.html.

13 42 U.S.C. § 17932(h).

14 42 U.S.C. § 17932(e)2, (3), www.law.cornell.edu/uscode/html/uscode42/usc_sec_42_00017932----000-.html.

15 42 U.S.C. § 17932(h), www.law.cornell.edu/uscode/html/uscode42/usc_sec_42_00017932----000-.html.

16 42 U.S.C. § 1320d-5, www.law.cornell.edu/uscode/html/uscode42/usc_sec_42_00001320---d005-.html.

17 42 U.S.C. § 17935(a), (b), www.law.cornell.edu/uscode/html/uscode42/usc_sec_42_00017935----000-.html.

18 42 CFR §§ 412, 413, 422, 495; 45 CFR §170.32/.

19 http://www.nhinwatch.com/.

20 42 U.S.C. § 17935(c). The accounting for disclosures does not take effect until at least 2014; www.law.cornell.edu/uscode/html/uscode42/usc_sec_42_00017935----000-.html.

21 42 U.S.C. § 1936, www.law.cornell.edu/uscode/html/uscode42/usc_sec_42_00017936----000-.html.

22 Pub. L. 110-233, 122 Stat. 881 (2008).

23 *Id.* at § 2.

24 *Id.*

25 *See generally id.* at §§ 101, 104, 200.

26 *Id.* at § 101.

27 *Id.*

28 *Id.*

29 *Id.*

30 *Id.*

31 *Id.*

32 *Id.* at § 102.

33 *Id.*

34 *Id.* at § 104.

35 As described in 42 U.S.C. § 1171(4)(B) (2006).

36 *Id.* at § 105.

37 *Id.* at tit. II.

38 *Id.* at § 202.

39 *Id.* at §§ 202-205.

40 *Id.* at § 202.

41 *Id.*

42 *Id.* at §§ 203-205.

43 *Id.* at § 206.

44 *Id.* Such medical records should be kept in a manner consistent with the practices mandated for employee entrance exams under 42 U.S.C. § 12112(d)(3)(B) (2006).

45 For example, a private right of action for employment discrimination may be available under Title VII of the Civil Rights Act. Additionally, 21 states have private rights of action for genetic discrimination.

46 GINA, at § 208.

CHAPTER FIVE

Financial Privacy

Banking and other financial records have long been treated with high levels of confidentiality. Medieval and early modern banks often kept the identity of their borrowers secret and would not reveal intimate financial details of their customers. One reason for this confidentiality was to encourage borrowers to report honestly to the lender about their other debts and ability to pay. Another priority in the financial sector is to assure security—thieves and fraudsters can target individuals or transactions if they have access to these details.

This chapter focuses on restrictions on how financial services firms may collect, use and disclose personal information. Financial institutions are also subject to a variety of special rules about when they must disclose personal information. For instance, banks and other financial institutions have a variety of reporting obligations under the anti-money-laundering laws. These required disclosures are discussed in Section 5.

The chapter begins with the Fair Credit Reporting Act (FCRA), which was enacted in 1970 and substantially updated by the Fair and Accurate Credit Transactions Act of 2003 (FACTA). It next discusses the privacy and security portions of the Gramm-Leach-Bliley Act of 1999 (GLBA), which supplies the general framework for confidentiality of records in the financial services sector. It concludes with the relevant portions of the Dodd-Frank Wall Street Reform and Consumer Protection Act of 2010. That law, passed in the wake of the financial crisis that struck in 2008, created a new regulatory agency, the Consumer Financial Protection Bureau (CFPB). The CFPB now has rule-making authority for the FCRA, as updated by FACTA, as well as for most financial institutions under GLBA, and shares enforcement authority for these with the FTC and banking regulators.

1. The Fair Credit Reporting Act

The FCRA was enacted in 1970 to regulate the consumer reporting industry and provide privacy rights in consumer reports. Specifically, FCRA mandates accurate and relevant data collection, provides consumers with the ability to access and correct their information, and limits the use of consumer reports to defined permissible purposes.[1]

The origins of the FCRA can be traced to the rise of consumer credit in the United States. In the post–World War II era, merchants began to share more in-depth customer data in order to facilitate lending to households. By the 1960s, consumer credit was critical, but increasingly, individuals were being harmed by inaccurate information that they could neither see nor correct. In response, Congress passed the FCRA, the first federal law to regulate the use of personal information by private businesses.[2]

FCRA amendments in 1996 strengthened consumer access and correction rights and included provisions for non-consumer-initiated transactions (also known as "prescreening"). The FCRA was further amended by FACTA, with provisions related to identity theft and other subjects.[3]

The FCRA regulates any "consumer reporting agency" (CRA) that furnishes a "consumer report." A CRA is any person or entity that compiles or evaluates personal information for the purpose of furnishing consumer reports to third parties for a fee. Three well-known examples of CRAs are Equifax, TransUnion LLC (TransUnion) and Experian Information Solutions. There are thousands of smaller CRAs that compile personal records, such as criminal records or driving histories, for other consumer reporting purposes, such as preemployment screening.

A consumer report is any communication by a CRA related to an individual that pertains to the person's:

- Creditworthiness
- Credit standing
- Credit capacity
- Character
- General reputation
- Personal characteristics
- Mode of living

and that is used in whole or in part for the purpose of serving as a factor in establishing a consumer's eligibility for credit, insurance, employment or other business purpose.

Users of consumer reports must meet four main requirements under the FCRA:

1. Third-party data for substantive decision making must be appropriately accurate, current and complete.
2. Consumers must receive notice when third-party data is used to make adverse decisions about them.
3. Consumer reports may be used only for permissible purposes.
4. Consumers must have access to their consumer reports and an opportunity to dispute them or correct any errors.

Additionally, users of consumer reports must comply with other requirements, such as record keeping, providing certifications to the CRAs and securely disposing of the consumer report data.

The FCRA also specifically requires CRAs to:

- Provide consumers with access to the information contained in their consumer reports, as well as the opportunity to dispute any inaccurate information
- Take reasonable steps to ensure the maximum possible accuracy of information in the consumer report
- Not report negative information that is outdated; in most cases this means account data more than seven years old or bankruptcies more than 10 years old
- Provide consumer reports only to entities that have a permissible purpose under the FCRA
- Maintain records regarding entities that received consumer reports
- Provide consumer assistance as required by FTC rules

As discussed below, the FCRA imposes obligations on organizations that are not CRAs, including "users" (lenders, insurers, employers and others who use consumer reports) and "furnishers" (lenders, retailers, and others who furnish credit history or other personal information to the CRAs). Additionally, as also discussed below, companies that extend credit to consumers, even if they do not use consumer reports to make credit decisions, are now required to implement a "Red Flag" program to detect and deter identity theft.

Violations of FCRA are enforced by the FTC, the CFPB and state attorneys general. Under Dodd-Frank, rule-making authority shifted from the FTC to the CFPB. Individuals also have a private right of action, with damages in recent years exceeding $100,000 in a number of cases. Noncompliance can include civil and criminal penalties. In addition to actual damages, violators are subject to statutory damages of at least $1,000 per violation, and at least $2,500 for willful violations.

1.1 Notice Requirements Under FCRA

In 2004 the FTC published a notice to all users of consumer reports of their obligations under the FCRA.[4] "Users" include employers who use consumer reports in employment decisions as well as lenders, insurers and others. CRAs are required to provide this notice of their obligations to users of consumer reports.

1. Users must have a permissible purpose. Congress has limited the use of consumer reports to protect consumers' privacy. All users must have a "permissible purpose" under the FCRA to obtain a consumer report. Such purposes include obtaining reports:

    - As ordered by a court or a federal grand jury subpoena
    - As instructed by the consumer in writing
    - For the extension of credit as a result of an application from a consumer, or the review or collection of a consumer's account
    - For employment purposes, including hiring and promotion decisions, where the consumer has given written permission

- For the underwriting of insurance as a result of an application from a consumer
- When there is a legitimate business need, in connection with a business transaction that is initiated by the consumer
- To review a consumer's account to determine whether the consumer continues to meet the terms of the account
- To determine a consumer's eligibility for a license or other benefit granted by a governmental instrumentality required by law to consider an applicant's financial responsibility or status
- For use by a potential investor or servicer, or current insurer, in a valuation or assessment of the credit or prepayment risks associated with an existing credit obligation
- For use by state and local officials in connection with the determination of child support payments, or modifications and enforcement thereof

  In addition, creditors and insurers may obtain certain consumer report information for the purpose of making "prescreened" unsolicited offers of credit or insurance (Section 604[c] of the act).

2. Users must provide certifications. Section 604(f) of the FCRA prohibits any person from obtaining a consumer report from a CRA unless the person has certified to the CRA the permissible purpose(s) for which the report is being obtained and certifies that the report will not be used for any other purpose.
3. Users must notify consumers when adverse actions are taken. The term adverse action is defined very broadly to include all business, credit and employment actions affecting consumers that can be considered to have a negative impact, such as denying or canceling credit or insurance, or denying employment or promotion. No adverse action occurs in a credit transaction where the creditor makes a counteroffer that is accepted by the consumer.

The FCRA also details a number of adverse actions that can be taken as result of obtaining or reviewing the information contained within a consumer credit report.

Adverse actions based on information obtained from a CRA. If a user takes any type of adverse action (as defined by the FCRA, action that is based, even in part, on information contained in a consumer report), the FCRA requires the user to notify the consumer. The notification may be done in writing, orally or by electronic means. It must include the following elements:

- The name, address and telephone number of the CRA (including a toll-free telephone number, if it is a nationwide CRA) that provided the report
- A statement that the CRA did not make the adverse decision and is not able to explain why the decision was made

- A statement setting forth the consumer's right to obtain a free disclosure of the consumer's file from the CRA if the consumer makes a request within 60 days
- A statement setting forth the consumer's right to dispute directly with the CRA the accuracy or completeness of any information provided by the CRA

Adverse actions based on information obtained from third parties that are not consumer reporting agencies. If a person denies (or increases the charge for) credit for personal, family or household purposes based either wholly or partly upon information from a person other than a CRA, and the information is the type covered by the FCRA, Section 615(b)(1) requires that the user clearly and accurately disclose to the consumer his or her right to be informed of the nature of the information that was relied upon, if the consumer makes a written request within 60 days of notification. The user must then provide the disclosure within a reasonable period of time following the consumer's written request.

Adverse actions based on information obtained from affiliates. If a person takes an adverse action involving insurance, employment or a credit transaction initiated by the consumer, based on the type of information covered by the FCRA, and this information was obtained from an entity affiliated with the user of the information by common ownership or control, Section 615(b)(2) requires the user to notify the consumer of the adverse action. The notice must inform the consumer that he or she may obtain a disclosure of the nature of the information relied upon by making a written request within 60 days of receiving the adverse action notice. If the consumer makes such a request, the user must disclose the nature of the information no later than 30 days after receiving the request. If consumer report information is shared among affiliates and then used for an adverse action, the user must make a similar adverse action disclosure.

1.2 Disclosures Under FCRA

The FCRA requires disclosure by all persons who use credit scores in making or arranging loans secured by residential real property. These persons must provide credit scores and other information about credit scores to applicants. Further, in some instances the person must provide a risk-based pricing notice to the consumer in accordance with regulations jointly prescribed by the CFPB (formerly the FTC) and the Federal Reserve Board. These notices are required if a consumer report is used by an individual or organization in connection with an application for credit or a grant, extension or provision of credit to a consumer on terms that are less favorable than the most favorable terms available to a substantial proportion of consumers acquiring loans from or through that person.

1.2.1 Consumer Reports and Employment

The FCRA imposes certain additional obligations on organizations that intend to use consumer report information for employment purposes. The user of such information must:

- Make a clear and conspicuous written notification to the consumer before the report is obtained, in a document that consists solely of the disclosure that a consumer report may be obtained by the employer.
- Obtain prior written consumer authorization in order to obtain a consumer report. Authorization to access reports during the term of employment may be obtained at the time of employment.
- Certify to the CRA that the above steps have been followed, that the information being obtained will not be used in violation of any federal or state equal opportunity law or regulation, and that, if any adverse action is to be taken based on the consumer report, a copy of the report and a summary of the consumer's rights will be provided to the consumer.
- Before taking an adverse action, provide a copy of the report to the consumer as well as the summary of the consumer's rights. (The user should receive this summary from the CRA.) An adverse action notice should be sent after the adverse action is taken.

An adverse action notice also is required in employment situations if credit information (other than transactions and experience data) obtained from an affiliate is used to deny employment.

1.3 Employee Investigations

The FCRA provides special procedures for investigations of suspected misconduct by an employee or for compliance with federal, state or local laws and regulations or the rules of a self-regulatory organization, and compliance with written policies of the employer. These investigations are not treated as consumer reports as long as (1) the employer or its agent complies with the procedures set forth in the act, (2) no credit information is used and (3) a summary describing the nature and scope of the inquiry is provided to the employee if an adverse action is taken based on the investigation.

1.4 Investigative Consumer Reports

Investigative consumer reports contain information about a consumer's character, general reputation, personal characteristics and mode of living. This information is obtained through personal interviews by an entity or person that is a CRA.

Consumers who are the subjects of such reports are given special rights under the FCRA. If a user intends to obtain an investigative consumer report, Section 606 of the act requires that the user of the report disclose its use to the consumer. The disclosure is subject to the following requirements:

- The consumer must be informed that an investigative consumer report may be obtained.
- The disclosure must be in writing and must be mailed or otherwise delivered to the consumer some time before but not later than three days after the date on which the report was first requested.

- The disclosure must include a statement informing the consumer of his or her right to request additional disclosures of the nature and scope of the investigation, and the summary of consumer rights required by the FCRA. The summary of consumer rights will be provided by the CRA that conducts the investigation.
- The user must certify to the CRA that the required disclosures have been made and that the user will make the necessary disclosure to the consumer.
- Upon written request of a consumer made within a reasonable period of time after the required disclosures, the user must make a complete disclosure of the nature and scope of the investigation.
- The nature and scope disclosure must be made in a written statement that is mailed or otherwise delivered to the consumer no later than five days after the date on which the request was received from the consumer or the report was first requested, whichever is later.

1.5 Medical Information Under FCRA

FCRA limits the use of medical information obtained from CRAs, other than payment information that appears in a coded form and does not identify the medical provider. If medical information is to be used for an insurance transaction, the consumer must provide consent to the user of the report, or the information must be coded. If the report is to be used for employment purposes—or in connection with a credit transaction, except as provided in regulations issued by the banking and credit union regulators—the consumer must provide specific written consent and the medical information must be relevant. Any user who receives medical information shall not disclose the information to any other person, except where necessary to carry out the purpose for which the information was disclosed, or as permitted by statute, regulation or order.

1.6 "Prescreened" Lists

FCRA permits creditors and insurers to obtain limited consumer report information for use in connection with firm unsolicited offers of credit or insurance, under certain circumstances and conditions. This practice is known as "prescreening" and typically involves obtaining from a CRA a list of consumers who meet certain preestablished criteria. If any person intends to use prescreened lists, that person must (1) before the offer is made, establish the criteria that will be relied upon to make the offer and to grant credit or insurance, and (2) maintain such criteria on file for a three-year period beginning on the date on which the offer is made to each consumer. In addition, any user must include with each written solicitation a clear and conspicuous statement that:

- Information contained in a consumer's CRA file was used in connection with the transaction.
- The consumer received the offer because he or she satisfied the criteria for creditworthiness or insurability used to screen for the offer.

- Credit or insurance may not be extended if, after the consumer responds, it is determined that the consumer does not meet the criteria used for screening or any applicable criteria bearing on creditworthiness or insurability, or the consumer does not furnish required collateral.
- The consumer may prohibit the use of information in his or her file in connection with future prescreened offers of credit or insurance by contacting the notification system established by the CRA that provided the report. The statement must include the address and toll-free telephone number of the appropriate notification system.

Beginning in 2005, the companies that send prescreened solicitations of credit or insurance were required to supply simple and easy-to-understand notices explaining the consumer's right to opt out of receiving such offers. The FTC issued a rule requiring a layered notice with opt-out rights included on the first page. The FTC also issued a new consumer education brochure concerning prescreening.

2. The Fair and Accurate Credit Transactions Act

In 2003 Congress passed FACTA, which made substantial amendments to the FCRA.[5] FACTA preempts stricter state laws in most areas, although states retain some powers to enact laws addressing identity theft. FACTA enacted a number of consumer protections. It requires truncation of credit and debit card numbers, so that receipts do not reveal the full credit or debit card number. It gives consumers new rights to an explanation of their credit scores. It also gives individuals the right to request a free annual credit report from each of the three national consumer credit agencies—Equifax, TransUnion and Experian. Along with other identity theft protections, FACTA requires regulators to promulgate a Disposal Rule and a Red Flags Rule.

In 2010, the FTC issued new rules updating the manner of disclosure required by the companies advertising "free credit reports." The updates "include prominent disclosures designed to prevent consumers from confusing these 'free' offers with the federally mandated free annual file disclosures." Such a disclosure must be "easily readable," and the rules give examples of fonts that are, and are not, easily readable.[6] The FTC's complete set of regulations is available at www.ftc.gov/credit.

2.1 The Disposal Rule

The Disposal Rule requires any individual or entity that uses a consumer report, or information derived from a consumer report, for a business purpose to dispose of that consumer information in a way that prevents unauthorized access and misuse of the data. Consumer reports can be electronic or written. The rule applies to both small and large organizations, including consumer reporting agencies, lenders, employers, insurers, landlords, car dealers, attorneys, debt collectors and government agencies.

"Disposal" includes any discarding, abandonment, donation, sale or transfer of information. The standard for disposal requires practices that are "reasonable" to protect against unauthorized access to or use of the consumer data. Factors to consider include the sensitivity of information being disposed of, the costs and benefits of various disposal methods, and available technology.[7] Examples of acceptable, reasonable measures include developing and complying with policies to:

- Burn, pulverize, or shred papers containing consumer report information so that the information cannot be read or reconstructed
- Destroy or erase electronic files or media containing consumer report information so that the information cannot be read or reconstructed
- Conduct due diligence and hire a document destruction contractor to dispose of material specifically identified as consumer report information consistent with the rule

Enforcement of the Disposal Rule is by the FTC, the federal banking regulators and the CFPB. Violators may face civil liability as well as federal and state enforcement actions. Financial institutions that are subject to both the FACTA Disposal Rule and the Gramm-Leach-Bliley Safeguards Rule (discussed in Section 3 below) should incorporate required disposal practices into the information security program that the Safeguards Rule mandates. They should also be aware of any state disposal rules that may impose broader requirements.

2.2 The Red Flags Rule

The Red Flags Rule was originally promulgated under FACTA. Section 114 of the act required agencies that regulate financial entities to develop a set of rules to mandate the detection, prevention and mitigation of identity theft. The FTC, together with federal banking agencies, authored the Red Flags Rule.[8] As with the rest of the FCRA and FACTA, the CFPB has now gained rule-making and enforcement authority.

The rule requires certain financial entities to develop and implement written identity theft detection programs that can identify and respond to the "red flags" that signal identity theft. Specifically, the rule applies to financial institutions and creditors. "Financial institution" is defined as all banks, savings and loan associations and credit unions. It also includes all other entities that hold a "transaction account" belonging to a consumer. Due to confusion over which entities qualify as covered "creditors," however, enforcement of the rule was delayed several times until a clarification was published in 2010.[9]

The Red Flag Program Clarification Act of 2010 was passed in response to concern that the definition of "creditor" extended to implicate unintended entities, such as attorneys and health providers, simply because they allow customers to pay their bills after the time of service.[10] The clarification narrows the previously broad definition of "creditor," as well as the circumstances under which they are covered by the rule. It eliminates entities that extend credit only "for expenses incidental to a service." The rule still applies to entities that, regularly and in the course of business:

- Obtain or use consumer reports in connection with a credit transaction
- Furnish information to consumer reporting agencies in connection with a credit transaction
- Advance funds to or on behalf of someone, except for expenses incidental to a service provided by the creditor to that person

The new law also authorizes regulations that apply the rule to businesses whose accounts should be "subject to a reasonably foreseeable risk of identity theft." The rule does not provide a checklist for specific "red flags" that must be included in the identity theft detection programs. Rather, the program should generally identify relevant patterns, practices and specific forms of activity that are red flags of possible identity theft, incorporate these flags into the program and update the program regularly to reflect changes in risks. Each organization is required to develop its own list of red flags, but examples cited by the FTC include alerts, notifications or warnings from a consumer reporting agency; suspicious identification documents; suspicious personal identifying data; and unusual use of a covered account.

3. Gramm-Leach-Bliley Act

Title V of the Financial Services Modernization Act of 1999 led to the promulgation of both a Privacy Rule and a Safeguards Rule.[11] The act, also known as the Gramm-Leach-Bliley Act (GLBA) was major legislation that reflected and codified the consolidation of the U.S. banking, securities and insurance industries in the late 1990s. As previously separate types of financial institutions began to merge, substantial concerns arose over how consumer data would be collected, used and shared among the newly formed holding companies and their subsidiaries within the financial sector.

These privacy provisions were spurred by enforcement actions against major banks for controversial data practices. Prior to GLBA's passage, a number of leading financial institutions were found to have sold detailed customer information, including account numbers and other highly sensitive data, to telemarketing firms. Subsequently, the firms used the account numbers to charge customers for unsolicited services.

One of the most prominent cases involved U.S. Bancorp and the telemarketing firm MemberWorks.[12] The Minnesota attorney general's office brought suit in 1999, as Congress was considering GLBA. The suit resulted in a $3 million settlement for allegations that the bank had sent detailed customer information to the telemarketing firm, including account numbers and related information that enabled the marketer to directly withdraw funds from the customer account. The allegations also stated that the marketing firm was using a "negative option," where customers were charged automatically for services unless they later sent a specific request not to be billed.

The U.S. Bancorp/MemberWorks case focused popular and regulatory attention on the prevalence of data-sharing relationships between banks with third-party marketers. A group of 25 attorneys general brought additional actions against major financial institutions in an attempt to address these practices. Congress responded to these events by including significant privacy and security protections for consumers in GLBA and mandating further rule-making on privacy and security by the Federal Trade Commission, federal banking regulators and state insurance regulators. Financial institutions were required to substantially comply with GLBA's requirements in 2001.

The passage of GLBA led to major changes in the structure of the financial services industry, and provided for the creation of new financial service holding companies that offer a full range of financial products. It eliminated legal barriers to affiliations among banks, securities firms, insurance companies and other financial services companies. Under GLBA's privacy provisions, financial institutions are required to:

- Store personal financial information in a secure manner
- Provide notice of their policies regarding the sharing of personal financial information
- Provide consumers with the choice to opt out of sharing some personal financial information

3.1 Scope and Enforcement of GLBA

GLBA applies to "financial institutions" (FI), which are defined broadly as any U.S. companies that are "significantly engaged" in financial activities. Financial institutions include entities such as banks, insurance providers, securities firms, payment settlement services, check cashing services, credit counselors and mortgage lenders, among others.

GLBA regulates FI management of "nonpublic personal information," defined as "personally identifiable financial information (i) provided by a consumer to a financial institution, (ii) resulting from a transaction or service performed for the consumer, or (iii) otherwise obtained by the financial institution." Excluded from the definition are publicly available information and any consumer list that is derived without using personally identifiable financial information.[13]

This encompasses a wide range of information that is not exclusively financial in nature. For example, the name of a financial institution's customer is considered nonpublic personal financial information, covered under the act, because it indicates the existence of a relationship between the institution and the consumer that is financial in nature.

GLBA requires financial institutions to protect consumers' nonpublic personal information under privacy rules that were promulgated originally by the FTC and FI regulators. In 2011, with the passage of the Dodd-Frank Act, the CFPB assumed this rule-making power, with exceptions for the Securities and Exchange Commission and the Commodity Futures Trading Commission.

As enacted in 1999, federal financial regulators enforced GLBA for the institutions in their jurisdiction, such as for the Federal Reserve, Office of the Comptroller of the Currency, Federal Deposit Insurance Corporation and Securities and Exchange Commission. Banking and related financial institutions that fail to comply with GLBA requirements may be subject to penalties under the Financial Institutions Reform, Recovery and Enforcement Act (FIRREA). FIRREA penalties range from up to $5,500 for violations of laws and regulations, to up to $27,500 if violations are unsafe, unsound or reckless, to up to $1.1 million for "knowing" violations. For financial institutions not within the jurisdiction of one of the other agencies, the FTC originally had enforcement authority. Under the Dodd-Frank Act, the CFPB also now has enforcement authority for the GLBA Privacy and Safeguards Rules, under its general enforcement powers, discussed further below in Section 4.

At the state level, state attorneys general can enforce GLBA. Stricter state laws are not preempted under GLBA.[14] The validity of stricter state laws, however, can be subject to challenge because there is limited preemption under FCRA, so courts would need to determine which federal financial privacy statute governs for a particular state law. Although there is no private right of action under GLBA, failure to comply with certain notice requirements may be considered a deceptive trade practice by state and federal authorities. Some states also have private rights of action for this type of violation.

GLBA's privacy protections generally apply to "consumers," or individuals who obtain financial products or services from a financial institution to be used primarily for personal, family or household purposes. Many of the act's requirements relate to the subset of consumers who are also "customers"—consumers with whom the organization has an ongoing relationship. Financial services companies that do not have such "consumer customers" are not subject to some of GLBA's requirements, such as those related to notice.

Major components of the GLBA Privacy Rule provide that financial institutions must:

1. Prepare and provide to customers clear and conspicuous notice of the financial institution's information-sharing policies and practices. These notices must be provided when a customer relationship is established and annually thereafter.
2. Clearly provide customers the right to opt out of having their nonpublic personal information shared with nonaffiliated third parties (subject to a number of significant exceptions, including for joint marketing and processing of consumer transactions).
3. Refrain from disclosing to any nonaffiliated third-party marketer, other than a consumer reporting agency, an account number or similar form of access code to a consumer's credit card, deposit or transaction account.
4. Comply with regulatory standards established by certain government authorities to protect the security and confidentiality of customer records and information, and protect against security threats and unauthorized access to or certain uses of such records or information.

3.2 GLBA and Privacy Notices

The GLBA Privacy Rule establishes a standard for privacy notices under which a financial institution must provide initial and annual privacy notices to consumers on nine categories of information, and must process opt-outs within 30 days. The privacy notice itself must be a clear, conspicuous and accurate statement of the company's privacy practices and must include the following:

- What information the financial institution collects about its consumers and customers
- With whom it shares the information
- How it protects or safeguards the information
- An explanation of how a consumer may opt out of having his information shared through a reasonable opt-out process[15]

Provided that this notice standard is met, a financial institution may share any information it has with its affiliated companies and joint marketing partners, which are other financial institutions with whom the entity jointly markets a financial product or service.[16] In addition, other than for defined exceptions, a financial institution may also share consumer information with nonaffiliated companies and other third parties, but only after disclosing information-sharing practices to customers and providing them with the opportunity to opt out.

It should be noted that the GLBA prohibits financial institutions from disclosing consumer account numbers to nonaffiliated companies for purposes of telemarketing and direct mail marketing (including through e-mail), even if the consumer has not opted out of sharing the information for marketing purposes. Also, a financial institution must ensure that service providers will not use provided consumer data for anything other than the intended purpose.

There are certain situations in which the consumer has no right to opt out. For example, a consumer cannot opt out if:

- A financial institution shares information with outside companies that provide essential services like data processing or servicing accounts
- The disclosure is legally required
- A financial institution shares customer data with outside service providers that market the financial company's products or services

In 2009, eight federal regulatory agencies issued a model short privacy notice.[17] The model notice implemented the Financial Services Regulatory Relief Act of 2006, which requires the agencies to propose a succinct and comprehensible model form that allows consumers to easily compare the privacy practices of different financial institutions.[18] Financial institutions that use the model notice satisfy the disclosure requirements for notices, but they are not required to use it.

3.3 The GLBA Safeguards Rule

Along with privacy standards and rules, GLBA requires financial institutions to maintain security controls to protect the confidentiality and integrity of personal consumer information, including both electronic and paper records. The regulatory agencies established such standards in the form of a final rule, the Safeguards Rule, that became effective in 2003.[19]

The GLBA Safeguards Rule requires financial institutions to develop and implement a comprehensive "information security program," which is defined as a program that contains "administrative, technical and physical safeguards" to protect the security, confidentiality and integrity of customer information.[20] The program must be appropriate for the size, complexity, nature and scope of the activities of the institution. Thus, similar to the GLBA Privacy Rule, the Safeguards Rule distinguishes the concepts of security, confidentiality and integrity, but suggests that all three concepts are integral to a complete understanding of security.

The information security program required under the rule must contain certain elements, including a designated employee to coordinate the program, audit systems to determine risks, and certain procedures to take with service providers to assure that the security of the information is maintained.

Under the GLBA Safeguards Rule, a financial institution must provide the following three levels of security for consumer information:

1. Administrative security, which includes program definition, management of workforce risks, employee training and vendor oversight
2. Technical security, which covers computer systems, networks and applications in addition to access controls and encryption
3. Physical security, which includes facilities, environmental safeguards, business continuity and disaster recovery

Pursuant to the Safeguards Rule, the administrative, technical and physical safeguards to be implemented must be reasonably designed to (1) insure the security and confidentiality of customer information, (2) protect against any anticipated threats or hazards to the security or integrity of the information and (3) protect against unauthorized access to or use of the information that could result in substantial harm or inconvenience to any customer.[21] Maintaining the security of this information essentially means protecting the confidentiality and integrity of information, and restricting access to it.

The Safeguards Rule does allow for flexibility in implementing a security program, stating that the program must contain safeguards that are "appropriate" to the entity's size and complexity, the nature and scope of the entity's activities, and the sensitivity of any customer information at issue.[22] The Safeguards Rule requires that certain basic elements be included in a security program. Each institution must:

1. Designate an employee to coordinate the safeguards
2. Identify and assess the risks to customer information in each relevant area of the company's operation, and evaluate the effectiveness of the current safeguards for controlling those risks
3. Design and implement a safeguard program and regularly monitor and test it
4. Select appropriate service providers and enter into agreements with them to implement safeguards
5. Evaluate and adjust the program in light of relevant circumstances, including changes in business arrangements or operations, or the results of testing and monitoring of safeguards[23]

3.4 California SB-1

California SB-1, also known as the California Financial Information Privacy Act, expands the financial privacy protections afforded under the federal Gramm-Leach-Bliley Act.[24] SB-1 increases the disclosure requirements of financial institutions and grants consumers increased rights with regard to the sharing of information. Violation of SB-1 in cases of negligent noncompliance can be punished with statutory damages of $2,500 per consumer, up to a cap of $500,000 per occurrence. In cases of willful noncompliance, there is no $500,000 damage cap.

Under the legislation, opt-in and opt-out requirements exist for financial institutions as follows: Written opt-in consent is required for a financial institution to share personal information with nonaffiliated third parties. Opt-in provisions must be presented on a form titled "Important Privacy Choices for Consumers" and be written in simple English. Additionally, SB-1 grants consumers the ability to opt out of information sharing between their financial institutions and affiliates not in the same line of business. A financial institution does not, however, need to obtain consumer consent in order to share nonmedical information with its wholly owned subsidiaries engaged in the same line of business—insurance, banking or securities—if they are regulated by the same functional regulator.

4. Dodd-Frank Wall Street Reform and Consumer Protection Act

In response to the financial crisis that became acute in 2008, Congress enacted the Dodd-Frank Wall Street Reform and Consumer Protection Act, which was signed into law in June 2010. Along with numerous other reforms, Title X of the act created the new Consumer Financial Protection Bureau (CFPB) as an independent bureau within the Federal Reserve.

The CFPB oversees the relationship between consumers and providers of financial products and services. It holds broad authority to examine, write regulations and bring enforcement actions concerning businesses that provide financial products or services, including service providers.[25] The CFPB assumes rule-making authority for specific existing laws related to financial privacy and other consumer issues, such as the FCRA, GLBA and Fair Debt Collection Practices Act.[26] It has enforcement authority over all nondepository financial institutions,[27] and over all depository institutions with more than $10 billion in assets.[28] For depository institutions with assets of $10 billion or less, CFPB promulgates rules but enforcement power remains with banking regulators.[29]

One potentially important innovation in the act is a change in the usual language about "unfair and deceptive" acts or practices. As discussed in multiple places in this book, the FTC and state attorneys general have long had the power to enforce against unfair and deceptive acts and practices. The CFPB also can now bring enforcement actions for unfairness and deception. In addition, the CFPB has a new power to enforce against "abusive acts and practices." An abusive act or practice:

- *Materially interferes with the ability of a consumer to understand a term or condition of a consumer financial product or service or*
- *Takes unreasonable advantage of—*
  - *A lack of understanding on the part of the consumer of the material risks, costs, or conditions of the product or service;*
  - *The inability of the consumer to protect its interests in selecting or using a consumer financial product or service; or*
  - *The reasonable reliance by the consumer on a covered person to act in the interests of the consumer.*[30]

Because this is new statutory language, the precise meaning of "abusive act or practice" will only become known over time. By its terms, however, enforcement actions for abusive acts or practices may well apply to privacy notices and other aspects of privacy and security protections by financial institutions.

CFPB enforcement authority includes the ability to conduct investigations and issue subpoenas, hold hearings and commence civil actions against offenders.[31] Civil penalties vary from $5,000 per day for federal consumer privacy law violations to $25,000 per day for reckless violations, and $1 million for knowing violations.[32] Further, state attorneys general are also authorized to bring civil actions in enforcement of the law or regulations.[33]

5. Required Disclosure Under Anti-Money-Laundering Laws

The privacy and security rules discussed above typically restrict uses and disclosures of personal information. Financial institutions are also subject to a variety of requirements to retain records and, in some instances, disclose personal financial information to the government. Financial institutions in general have intricate accounting and control systems to document transactions and reduce the risk of fraud. Banks have also long been closely supervised by the government, to ensure the safety and soundness of the banks and for other reasons. Financial institutions thus have more detailed record retention rules than most other kinds of companies.

In recent decades, anti-money-laundering laws have become a major additional basis for record retention and mandatory disclosure to the government. U.S. anti-money-laundering laws stem from the Bank Secrecy Act of 1970, which targeted organized crime groups and others who used large cash transactions. The laws became stricter as part of the USA Patriot Act of 2001, with its focus on antiterrorism efforts. The fundamental goal of anti-money-laundering laws is to "follow the money."[34] The idea of thorough record keeping is that it will help detect and deter illegal activity, and provide evidence for proving illegality.[35]

5.1 The Bank Secrecy Act of 1970

The Bank Secrecy Act of 1970 (BSA), also known as the Currency and Foreign Transactions Reporting Act of 1970, authorizes the U.S. treasury secretary to issue regulations that impose extensive record-keeping and reporting requirements on financial institutions.[36] Specifically, financial institutions must keep records and file reports on certain financial transactions, including currency transactions in excess of $10,000, which may be relevant to criminal, tax or regulatory proceedings.

The BSA applies broadly to its own definition of "financial institutions," which uses different language than GLBA and so may differ in some cases. The BSA applies to banks, securities brokers and dealers, money services businesses, telegraph companies, casinos, card clubs and other entities subject to supervision by any state or federal bank supervisory authority. The scope of covered institutions has expanded over time, to address the problem that criminals have an incentive to exploit whatever institutions are not already covered by the anti-money-laundering laws.

The BSA contains regulations relating to currency transactions, transportation of monetary instruments and the purchase of currency-like instruments. For example, the BSA generally requires currency transactions over $10,000 to be reported to the IRS per the regulations, using a Currency Transaction Report, Form 4789. Similarly, the BSA regulations cover purchases of bank checks, drafts, cashier's checks, money orders or traveler's checks for $3,000 or more in currency. The rules require that the entity collect and report information, including the name and address and Social Security number of the purchaser, the date of purchase, type of instrument, and serial numbers and dollar amounts of the instruments.

The BSA regulates certain wire transfers, including funds transfers and transmittals of funds by financial institutions. Certain funds transfers are exempted from the regulation, however, including funds transfers governed by the Electronic Fund Transfer Act and those made through an automated clearinghouse, ATM or point-of-sale system.

5.1.1 Record Retention Requirements

As part of the overall anti-money-laundering strategy, financial institutions are required to retain categories of records for use in investigations or enforcement actions. Financial institutions are required to maintain records of all extensions of credit in excess of $10,000, but this does not include credit secured by real property. Not all records must be maintained—only those with a "high degree of usefulness."[37] Records that are maintained must include the borrower's name and address, credit amount, purpose of credit and date of credit. Such records must be maintained for five years. As to deposit account records, a financial institution must keep the depositor's taxpayer identification number, signature cards and checks in excess of $100 that are drawn or issued and payable by the bank; with regard to certificates of deposit, the financial institution must obtain the customer name and address, a description of the CD and the date of the transaction. For wire transfers or direct deposits, a financial institution must maintain all deposit slips or credit tickets for transactions over $100.[38] Additionally, the BSA includes detailed rules regarding information that banks must retain in connection with payment orders.

5.1.2 Suspicious Activity Reports

Financial institutions must file a Suspicious Activity Report (SAR) in defined situations. The rationale is that SARs can alert government agencies to potentially suspicious transactions. A SAR must be filed with the Department of Treasury's Financial Crimes Enforcement Network in the following circumstances: (1) when a financial institution suspects that an insider is committing (or aiding the commission of) a crime, regardless of dollar amount; (2) when the entity detects a possible crime involving $5,000 or more and has a substantial basis for identifying a suspect; (3) when the entity detects a possible crime involving $25,000 or more (even if it has no substantial basis for identifying a suspect); and (4) when the entity suspects currency transactions aggregating $5,000 or more that involve potential money laundering or a violation of the act.[39]

5.1.3 BSA Enforcement

Penalties for violations of the BSA and its regulations include the following: civil penalties, including fines up to the greater of $25,000 or the amount of the transaction (up to a $100,000 maximum), as well as penalties for negligence ($500 per violation); additional penalties up to $5,000 per day for failure to comply with regulations; penalties of up to $25,000 per day for failure to comply with the information-sharing requirements of the USA Patriot Act; and penalties up to $1 million against financial institutions that fail to comply with due diligence requirements; and criminal penalties up to a $100,000 fine and/or one-year imprisonment and up to a $10,000 fine and/or five-year imprisonment.[40]

5.2 The International Money Laundering Abatement and Anti-Terrorist Financing Act of 2001

As part of the USA Patriot Act, the International Money Laundering Abatement and Anti-Terrorist Financing Act of 2001 expanded the reach of the BSA and made other significant changes to U.S. anti-money-laundering laws. The act gave the treasury secretary the ability to promulgate broad rules to implement modified "Know Your Customer" requirements and to otherwise deter money laundering.

For covered financial services companies, the major USA Patriot Act compliance issues can be grouped into the following categories:

- Information-sharing regulations and participation in the cooperative efforts to deter money laundering, as required by Section 314
- Know Your Customer rules, including the identification of beneficial owners of accounts—procedures required by Section 326
- Development and implementation of formal money-laundering programs as required by Section 352
- Bank Secrecy Act expansions, including new reporting and record-keeping requirements for different industries (such as broker-dealers) and currency transactions

6. Conclusion

Financial institutions are subject to a wide range of government regulations. The FCRA in 1970 was the first major national data privacy law in the United States, applying notably to credit reporting agencies, extensions of credit and purchases of insurance. The overhaul of the financial system in Gramm-Leach-Bliley in 1999 included the GLBA privacy and safeguards requirements. FACTA updated the credit reporting rules in 2003. These laws, taken together, mean that financial institutions today must carefully examine their practices with personal information, and ensure compliance. As shown by the anti-money-laundering laws, financial institutions at the same time are subject to requirements to retain personal information and disclose it under certain circumstances. The potential complexity of complying with these multiple requirements suggests the usefulness of an overall information management plan for financial institutions, updated over time to meet changing market and regulatory requirements.

Endnotes

1 *See generally* EPIC, "The Fair Credit Reporting Act (FCRA) and the Privacy of Your Credit Report," http://epic.org/privacy/fcra/; for a slightly different drafting of the principles see Federal Trade Commission, "Fair Information Principles," www.ftc.gov/reports/privacy3/fairinfo.htm.

2 *See generally* EPIC, "The Fair Credit Reporting Act (FCRA) and the Privacy of Your Credit Report," http://epic.org/privacy/fcra/.

3 White House Fact Sheet: President Bush Signs the Fair and Accurate Credit Transactions Act of 2003, Dec. 4, 2003, http://georgewbush-whitehouse.archives.gov/news/releases/2003/12/20031204-3.html; also see National Consumer Law Center, Analysis of the Fair and Accurate Credit Transactions Act of 2003, Pub. L. No. 108-159 (2003): Summary of FACTA Changes to the FCRA, www.creditinfocenter.com/forums/credit-repair/224021-summary-facta-changes-fcra.html.

4 www.ftc.gov/os/2004/11/041119factaapph.pdf.

5 16 C.F.R. Part 682.

6 16 C.F.R. Part 610.

7 www.ftc.gov/opa/2005/06/disposal.shtm.

8 16 C.F.R. Part 681.

9 www.ftc.gov/opa/2010/05/redflags.shtm.

10 S. 3987 (111th).

11 Gramm-Leach-Bliley Act, 15 U.S.C, Subchapter I, Sec. 6801-6809 (1999). Also see FTC, "In Brief: The Financial Privacy Requirements of the Gramm-Leach-Bliley Act," http://business.ftc.gov/documents/bus53-brief-financial-privacy-requirements-gramm-leach-bliley-act.

12 "Consumer Watch: U.S. Bancorp Pays $3 Million in Privacy Case Settlement," Market Watch, July 1, 1999, www.marketwatch.com/story/consumerwatch-us-bancorp-pays-3-million-in-privacy-case-settlement.

13 Gramm-Leach-Bliley Act, 15 U.S.C., Subchapter I, Sec. 6809.

14 In Vermont, the state's Department of Banking, Insurance, Securities, and Health Care Administration adopted opt-in provisions for information sharing. To comply with the regulation, some companies have treated all Vermont residents as having opted-out under GLBA.

15 Providing a toll-free telephone number or a detachable form with a preprinted address is "reasonable"; requiring someone to write a letter as the only way to opt out is not.

16 The GLBA does not give consumers the right to opt out when the financial institution shares other information with its affiliates. Consumers have this right under the FCRA.

17 www.ftc.gov/opa/2009/11/glb.shtm.

18 www.gpo.gov/fdsys/pkg/BILLS-109s2856enr/pdf/BILLS-109s2856enr.pdf.

19 16 C.F.R. § 314, www.ftc.gov/os/2002/05/67fr36585.pdf.

20 16 C.F.R. § 314.1(a).

21 *Id.*

22 16 C.F.R. § 314.3(a).

23 16 C.F.R. § 314.4.

24 Cal. Fin. Code § 4050 *et seq.*

25 Dodd-Frank Act § 1022.

26 *Id.* at § 1002(12).

27 *Id.* at § 1002(5); (15).

28 *Id.* at § 1025.

29 *Id.* at § 1026.

30 *Id.* at § 5531.

31 *Id.* at § 1052(b)-(c).

32 *Id.* at § 1055.

33 *Id.* at §§ 1041-1042.

34 www.fincen.gov/about_fincen/wwd/.

35 Peter P. Swire, "Financial Privacy and the Theory of High-Tech Government Surveillance," *Washington U. L. Q.* 77: 461 (1999).

36 Financial Recordkeeping and Reporting of Currency and Foreign Transactions Act of 1970, 31 U.S.C. 1051. In addition to the federal Bank Secrecy Act and other regulations that require reporting to the U.S. government, many states also provide for the disclosure of banking records and financial transaction data to state and local law enforcement agencies.

37 12 U.S.C. 1829(b).

38 See 31 C.F.R. 103.33; 31 C.F.R. 103.34; 31 C.F.R. 103.38.

39 See 12 C.F.R. 21.11; 12 C.F.R. 208.62; 12 C.F.R. 353.3.

40 1 C.F.R. Part 5321.

CHAPTER SIX

Education Records

Education records, for institutions that receive federal funding, have privacy protections under U.S. law. The logic is that grades, disciplinary actions and other school information about a particular student deserve privacy protection. This chapter discusses the Family Educational Rights and Privacy Act of 1974 (FERPA) and the Protection of Pupil Rights Amendment of 1978 (PPRA), as amended.

1. An Overview of FERPA

FERPA is a federal statute that provides students with control over disclosure and access to their education records.[1] FERPA is also referred to as the Buckley Amendment, in reference to Senator James Buckley, who supported its enactment. The statute generally prevents schools from divulging education record information, such as grades and behavior, to parties other than the student, without that student's consent.[2] FERPA provides for major aspects of Fair Information Practice Principles, including notice, consent, access and correction, security and accountability.

FERPA applies to all educational institutions that receive federal funding.[3] Such funding exists for virtually all public and most private schools, especially at the postsecondary level. Specifically, the statute protects the rights of students by providing them with the right to:

- Control the disclosure of their education records to others
- Review and seek amendment of their own education records
- Receive annual notice of their rights under FERPA
- File complaints with the Department of Education (there is no private right of action permitted under FERPA)

"Education record" has a broad meaning. FERPA defines it to include all records that are directly related to the student and maintained by the school or by a party on behalf of the school.[4] This extends beyond grades and other academic records to include financial aid records, disciplinary records and others related to the student.

FERPA defines "record" as "any information recorded in any way, including, but not limited to, handwriting, print, computer media, video or audio tape, film, microfilm, and microfiche."[5] All electronic records and e-mails are covered by the term "computer media."

There are several exceptions to the definition of educational record; however, these may be protected under other privacy laws. The following records are not considered "education records" under FERPA:

- **Campus police records** created and maintained by school campus police for law enforcement purposes.[6] However, if the records are shared between campus police and other campus administrators, these are considered education records.
- **Employment records**, when the employee is not a student at the university.[7]
- **Treatment records**, or health records, subject to several requirements.[8] Generally, records that are created or maintained by a professional health practitioner for the purpose of treating a student, and not disclosed to anyone except those providing the treatment, are considered treatment records.
- **Applicant records** of those who are not enrolled in the university.
- **Alumni records** created by a school after the individual is no longer a student.
- **Grades on peer-graded papers**, before they are collected and recorded by a faculty member or other university representative.[9]

Disclosure of education records is permitted only if one of the following conditions is met:

- The information is not "personally identifiable."
- The information is "directory information" whose release the student has not blocked.
- The student has provided consent.
- The disclosure is made to the student him/herself.
- A statutory exception applies, such as for health or safety purposes.

FERPA's definition of "personally identifiable information" is similar to other statutory definitions. It includes, but is not limited to:

- The student's name
- The name of the student's parent or other family members
- The student or student's family's address
- Personal identifiers such as the Social Security number or student number
- Other identifiers, such as date of birth
- Other information that, alone or in combination, can be linked to a student and would allow the student to be identified with reasonable certainty
- Information requested by a person whom the school reasonably believes knows the identity of the student to which the education record is linked[10]

Personally identifiable information may still be disclosed if it is determined to be "directory information."[11] Directory information is defined by FERPA as information in an education record that a student would not generally consider an invasion of privacy or harmful if disclosed. FERPA does not define "directory information" but rather allows individual educational institutions to create their own definition. Typical examples include name, date of birth, address, e-mail address, telephone number and field of study.

Educational institutions are permitted to use these items to create their own directory of information. They must first, however, provide students with an opportunity to opt out, or block the release of their directory information. Students cannot use this opt-out to prevent the release of information that falls under a FERPA exception. Lacking student consent, a school is also prohibited from disclosing directory information if a student's Social Security number or other nondirectory information is used alone or with other data elements to identify that student or his records. Other than the exceptions noted above, nondirectory information such as grade point average (GPA), grades or transcripts and academic standing is never released without student consent.

Valid student consent to disclosure must be signed (by hand or electronically), dated and written. It must also identify:

- The record(s) to be disclosed
- The purpose of disclosure
- To whom the disclosure is being made

Under several statutory exceptions a school is authorized to disclose personally identifiable information from an education record without student consent. Educational institutions need meet only one exception for the disclosure to be valid. However, schools must use reasonable methods to verify the identity of the party they disclose the information to. "Reasonable methods" include password access, security questions, smart card access and PINs, among other methods.

Exceptions to the FERPA consent requirements include the following:

- Disclosure to school officials who have determined a "legitimate and educational interest" in the records. A "legitimate educational interest" exists if the record is relevant and necessary to the school official's responsibilities. This includes school employees and board members as well as third-party vendors (1) to whom the school outsources duties and (2) who are under the direct control of the school regarding use and maintenance of the record. These third parties are not permitted to disclose record information to any other party without consent, and cannot use the record for any other purpose than for which the disclosure was made.

  The "legitimate educational interest" does not have to be academic, just related to any appropriate school function. Also, reasonable security controls must be in place to ensure that access is provided only to the records in which the party has a legitimate educational interest.

- Disclosure to educational institutions in which a student seeks or intends to enroll, or is currently enrolled, when the disclosure is for a purpose related to the student's enrollment or transfer.

- Disclosure in connection with financial aid that the student has received or for which the student will apply, when the purpose of the disclosure is to determine the student's eligibility for, conditions to or amount of financial aid.
- Disclosure to organizations doing research studies for, or on behalf of, educational institutions for the purpose of developing predictive tests, administering student aid programs or improving school instruction.
- Disclosure to accrediting organizations to fulfill accrediting duties.
- Disclosure to the alleged victim of a forcible or nonforcible sex offense.
- Disclosure of information related to sex offenders and others when the information is provided to the school under federal registration and disclosure requirements.
- Disclosure to a person or entity that is verified as the party that provided or created that record. For example, if a student transfers high schools, the second school can disclose a student's transcript to the original school to verify its authenticity.
- Disclosure to law enforcement or otherwise to comply with a judicial order or subpoena. The school must make reasonable efforts to notify the student prior to the disclosure unless it is a legal matter that orders nondisclosure.
- Disclosure to appropriate parties in connection with a "health or safety emergency," if knowledge of this information is necessary to protect the health or safety of the student or others. The threat of harm must be "articulable and significant," and the school can take the totality of the circumstances into account in making this determination. Information can be disclosed to any individual with the ability to assist in the situation—this includes parents, law enforcement, school officials, spouse or partner and other educational institutions, among others.

A school is safe from federal scrutiny of its health and safety emergency determination as long as, based on the information available at the time, there is rational basis for the determination. In that case, the Department of Education will not question the determination.

FERPA also provides students with the right to access and review their education records. Once a student has issued a request, the educational institute must provide access to the records within 45 days of that request. It also must respond to reasonable requests from students for explanations of the records. As with other disclosures to third parties, the educational institution must use reasonable measures to verify the identity of the student making the record request.

There are several exceptions to the right of inspection. Students do not have the right to inspect the financial records of their parents, confidential letters of recommendation (if the student has waived the right to inspect those documents), treatment records, attorney-client privileged information or records excluded from the definition of education records (such as law enforcement records). Also, when the request pertains to a record containing information about more than one student, the requesting students may access only the parts pertaining to themselves.[12]

Students can request corrections to their education records if they believe the records to be inaccurate, misleading or in violation of their privacy.[13] This access is intended to allow students to address incorrect records and is not for other purposes. If the request is granted, the records must be corrected within a reasonable time. If the request is denied, the student has a right to request a hearing, which must meet several requirements:

- The student must receive prior and reasonable notice of the time, place and date.
- It must be held within a reasonable time after the request is made.
- It must be conducted by a party without a direct interest in the outcome.
- The student must be afforded a "full and fair" opportunity to present his/her case, with or without assistance or representation.
- The decision must be based on the evidence presented at the hearing, delivered, in writing, within a reasonable amount of time after the hearing, and must contain a summary and explanation for the decision. If the hearing affirms the student's request, the education record must be amended and the student must be notified in writing; however, if the request is denied, the institution must notify the student of his/her right to place a written statement in the file about the contested record. The statement must then be maintained and disclosed with any release of the contested record.

2. FERPA and the Protection of Pupil Rights Amendment

FERPA applies only to information stored in "education records," defined above as information that (1) directly relates to a student and (2) is maintained by the educational institution or on behalf of the institution. All other general student information that falls outside of this definition is not covered by FERPA's consent and disclosure requirements. This has traditionally allowed schools to sell student directory information to commercial entities such as banks or credit card companies, unless a parent or student opts out.[14]

Congress responded to concerns about the collection and disclosure of student information for commercial purposes by amending FERPA in 1978 with the Protection of Pupil Rights Amendment (PPRA). PPRA provides certain rights to parents of minors with regard to the collection of sensitive information from students through surveys. These areas include:

- Political affiliations
- Mental and psychological problems potentially embarrassing to the student and his/her family
- Sex behavior and attitudes
- Illegal, antisocial, self-incriminating and demeaning behavior
- Critical appraisals of other individuals with whom respondents have close family relationships
- Legally recognized privileged or analogous relationships, such as those of lawyers, physicians and ministers
- Religious practices, affiliations or beliefs of the student or student's parent
- Income (other than that required by law to determine eligibility for participation in a program or for receiving financial assistance under such program)[15]

The No Child Left Behind Act of 2001 broadened the PPRA to limit the collection and disclosure of student survey information.[16] The amended PPRA now requires schools to:

- Enact policies regarding the collection, disclosure or use of personal information about students for commercial purposes[17]
- Allow parents to access and inspect surveys and other commercial instruments before they are administered to students[18]
- Provide advance notice to parents about the approximate date when these activities are scheduled[19]
- Provide parents the right to opt out of surveys or other sharing of student information for commercial purposes[20]

PPRA requirements apply to all elementary and secondary schools that receive federal funding; however, the statute does not apply to postsecondary schools.

3. Conclusion

U.S. law provides the major Fair Information Practice Principles related to education records that schools receiving federal funding must abide by. Such educational institutions therefore must examine their practices to ensure compliance with these relatively detailed rules. High schools and universities, in addition, should remain alert to the change in legal status that occurs when a student becomes an adult at the age of 18. At that point, the student is the person in control of rights connected to education records, including grades, rather than the parents.

Endnotes

1 20 U.S.C. § 1232g.

2 20 U.S.C. § 1232g, 34 CFR 99.

3 20 U.S.C. § 1221 (2000).

4 20 U.S.C. § 1232g(a)(4)(A).

5 34 C.F.R. § 99.3.

6 20 U.S.C. § 1232g(a)(4)(B)(ii).

7 20 U.S.C. § 1232g(a)(4)(B)(iii).

8 20 U.S.C. § 1232g(a)(4)(B)(iv).

9 *Owasso Independent School District v. Falvo,* 534 U.S. 426 (2002).

10 34 C.F.R. § 99.3 ("Personally identifiable information").

11 20 U.S.C. § 1232g(a)(5)(A)-(B).

12 20 U.S.C. § 1232g(a)(1)(A). See also 34 C.F.R. § 99.12(a).

13 20 U.S.C. § 1232g(a)(2).

14 Lynn M. Daggett, "FERPA in the Twenty-First Century: Failure to Effectively Regulate Privacy for All Students," *Cath. U. L. Rev.* 58 (2008): 59, 100, n. 238.

15 PPRA.

16 No Child Left Behind Act, Pub. L. No. 107-110 § 1061, 115 Stat. 1425, 2083 (2002).

17 20 U.S.C. § 1232h(c).

18 20 U.S.C. § 1232h(c)(1)(F).

19 20 U.S.C. § 1232h(c)(2)(B).

20 20 U.S.C. § 1232h(c)(2)(B).

CHAPTER SEVEN

Telecommunications and Marketing

Telecommunications involves very important privacy issues. One set of privacy telecommunications issues concerns specific communications channels and methods such as telemarketing, electronic mail and faxes. For these channels, U.S. law has specific rules that regulate how organizations can communicate with individuals for direct marketing and related purposes. Another set of issues concerns the rules that apply to personal information collected by the telecommunications companies themselves in the course of providing their services. Telephone and cable companies, for instance, can potentially learn a great deal about the phone calls people make or the television shows they watch. This chapter examines the statutes that govern the *commercial* use of that type of telephone and cable activity. Chapter 10 examines rules for *government* access to the communications, under wiretap and other statutes, which provide lawful access for the government to that data, subject to search warrants and other restrictions.

1. Regulations Governing Telemarketing

U.S. federal and state laws place legal limits on the manner in which organizations can call individuals for marketing and fund-raising purposes. One traditional privacy tort action is "intrusion on seclusion," which imposes liability on "one who intentionally intrudes, physically or otherwise, upon the solitude or seclusion of another or his private affairs or concerns."[1] To succeed in an intrusion tort claim, the plaintiff must show that "the intrusion would be highly offensive to a reasonable person."[2] In contrast with intrusion tort requirements, telemarketing regulations in the United States address milder intrusions, which do not require a showing of "highly offensive" intrusion. Instead, legislators and regulators have issued regulation in response to complaints by families about deceptive marketing as well as unwanted marketing calls. Telemarketing laws in the United States provide considerable detail about what types of "intrusions" are permitted under federal law.

The Federal Trade Commission (FTC) first issued its Telemarketing Sales Rule (TSR) in 1995, implementing the Telemarketing and Consumer Fraud and Abuse Prevention Act. It has since amended the TSR in 2003, 2008 and 2010. The Federal Communications Commission (FCC) has issued regulations under the Telephone Consumer Protection Act of 1991,[3] and updated them most recently in 2012 to address robocalls. The agencies have coordinated closely in their requirements. The focus of this discussion will be on the FTC rule. This chapter first examines who can receive such calls consistent with the Do Not Call list, and then turns to the rules governing how telemarketing calls can be made.

*The **Telemarketing Sales Rule** defines telemarketing as "a plan, program, or campaign which is conducted to induce the purchase of goods or services or a charitable contribution, by use of one or more telephones and which involves more than one interstate telephone call."*[4]

The Telephone Consumer Protection Act prohibits automatic telephone dialing systems from making calls to any cell phone or other service "for which the called party is charged for the call."[5] This provision was passed to ensure that consumers are not charged for unsolicited calls.

1.1 Who Can Be Called: The U.S. National Do Not Call Registry

The U.S. National Do Not Call (DNC) Registry is perhaps the best known of the FTC's TSR requirements and remains the most popular consumer program ever to be implemented by the FTC.[6] The program provides a means for U.S. residents to register residential and wireless phone numbers that they do not wish to be called for telemarketing purposes (with specific exceptions, below).

The FTC, the FCC and state attorneys general enforce the DNC Registry, which now contains over 200 million participating phone numbers—and is still growing.[7] Violations of the rule can lead to civil penalties of up to $16,000 per violation.[8] In addition, violators may be subject to nationwide injunctions that prohibit certain conduct, and may be required to pay redress to injured consumers.

The DNC Registry provisions took effect in 2003 and require sellers and telemarketers to access the registry prior to making any phone-based solicitations. They are also required to update their call lists every 31 days with new registry information.

The registry is accessed via an automated website at www.telemarketing.donotcall.gov. Only sellers, telemarketers and their service providers may access the registry. Each seller must establish a profile by providing identifying information about the organization. The seller then receives a unique Subscription Account Number (SAN) upon payment of the appropriate fee.

Telemarketers accessing the registry on behalf of seller-clients are required to identify the seller-clients and provide the seller-client's unique SAN. (Telemarketers access the registry, at no cost, through the use of their seller-client's unique SANs—their access is limited to the area codes requested and paid for by the seller-client.)

The FTC's guidance[9] specifically states that:

> *Even though they are not required by law to do so, telemarketers and service providers may gain access to the national registry on their own behalf, but they must pay a separate fee for*

that ability. But before placing calls on behalf of a seller-client, telemarketers are required to ensure that their seller-client has a valid SAN.

In other words, each SAN belongs to a specific seller, and SANs are not transferable.

Note that it is a violation of the TSR to place any call to a consumer (absent an exception) unless the registry is checked. In other words, even a call to a consumer whose phone number is not on the registry is a violation of the TSR if the registry was not checked prior to the call.

1.1.1 Exceptions to the DNC Rules

DNC rules apply to for-profit organizations and cover charitable solicitations placed by for-profit telefunders. DNC rules do *not* apply to:

- Nonprofits calling on their own behalf
- Calls to customers with an existing relationship within the last 18 months
- Inbound calls, provided that there is no "upsell" of additional products or services[10]
- Most business-to-business calls

1.1.1.1 Existing Business Relationship Exception

Sellers (and telemarketers calling on their behalf) may call a consumer with whom a seller has an established business relationship (EBR), provided the consumer has not asked to be on the seller's entity-specific do-not-call list. The TSR recognizes two distinct types of relationships: "customers" and "prospects."

An EBR exists with a customer if the consumer has purchased, rented or leased the seller's goods or services (or completed a financial transaction with the seller) within 18 months preceding a telemarketing call. The 18-month period runs from the date of the last payment, transaction or shipment between the consumer and the seller.

An EBR exists with a prospect if the consumer has made an application or inquiry regarding the seller's goods and services. This EBR runs for three months from the date of the person's inquiry or application.

1.1.1.2 Exception Based on Consent

The TSR allows sellers and telemarketers to call consumers who consent to receive such calls. This consent must be in writing, must state the number to which calls may be made and must include the consumer's signature. (A valid electronic signature is acceptable.)

Note that the seller's request for consent must be "clear and conspicuous." If in writing, the request "cannot be hidden; printed in small, pale, or non-contrasting type; hidden on the back or bottom of the document; or buried in unrelated information where a person would not expect to find such a request."[11] If online, the "please call me" button may not be prechecked. The FTC's guidance also states: "In the FTC's enforcement experience, sweepstakes entry forms often have been used in a deceptive manner to obtain 'authorization' from a consumer to incur a charge or some other detriment. Authorization or permission obtained through subterfuge is ineffective. The FTC scrutinizes any use of such sweepstakes entry forms as a way to get a consumer's permission to place telemarketing calls to her number."[12]

1.1.1.3 The Do-Not-Call Safe Harbor

The TSR has a "DNC Safe Harbor" that sellers and telemarketers can use to reduce the risk of liability. Per the guidance,[13]

- *[I]f a seller or telemarketer can establish that as part of its routine business practice, it meets the following requirements, it will not be subject to civil penalties or sanctions for erroneously calling a consumer who has asked not to be called, or for calling a number on the National Registry:*
- *The seller or telemarketer has established and implemented written procedures to honor consumers' requests that they not be called, [and]*
- *The seller or telemarketer has trained its personnel, and any entity assisting in its compliance, in these procedures, [and]*
- *The seller, telemarketer, or someone else acting on behalf of the seller . . . has maintained and recorded an entity-specific Do Not Call list, [and]*
- *The seller or telemarketer uses, and maintains records documenting, a process to prevent calls to any telephone number on an entity-specific Do Not Call list or the National Do Not Call Registry. This, provided that the latter process involves using a version of the National Registry from the FTC no more than 31 days before the date any call is made, [and]*
- *The seller, telemarketer, or someone else acting on behalf of the seller. . . monitors and enforces compliance with the entity's written Do Not Call procedures, [then]*
- *The call is a result of error.*

This DNC Safe Harbor provides an important protection for sellers and telemarketers because violations of the TSR can result in civil penalties of up to $16,000 per call.[14]

1.2 Rules Governing How Calls Can Be Made Under Telemarketing Laws

The TSR provides detailed rules about many aspects of how telemarketing calls can be made. The vast majority of telemarketing calls are from legitimate businesses trying to achieve their business goals while satisfying consumers. The telemarketing field, however, has also been plagued with a history of intrusive and fraudulent callers. Such callers sometimes intrude repeatedly on consumers, making frequent calls at inappropriate hours and in other ways that bother consumers. Such callers also sometimes take advantage of their anonymity and physical distance from consumers to try to defraud consumers. This combination of intrusiveness and fraud has led to periodic TSR updates to address new forms of problems for consumers.

The TSR requires covered organizations to:

- Call only between 8 a.m. and 9 p.m.
- Screen and scrub names against the national DNC list
- Display caller ID information
- Identify themselves and what they are selling
- Disclose all material information and terms[15]
- Comply with special rules for prizes and promotions
- Respect requests to call back
- Retain records for at least 24 hours
- Comply with special rules for automated dialers

Under the rules, telemarketing is defined as "a plan, program, or campaign . . . to induce the purchase of goods or services or a charitable contribution" involving more than one interstate telephone call.[16] With some exceptions, all businesses or individuals that engage in telemarketing must comply with the TSR (or the FCC counterpart) as well as applicable state laws.[17] Neither the TSR nor the FCC rules preempt state law. As the FTC notes, compliance is required both of "telemarketers," entities that initiate or receive telephone calls to or from consumers, and "sellers," the entities that provide or arrange to provide the goods and services being offered.

1.2.1 Entity-specific Suppression Lists

The TSR prohibits any seller (or telemarketer calling on the seller's behalf) from calling any consumer who has asked not to be called again. Sellers and telemarketers are required to maintain internal suppression lists to respect these do-not-call requests.

The TSR does provide some latitude for companies that have distinct corporate divisions. In general, such divisions are considered separate sellers under the rule.

The FTC specifies two factors that should be used to determine whether do-not-call requests should be shared among divisions:

- (1) whether there is substantial diversity between the operational structure of the divisions and
- (2) whether the goods or services sold by the divisions are substantially different from each other.

If a consumer tells one division of a company not to call again, a distinct corporate division of the same company may still make calls to that consumer. If the divisions are not distinct, however, the seller may not call the consumer even to offer different goods or services.

1.2.2 Required Disclosures

The TSR requires that, at the beginning of the call, before delivering any sales content, telemarketers disclose:

- The identity of the seller
- That the purpose of the call is to sell goods or services

- The nature of those goods or services
- In the case of a prize promotion, that no purchase or payment is necessary to participate or win, and that a purchase or payment does not increase the chances of winning

The FTC has issued guidance on how and when these four basic disclosures must be made. For example, disclosures must be truthful. A company cannot say it is making a "courtesy call" to the consumer if the purpose of the call is telemarketing.

If a call has multiple purposes (such as the sale of different types of products or different overall purposes), disclosures have to be given for all sales purposes. The following examples are from the FTC's "Complying with the TSR" guide:[18]

> *Say a seller calls a consumer to determine whether he or she is satisfied with a previous purchase and then plans to move into a sales presentation if the consumer is satisfied. Since the seller plans to make a sales presentation in at least some of the calls (the seller plans to end the call if the consumer is not satisfied), four disclosures must be made promptly during the initial portion of the call and before inquiring about customer satisfaction.*
>
> *However, a seller may make calls to welcome new customers and ask whether they are satisfied with goods or services they recently purchased. If the seller doesn't plan to sell anything to these customers during any of these calls, the four oral disclosures are not required. That's the case even if customers ask about the sellers' other goods or services, and the seller responds by describing the goods or services. Because the seller has no plans to sell goods or services during these calls, the disclosures are not required.*

1.2.3 Misrepresentations and Material Omissions

The TSR prohibits misrepresentations during the sales call. Telemarketers must provide accurate and complete information about the products and services being offered. They may also not omit any material facts about the products or services. There are six broad categories of information that must always be disclosed:

1. Cost and quantity
2. Material restrictions and conditions
3. No-refund policy details (if applicable)
4. Prize and promotion details (such as odds of winning and value of the prize)
5. Credit card loss prevention program disclosures (for sellers offering this service)
6. Negative option feature details (if the seller uses a negative option)

The rule also was amended to require specific disclosures when a telemarketer accepts payment by means other than a credit card or debit card, such as phone or utility billing. In this case, the seller must obtain "express verifiable authorization." In amending the rule, the commission noted that many new payment methods lacked basic consumer protection provisions that exist in credit card transactions. Because the consumers may not have protections against, for example, unauthorized charges, or recourse in the event they are dissatisfied with the goods or services, the TSR now requires telemarketers to meet a higher standard for proving authorization when consumers use new payment methods.

1.2.4 Transmission of Caller ID Information

The TSR requires entities that make telemarketing calls to transmit accurate call identification information so that it can be presented to consumers with caller ID services. In particular, each telemarketer may transmit its own name and phone number or it may substitute the name of the seller on whose behalf the telemarketer is making the call. The telemarketer may also substitute the seller's customer-service telephone number for its number, provided that the seller's number is answered during normal business hours.

Telemarketers are not liable if, for some reason, caller ID information does not reach a consumer, provided that the telemarketer has arranged with its carrier to transmit this information in every call. The FTC guidance[19] states that "telemarketers who can show that they took all available steps to ensure transmission of Caller ID information in every call will not be liable for isolated inadvertent instances when the Caller ID information fails to make it to the consumer's receiver. Nevertheless, a telemarketer's use of calling equipment that is not capable of transmitting Caller ID information is no excuse for failure to transmit the required information."

1.2.5 Prohibition on Call Abandonment

The TSR expressly prohibit telemarketers from abandoning an outbound telephone call with either "hang-ups" or "dead air." Under the TSR, an outbound telephone call is "abandoned" if a person answers it and the telemarketer does not connect the call to a live sales representative within two seconds of the person's completed greeting.

Abandoned calls often result from a telemarketer's use of predictive dialers to call consumers. Predictive dialers promote telemarketers' efficiency by simultaneously calling multiple consumers for every available sales representative. This maximizes the amount of time telemarketing sales representatives spend talking to consumers and minimizes representatives' downtime. But it also means that some calls are abandoned: Consumers are either hung up on or kept waiting for long periods until a representative is available.

The use of prerecorded-message telemarketing, where a sales pitch begins with or is made entirely by a prerecorded message, also violates the TSR because the telemarketer is not connecting the call to a live sales representative within two seconds of the called person's completed greeting.[20] For a company to use prerecorded sales messages, it must have the prior express consent (opt-in) of the consumer.

1.2.6 Abandonment Safe Harbor

According to the FTC guidance, the abandoned call Safe Harbor provides that a telemarketer will not face enforcement action for violating the call abandonment prohibition if the telemarketer:

- Uses technology that ensures abandonment of no more than three percent of all calls answered by a live person, measured per day per calling campaign

- Allows the telephone to ring for 15 seconds or four rings before disconnecting an unanswered call
- Plays a recorded message stating the name and telephone number of the seller on whose behalf the call was placed whenever a live sales representative is unavailable within two seconds of a live person answering the call
- Maintains records documenting adherence to the preceding three requirements

To take advantage of the Safe Harbor, a telemarketer must first ensure that a live representative takes the call in at least 97 percent of the calls answered by consumers. Any calls answered by machine, calls that are not answered at all and calls to nonworking numbers do not count in this calculation.

This three percent rule applies to each day and each calling campaign. The FTC does not allow a telemarketer to average abandonment rates, even if it is running simultaneous calling campaigns on behalf of different sellers. The Safe Harbor also requires the telemarketer to let the phone ring at least four times (or for 15 seconds). This requirement is designed to ensure that consumers have sufficient time to answer a call.

For the small number of calls that are abandoned, the TSR's Safe Harbor requires the telemarketer to play a recorded greeting, consisting of the company's name and phone number and a statement that the call was for telemarketing purposes. This recorded message may not contain a sales pitch.[21] The phone number provided in the message must also be one to which the consumer can call to be placed on the company's own do-not-call list.

Finally, to be within the Safe Harbor, the telemarketer must keep records that demonstrate its compliance with the other Safe Harbor provisions. The records must demonstrate both that the per-day, per-campaign abandonment rate has not exceeded three percent and that the ring time and recorded message requirements have been met.

1.2.7 Prohibition on Unauthorized Billing

The detailed rules in the TSR have been amended over time to address specific problems that consumers have experienced. For instance, the TSR strictly prohibits telemarketers from billing consumers for any goods or services without the consumer's "express, informed consent." If the consumer provides the billing account information to the telemarketer during the call, then express, informed consent can be obtained in any nondeceptive manner.

If, on the other hand, the telemarketer has obtained the consumer's account information from some other source ("pre-acquired account information"), the TSR imposes an array of specific requirements on how express, informed consent must be obtained. In particular, the TSR has special requirements for "free-to-pay conversion" offers (offers that begin with a free trial, but then convert to paid service at the end of the trial period). These rules are designed to combat the high incidence of unauthorized charges made to consumer accounts where consumers did not understand that the service provider would charge the consumer at the end of the trial period. If preacquired account information is used in connection with a free-to-pay conversion offer, the telemarketer must:

- Obtain from the customer at least the last four digits of the account number to be charged
- Obtain the customer's express agreement to be charged for the goods or services using the account number for which the customer has provided at least the last four digits
- Make and maintain an audio recording of the entire telemarketing transaction

If preacquired account information is used in connection with any other type of transaction, the telemarketer must still (at minimum) identify the account with enough specificity for the consumer to understand which account will be charged, and obtain the consumer's express agreement to be charged using that account number.

1.2.8 New FCC Robocall Rules

On February 15, 2012, the FCC revised its rules governing prerecorded calls (robocalls) to reconcile its rule with the TSR.[22] First, the FCC revised its established business relationship exemption for robocalls. Now, even if a company has an established business relationship with a consumer, it is required to receive "prior express written consent" for all robocalls to residential lines. The rules allow for a 12-month adoption period. Companies can obtain consent through several methods, such as e-mail, website form, text message, telephone keypress (e.g., "press one") and/or voice recording.

The rules also include a provision that allows consumers to "opt out of future robocalls during a robocall." Additionally, the revisions increase harmonization with the FTC's rules to require "assessment of the call abandonment rate to occur during a single calling campaign over a 30-day period, and if the single calling campaign exceeds a 30-day period, we require that the abandonment rate be calculated each successive 30-day period or portion thereof during which the calling campaign continues." Finally, also consistent with the FTC, robocalls to residential lines made by healthcare-related entities governed by HIPAA are exempt from the above requirements.

1.2.9 Record-keeping Requirements

To make enforcement more effective, the TSR requires sellers and telemarketers to keep substantial records that relate to their telemarketing activities. In general, the following records must be maintained for two years from the date that the record is produced:

- Advertising and promotional materials
- Information about prize recipients
- Sales records
- Employee records
- All verifiable authorizations or records of express informed consent or express agreement

These records may be maintained in whatever manner, format or medium the company uses in the normal course of business. For example, the records may be maintained in electronic or paper formats. Additionally, the TSR requires only one copy of the records to be maintained. In particular, sellers and telemarketers can decide which party should maintain which records as part of the services contract. As the FTC's guidance states:[23]

> *Sellers and telemarketers do not have to keep duplicative records if they have a written agreement allocating responsibility for complying with the recordkeeping requirements. Without a written agreement between the parties, or if the written agreement is unclear as to who must maintain the required records, telemarketers must keep employee records, while sellers must keep the advertising and promotional materials, information on prize recipients, sales records, and verifiable authorizations.*

In the event of dissolution or termination of the business of a seller or telemarketer, the principal of the business must maintain all records of the business. In the event of a sale, assignment or other change in ownership of the seller or telemarketer's business, the successor business must maintain the records.

For each type of record listed above, the TSR includes lists of the information that must be retained. For example, sales records must include: (1) the name and last known address of each customer, (2) the goods or services purchased, (3) the date the goods or services were shipped or provided and (4) the amount the customer paid for the goods or services.

Similarly, for all current and former employees directly involved in telephone sales, records must include (1) the name (and any fictitious name used), (2) the last known home address and telephone number and (3) the job title(s) of each employee. Additionally, if fictitious names are used by employees, the TSR also requires that each fictitious name be traceable to a specific employee.

1.2.10 Other Provisions

The TSR also includes specific regulations designed to address:

- Credit card laundering
- Telemarketing sales of credit repair programs, loss recovery services and advance loans
- "Telefunding" activities (for-profit companies that call on behalf of charitable organizations)

The TSR includes significant enforcement provisions. As noted earlier, the TSR can be enforced by the FTC, the state attorneys general or private individuals.[24] The FTC has aggressively enforced the TSR. As noted above, violations of the TSR are punishable by civil penalties of up to $16,000 per call. The FCC and state attorneys general also actively enforce their counterpart regulations. Additionally, some states may have their own versions of telemarketing sales rules that carry additional penalties and may have different requirements. For example, Louisiana's Public Service Commission's Do Not Call General Order has different allowed time frames for making calls, limits established business relationships to six months and has established its own penalties for violators.

1.3 State Telemarketing Legislation

States have enacted telemarketing laws as well, creating additional legal requirements for telemarketers. For example, more than half the states require that telemarketers obtain a license or register with the state.[25] States can also create their own DNC lists, with differing exceptions, fines or methods of consumer enrollment from their federal counterpart.[26] Some states require that telemarketers identify themselves at the beginning of the call, or that the telemarketer terminate the call without rebuttal if the recipient of the call so desires.[27] Finally, states may require that a written contract be created for certain transactions.[28]

2. Fax Marketing

Much the way that consumers may not wish to receive telemarketing calls at dinner time, owners of fax machines can have concerns about a high volume of incoming unsolicited faxes. Such faxes can tie up phone lines and impose printing costs on the recipients. In response to this concern, Congress enacted the Telephone Consumer Protection Act of 1991 (TCPA).[29] The TCPA is enforced by the FCC and prohibits unsolicited commercial fax transmissions. Penalties include a private right of action and statutory damages of up to $500 per fax.[30]

As originally implemented, the act required consent for commercial faxing. Many companies believed that this consent could be implied by an existing business relationship, although that was not specified in the regulations; however, the FCC received many complaints about unwanted faxes.

To address these complaints, in 2003, the FCC revised the TCPA regulations and required fax senders to document that they had consent to send faxes by obtaining signed, written authorizations from all prospective recipients. The authorizations had to include the numbers to which faxes could be sent. Due to concerns about the costs and difficulty of obtaining authorizations from customers, the FCC stayed implementation of these regulations to allow companies to send faxes to existing customers while obtaining the necessary consents.

Congress responded to this situation by passing the Junk Fax Prevention Act of 2005 (JFPA). The JFPA specifically provides that consent can be inferred from an existing business relationship (EBR), and it permits sending of commercial faxes to recipients based on an EBR, as long as the sender offers an opt-out in accordance with the act.

2.1 Existing Business Relationships

For purposes of the JFPA, "existing business relationship" has the same definition as it does in the FTC's Do Not Call rule. Specifically, an existing business relationship exists if the fax recipient has entered into a purchase or services transaction with the sender within the past 18 months or if the recipient has made an inquiry or application with the sender during the past three months. The JFPA permits faxes to both consumers and businesses, if the EBR exists.

The JFPA also imposes requirements on how fax numbers can be obtained. Senders wishing to rely on the EBR may collect fax numbers from new customers only (1) through the voluntary communication of the fax number from the customer within the context of the business relationship, or (2) from a directory or Internet site where recipients have voluntarily agreed to make fax numbers available for public distribution. EBR customer fax numbers possessed prior to the effective date are not subject to this requirement.

2.2 State Fax Marketing Laws

Some states have enacted their own laws regulating unsolicited commercial fax transmissions. Notably, California attempted to eliminate the TCPA's EBR exception with legislation applicable to unsolicited faxes sent to or from a fax machine located within the state.[31] The law, however, was declared unconstitutional when applied to interstate fax transmissions due to the TCPA's preemption of interstate regulation.[32]

3. Controlling the Assault of Non-Solicited Pornography and Marketing Act of 2003

Along with the rules governing commercial telemarketing and faxes, Congress has created rules for unsolicited commercial electronic mail in the Controlling the Assault of Non-Solicited Pornography and Marketing (CAN-SPAM) Act of 2003.[33] The act applies to anyone who advertises products or services by electronic mail directed to or originating from the United States. The law covers the transmission of commercial e-mail messages whose primary purpose is advertising or promoting a product or service.

CAN-SPAM was never intended to eliminate unsolicited commercial e-mail, but rather to provide a mechanism for legitimate companies to send e-mails to prospects and respect individual rights to opt out of unwanted communications. Spam-filtering software is still widely used to screen out as much of the continuing spam as possible. The act nonetheless has fulfilled an important purpose. It has created the rules of the road for how legitimate organizations send e-mails, including clear identification of the sender and a simple unsubscribe or opt-out. The CAN-SPAM Act:

- Prohibits false or misleading headers
- Prohibits deceptive subject lines
- Requires commercial e-mails to contain a functioning, clearly and conspicuously displayed return e-mail address that allows the recipient to contact the sender
- Requires all commercial e-mails to include clear and conspicuous notice of the opportunity to opt out along with a cost-free mechanism for exercising the opt-out, such as by return e-mail or by clicking on an opt-out link
- Prohibits sending commercial e-mail (following a grace period of 10 business days) to an individual who has asked not to receive future e-mail
- Requires all commercial e-mail to include (1) clear and conspicuous identification that the message is a commercial message (unless the recipient has provided prior affirmative consent to receive the e-mail) and (2) a valid physical postal address of the sender (which can be a post office box)

- Prohibits "aggravated violations" relating to commercial e-mails such as (1) address harvesting and dictionary attacks, (2) the automated creation of multiple e-mail accounts and (3) the retransmission of commercial e-mail through unauthorized accounts
- Requires all commercial e-mail containing sexually oriented material to include a warning label (unless the recipient has provided prior affirmative consent to receive the e-mail)

CAN-SPAM is enforced primarily by the FTC and carries penalties of fines of up to $16,000 per violation.[34] In addition, deceptive commercial e-mail is subject to laws banning false or misleading advertising. The FTC has the authority to issue regulations implementing the CAN-SPAM Act and did so in 2008 to clarify a number of statutory definitions.[35]

CAN-SPAM distinguishes commercial e-mail messages from "transactional or relationship messages," which are messages whose primary purpose is to:

- Facilitate or confirm an agreed-upon commercial transaction
- Provide warranty or safety information about a product purchased or used by the recipient
- Provide certain information regarding an ongoing commercial relationship
- Provide information related to employment or a related benefit plan
- Deliver goods or services to which the recipient is entitled under the terms of an agreed-upon transaction

CAN-SPAM contains a number of requirements generally applicable to the sender of a commercial e-mail message. A "sender" is anyone who initiates an e-mail message and whose product or service is advertised or promoted by the message. More than one person may be deemed to have initiated a message. The FTC issued a regulation in 2008 clarifying that the entity identified in the "from" line can generally be considered the single sender, so long as there is compliance with the other provisions of CAN-SPAM.[36] The 2008 regulation also provides additional detail on (1) a prohibition on having the e-mail recipient pay a fee to opt out, (2) the definition of "valid physical postal address" and (3) the application of the term *person* to apply beyond natural persons.

CAN-SPAM grants enforcement authority to the FTC and other federal regulators, along with state attorneys general and other state officials. Internet service providers that have been adversely affected by a violation may sue violators for injunctive relief and monetary damages. Unlike a number of state spam laws that are now preempted, the act does not provide for a right of action for other parties. For those authorized to sue, the act provides for injunctive relief and damages up to $250 per violation, with a maximum award of $2 million. The act further provides that a court may increase a damage award up to three times the amount otherwise available in cases of willful or aggravated violations. Certain egregious conduct is punishable by up to five years imprisonment.

CAN-SPAM preempts most state laws that restrict e-mail communications, although state spam laws are not superseded by CAN-SPAM to the extent such laws prohibit false or deceptive activity.

3.1 Wireless Message Rules Under CAN-SPAM

In addition to the e-mail rules discussed above, the FCC has issued rules implementing the CAN-SPAM Act with regard to mobile service commercial messages (MSCMs).

The CAN-SPAM Act defines an MSCM as "a commercial electronic mail message that is transmitted directly to a wireless device that is utilized by a subscriber of a commercial mobile service." The message must have (or utilize) a unique electronic address that includes "a reference to an Internet domain." The FCC also notes in its commentary that the rule is designed to apply only to mail addresses designed by carriers for mobile services messaging. The FCC's rules cover messages sent using Internet-to-phone short message service (SMS) technology, but do not cover phone-to-phone messages.[37]

The FCC rule defers to the FTC rules and interpretation regarding the definitions of "commercial" and "transactional" (with respect to the mail messages) as well as the mechanisms for determining the "primary purpose" of messages. Accordingly, the FCC rule must be analyzed in the context of the FTC regulatory framework for the CAN-SPAM Act.

3.2 Express Prior Authorization

The CAN-SPAM Act prohibits senders from sending any MSCMs without the subscriber's "express prior authorization." Express prior authorization must be obtained for each MSCM, regardless of sender or industry. The FCC requirements are quite detailed, and can be summarized as follows:

- "Express prior authorization" must be "express," meaning that the consumer has taken an affirmative action to give the authorization. Authorization may not be obtained in the form of a negative option. If the authorization is obtained via a website, the consumer must take an affirmative action, such as checking a box or hitting a button.
- The authorization must also be given prior to the sending of any MSCMs. There is no provision to grandfather existing authorizations that senders may have obtained. Because of the disclosure requirements in these authorizations, the FCC notes that senders who claim they have obtained authorization prior to the effective date of these rules will not be in compliance unless they can demonstrate that these existing authorizations have met each of the requirements in the rule.
- Consumers must not bear any cost with respect to the authorization or revocation processes.
- Each authorization must include certain required disclosures stating that:
    1. The subscriber is agreeing to receive MSCMs sent to his/her wireless device from a particular (identified) sender.
    2. The subscriber may be charged by his/her wireless provider in connection with the receipt of such messages.
    3. The subscriber may revoke the authorization at any time.

These disclosures must be clearly legible and in sufficiently large type (or volume, if given via audio). They must be presented in a manner that is readily apparent to the consumer. These disclosures must be separate from any other authorizations contained in another document. Additionally, if any portion of the authorization/disclosure is translated into another language, then all portions must be translated into that language.

- As noted above, the authorization must be specific to the sender and must clearly identify the entity that is being authorized to send the MSCMs. The FCC rule prohibits any sender from sending MSCMs on behalf of other third parties, including affiliates and marketing partners. Each entity must obtain separate express prior authorizations for the messages it sends.
- Authorization may be obtained in any format, oral or written, including electronic. Although writing is not required, the FCC requires that each sender of MSCMs must document the authorization and be able to demonstrate that a valid authorization (meeting all the other requirements) existed prior to sending the commercial message. The commentary notes that the burden of proof rests with the sender.
- With regard to revocations, senders must enable consumers to revoke authorizations using the same means that the consumers used to grant authorizations. (For example, if a consumer authorizes MSCMs electronically, the company must permit the consumer to revoke the authorization electronically.)
- Additionally, the MSCMs themselves must include functioning return e-mail addresses or another Internet-based mechanism that is clearly and conspicuously displayed for the purpose of receiving opt-out requests.
  Note: Consumers must not be required to view or hear any further commercial content during the opt-out process (other than institutional identification).
- The FCC rule maintains the CAN-SPAM-mandated 10-business-day grace period following a revoked authorization, after which messages cannot be sent.

3.3 The Wireless Domain Registry

To help senders of commercial messages determine whether those messages might be MSCMs (rather than regular commercial e-mail), the FCC has created a registry of wireless domain names (available on the FCC website).[38] It is updated on a periodic basis, as new domains are added.

Senders are responsible for obtaining this list and ensuring that the appropriate authorizations exist before sending commercial messages to addresses within the domains. In other words, the requirements listed above will apply to messages sent to any address whose domain name is included on the wireless domain name list.

According to the FCC guidance, messages that are not sent to an address for a wireless device, but only forwarded to a wireless device are not subject to FCC rules on MSCMs.[39]

With regard to the domain name list, all commercial mobile radio service providers are required under the rule to identify all electronic mail domain names that are dedicated for use by subscribers for wireless devices. The providers are also responsible for updating information on the domain name list to the FCC within 30 days before issuing any new or modified domain names.

4. The Telecommunications Act of 1996

The chapter thus far has examined marketing rules for telecommunications channels such as telephones, faxes and e-mails. The discussion now turns to rules affecting the telecommunications companies themselves in connection with personal information. The Telecommunications Act of 1996 was a major piece of legislation that reshaped numerous aspects of telecommunications markets.[40] Section 222 of the act governs the privacy of customer information provided to and obtained by telecommunications carriers. Prior to the act, carriers were permitted to sell customer data to third-party marketers without consumer consent. The statute imposed new restrictions on the access, use and disclosure of customer proprietary network information (CPNI).

CPNI is information collected by telecommunications carriers related to their subscribers. This includes subscription information, services used and network and billing information as well as phone features and capabilities. It also includes call log data such as time, date, destination and duration of calls. Personal information such as name, telephone number and address is not CPNI. The CPNI requirements apply to telecommunications carriers and voice-over-Internet protocol (VoIP) providers that are interconnected with telephone service, but not to Internet or cable service data.[41]

The act imposes requirements on carriers that limit access, use and disclosure of CPNI. Specifically, carriers can use and disclose CPNI only with customer approval or "as required by law."[42] However, carriers do not need approval to use, disclose or provide marketing offerings among service categories that customers already subscribe to. Carriers can also use CPNI for billing and collections, fraud prevention, customer service and emergency services.

The rules concerning opt-in and opt-out for use of CPNI have shifted over time. In 1998, the FCC issued a rule requiring carriers to obtain express consent from customers before using CPNI, even for the carriers' own marketing purposes. This rule was struck down in 1999 in *U.S. West, Inc. v. Federal Communications Commission.*[43] In that case, the Tenth Circuit found that the opt-in requirement violated the First Amendment speech rights of the carriers. Thus, the standard shifted to an opt-out system for carriers' own use of CPNI. In 2002, the FCC issued final rules requiring carriers to obtain express consent before CPNI could be shared with third parties, but allowed sharing of CPNI with joint venture or independent contractors unless customers opted out within 30 days of being notified. In 2007 the FCC issued new CPNI regulations governing carriers' use and sharing of CPNI.[44] The 2007 CPNI order requires customers to expressly consent, or opt in, before carriers can share their CPNI with joint venture partners and independent contractors for marketing purposes.

The 2007 CPNI order imposes requirements aimed at curbing pretexting, or gaining access to CPNI through fraudulent means. First, carriers must notify law enforcement when CPNI is disclosed in a security breach within seven business days of that breach. Second, customers must provide a password before they can access their CPNI via telephone or online account services. The order also establishes carrier CPNI compliance requirements. Carriers must certify their compliance with these laws annually, explain how their systems ensure compliance, and provide an annual summary of consumer complaints related to unauthorized disclosure of CPNI.

5. The Cable Television Privacy Act of 1984

The Cable Television Privacy Act of 1984 regulates the notice a cable television provider must furnish to customers, the ability of cable providers to collect personal information (PI), the ability of cable providers to disseminate PI and the retention and destruction of PI by cable television providers.[45] It also provides a private right of action for violations of the aforementioned provisions, and allows for actual or statutory damages, punitive damages and reasonable attorney's fees and court costs.[46] The act does not regulate the provision of broadband Internet services via cable because the act defines a "cable service" as "*one-way* transmission to subscribers of . . . video programming or . . . other programming service, and . . . subscriber interaction, if any, which is required for the selection or use of such video programming or other programming service."[47]

At the time of entering into an agreement to provide cable services, and on an annual basis thereafter, cable service providers are required to give subscribers a privacy notice that "clearly and conspicuously" informs subscribers of: (1) the nature of the PI collected, (2) how such information will be used, (3) the retention period of such information and (4) the manner by which a subscriber can access and correct such information.[48] The act further states that a cable TV service provider may only collect PI that is necessary to render cable services, or to detect the unauthorized reception of cable services.[49]

The act limits cable service providers' right to disseminate PI without the "written or electronic consent" of the subscriber, unless the disclosure is subject to a specified exception.[50] A number of exceptions to this provision do exist. Specifically, disclosures may be made (1) to the extent necessary to render services or conduct other legitimate business activities, (2) subject to a court order with notice to the subscriber or (3) if the disclosure is limited to names and addresses and the subscriber is given an option to opt out.[51]

Although the act does not specify a schedule for data retention or destruction, it does mandate that PI be destroyed when it is no longer needed for the purpose for which it was collected and there are no pending requests for access.[52]

The provision allowing for disclosures of PI subject to a court order with notice to the subscriber has been read as creating tension with the Electronic Communications Privacy Act of 1986 (ECPA), which allows such disclosures without notice to the consumer, as notice may negatively impact an ongoing investigation.[53] Courts have resolved this tension in favor of EPCA, due to its later enactment.[54]

6. The Video Privacy Protection Act of 1988

The Video Privacy Protection Act of 1988 (VPPA)[55] was passed in response to the disclosure and publication of then-Supreme Court nominee Robert Bork's video rental records.[56] Although the records revealed that Judge Bork watched innocuous films, the disclosure was considered a gross invasion of his privacy.

The act applies to "video tape service providers," who are defined as anyone "engaged in the business, in or affecting interstate or foreign commerce, of rental, sale, or delivery of prerecorded video cassette tapes or similar audio visual materials" as well as individuals who receive PI in the ordinary course of a videotape service provider's business or for marketing purposes.[57] Videotape service providers are prohibited from disclosing customer PI unless an enumerated exception applies.[58] Exceptions are provided for instances in which the disclosure (1) is made to the consumer themselves, (2) is made subject to the contemporaneous written consent of the consumer, (3) is made to law enforcement pursuant to a warrant, subpoena or other court order, (4) includes only the names and addresses of consumers, (5) includes only names, addresses and subject matter descriptions and the disclosure is used only for the marketing of goods or services to the consumers, (6) is for order fulfillment, request processing, transfer of ownership or debt collection, or (7) is pursuant to a court order in a civil proceeding and the consumer is granted a right to object.[59]

The act requires that PI be destroyed "as soon as practicable, but no later than one year from the date the information is no longer necessary for the purpose for which it was collected and there are no pending requests or orders for access to such information."[60]

The act affords a private right of action for violations and allows for actual or statutory damages, punitive damages, and reasonable attorney's fees and court costs.[61] Statutory damages are set at $2,500.[62] At least one case, however, suggests that the private right of action extends only to disclosure-related violations and not violations based merely on improper retention.[63] Additionally, the VPPA does not preempt more protective state laws, which may give rise to stricter penalties.[64]

Significant changes to the landscape of video delivery since the law was enacted in 1988 have created uncertainty surrounding what is covered by "prerecorded video cassette tapes or similar audio visual materials." As of early 2012, Netflix sought to amend the law to allow for one-time consumer consent, replacing the contemporaneity requirement.[65] Others, however, have suggested that a more comprehensive overhaul of the law is necessary.[66] Netflix stated that it desires to revise the law in order to provide social media integration for users.[67] Such social media integration previously resulted in Blockbuster settling a lawsuit resulting from the posting of customers' rentals from Blockbuster.com on Facebook via Facebook's beacon program in 2010.[68]

7. Conclusion

This chapter examined the legal rules that apply to important channels for marketing, including telephone marketing, fax marketing and commercial e-mail. It then considered the rules governing how the telecommunications companies can use personal information generated in the course of communications activities. Along with the Video Privacy Protection Act, special statutes apply to telephone and cable companies, because of their potential access to individuals' detailed communication and viewing information. Current law places significant limits on how these infrastructure companies can use and disclose personal information that flows through their systems. No similar statutes currently govern Internet service providers and website operators. Going forward, telephone, cable and video rental companies are likely to argue, in an era of convergence, that they are disadvantaged vis-à-vis the Internet-based business models.

Endnotes

1 Restatement of the Law (Second), Torts, § 652B.

2 *Id.*

3 15 U.S.C. §§ 6101-6108.

4 *Federal Register* 68, no, 19 (January 29, 2003): 4669, www.ftc.gov/os/2002/12/tsrfinalrule.pdf.

5 47 U.S.C. § 227(b)(1).

6 See generally, Federal Trade Commission, "The Amended TSR at a Glance," http://business.ftc.gov/documents/bus27-complying-telemarketing-sales-rule#Glance.

7 For example, in fiscal year 2011 over 8 million more numbers were added to the registry. See Federal Trade Commission, "Biennial Report to Congress Reporting on Fiscal Years 2010–2011" (December 2011), www.ftc.gov/os/2011/12/111230dncreport.pdf.

8 "New Rule Prohibiting Unwanted "Robocalls" to Take Effect on September 1," FTC File No. R411001, (Aug. 27, 2009), http://ftc.gov/opa/2009/08/robocalls.shtm.

9 Federal Trade Commission, "Q&A For Telemarketers & Sellers About DNC Provisions in TSR," under "Paying for Access: Who must pay the fee?," http://business.ftc.gov/documents/alt129-qa-telemarketers-sellers-about-dnc-provisions-tsr#paying.

10 Upselling is the sale of a product or service in addition to the product or service the customer has purchased.

11 Federal Trade Commission, " Complying with the Telemarketing Sales Rule," under "The Amended TSR at a Glance: The Written Permission to Call Exemption," http://business.ftc.gov/documents/bus27-complying-telemarketing-sales-rule#Glance.

12 Federal Trade Commission, " Complying with the Telemarketing Sales Rule," under "The Amended TSR at a Glance: The Written Permission to Call Exemption," http://business.ftc.gov/documents/bus27-complying-telemarketing-sales-rule#Glance.

13 Federal Trade Commission, "Complying with the Telemarketing Sales Rule," under "Protecting Consumers' Privacy: Do Not Call Safe Harbor," http://business.ftc.gov/documents/bus27-complying-telemarketing-sales-rule#safeharbor.

14 Federal Trade Commission, "Q&A For Telemarketers & Sellers About DNC Provisions in TSR" under "Coverage Under the TSR: Do the do not call provisions of the TSR cover calls soliciting money for charities?," http://business.ftc.gov/documents/alt129-qa-telemarketers-sellers-about-dnc-provisions-tsr.

15 Material terms may include cost, quantity, restrictions, limitations, conditions, no-refund policies, etc.

16 Intrastate calls are covered by the Federal Communications Commission's regulations under the Telephone Consumer Protection Act (47 U.S.C. § 227). These rules are similar to the TSR rules described herein.

17 Not all telemarketing activities are covered by the TSR. For example, most business-to-business calls are excluded from the rule. Additionally, the TSR applies only to entities subject to FTC jurisdiction, with other entities (such as banks) covered solely by the TCPA referenced in note 1. Finally, some types of calls are partially exempt from the rule. As discussed later in this Chapter, calls to existing customers are exempt from the Do Not Call Registry provisions. Inbound calls from customers are also excluded, although upselling during the call will bring it back within the scope of the rule with regard to disclosures, payment provisions, etc.

18 Federal Trade Commission, "Complying with the Telemarketing Sales Rule," under "The Amended TSR at a Glance: Multiple Purpose Calls," http://business.ftc.gov/documents/bus27-complying-telemarketing-sales-rule#Glance.

19 Federal Trade Commission, "Complying with the Telemarketing Sales Rule," under "The Amended TSR at a Glance: Transmitting Caller Id Information," http://business.ftc.gov/documents/bus27-complying-telemarketing-sales-rule#Glance.

20 47 C.F.R. § 64.1200(a)(6).

21 Including a sales message would violate the Federal Communication Commission's rules under the Telephone Consumer Protection Act (47 U.S.C. § 227) and FCC regulations at 47 C.F.R. Part 64.1200.

22 *In the Matter of Rules and Regulations Implementing the Telephone Consumer Protection Act of 1991, Report and Order*, CG Docket No. 02-278 (Feb 15, 2012) http://transition.fcc.gov/Daily_Releases/Daily_Business/2012/db0215/FCC-12-21A1.pdf.

23 Federal Trade Commission, "Complying with the Telemarketing Sales Rule," http://business.ftc.gov/documents/bus27-complying-telemarketing-sales-rule#whomustkeep.

24 Private individuals have to meet certain damage requirements to bring suit.

25 U.S. Small Business Administration, "Telemarketing Laws," www.sba.gov/content/telemarketing-laws.

26 For example, see Mississippi's Online DNC List registration, www.ms.gov/psc/nocall/ and Pennsylvania's Online DNC List registration, www.attorneygeneral.gov/dnc.aspx.

27 Kan. Stat. Ann. § 50-670.

28 Fla. Stat. § 501.059.

29 Telephone Consumer Protection Act (TCPA), 47 U.S.C. § 227 (1991), www.fcc.gov/cgb/policy/TCPA-Rules.pdf. Also see FCC, Telemarketing Policy, http://transition.fcc.gov/cgb/policy/telemarketing.html.

30 In 2003, the FCC approved a $5.3 million fine against Fax.com for violations of the act, http://hraunfoss.fcc.gov/edocs_public/attachmatch/DOC-242654A1.pdf; in 2001 a Hooters of Augusta (Ga.) was found to have violated the act and had to pay out over $1 million in a class action suit, www.keytlaw.com/faxes/hooterscase.htm.

31 California Business & Professions Code § 17538.43.

32 *Chamber of Commerce of the U.S. v. Lockyer*, 2006 WL 462482 (E. D. Cal. 2006).

33 The CAN-SPAM Act of 2003, 15 U.S.C. 7701, et seq., www.spamlaws.com/federal/can-spam.shtml.

34 Federal Trade Commission, "The CAN-SPAM Act: A Compliance Guide for Business," http://business.ftc.gov/documents/bus61-can-spam-act-compliance-guide-business.

35 Federal Trade Commission, "FTC Approves New Rule Provision Under the CAN-SPAM Act," May 12, 2008, www.ftc.gov/opa/2008/05/canspam.shtm.

36 16 CFR Part 316, www.ftc.gov/os/2008/05/R411008frn.pdf.

37 *In the Matter of Rules and Regulations Implementing the Controlling the Assault of Non-Solicited Pornography and Marketing Act of 2003; Rules and Regulations Implementing the Telephone Consumer Protection Act of 1991*, FCC 04-194, (Aug. 12, 2004), http://hraunfoss.fcc.gov/edocs_public/attachmatch/FCC-04-194A1.pdf.

38 Federal Communications Commission, "Domain Name Downloads," www.fcc.gov/cgb/policy/DomainNameDownload.html.

39 Federal Communications Commission, "Protecting Your Privacy," under "Protecting You From Unwanted Text Messages on Your Wireless Devices," www.fcc.gov/guides/protecting-your-privacy.

40 Telecommunications Act, 47 U.S.C. § 222 (1996).

41 Public Notice, Annual CPNI Certifications Due March 1, 2012, (Feb. 16, 2012), http://transition.fcc.gov/Daily_Releases/Daily_Business/2012/db0216/DA-12-170A1.pdf.

42 See ECPA discussion in Chapter 10.

43 *U.S. West, Inc. v. Federal Communications Commission*, 182 F.3d 1224 (10th Cir. 1999).

44 FCC Report and Order, 07-22 (April 2, 2007).

45 47 U.S.C. § 551 (2006).

46 *Id.* at § 551(a).

47 *Id.* at § 522(6)(A) (emphasis added).

48 *Id.* at § 551(a).

49 *Id.* at § 551(b).

50 *Id.* at § 551(c)(1).

51 *Id.* at § 551(c)(2).

52 *Id.* at § 551.

53 18 U.S.C. §§ 2703 & 2705.

54 See, e.g., In re Application of the United States of America for an Order Pursuant to 18 U.S.C. § 2703(D) Directed to Cablevision Systems Corp., 158 F.Supp.2d 644 (2001).

55 18 U.S.C. § 2710 (2006).

56 The Video Privacy Protection Act: Protecting Viewer Privacy in the 21st Century, 112th Cong. (2012) (statement of Rep. Watt), www.judiciary.senate.gov/pdf/12-1-31WattTestimony.pdf.

57 18 U.S.C. § 2710(a)(4) (2006).

58 *Id.* at § 2710(b)(1).

59 *Id.* at § 2710(b)(2).

60 *Id.* at § 2710(e).

61 *Id.* at § 2710(c).

62 *Id.*

63 *Sterk v. Redbox Automated Retail, LLC*, 2012 U.S. App. LEXIS 4570, *7 (7th Cir. 2012). ("The statute is not well drafted ... The biggest interpretive problem is created by the statute's failure to specify the scope of subsection (c), which creates the right of action on which this lawsuit is based. If (c) appeared after all the prohibitions, which is to say after (d) and (e) as well as (b), the natural inference would be that any violator of any of the prohibitions could be sued for damages. But instead (c) appears after just the first prohibition, the one in subsection (b), prohibiting disclosure.")

64 See, e.g., Conn. Gen. Stat. § 53-450; Maryland Code Art. 27 § 583.; Mich. L. § 445.1712.

65 H.R. 2471, 112th Cong. (2011).

66 See, e.g., The Video Privacy Protection Act: Protecting Viewer Privacy in the 21st Century, 112th Cong. (2012) (statement of Marc Rotenberg), www.judiciary.senate.gov/pdf/12-1-31RotenbergTestimony.pdf.

67 The Video Privacy Protection Act: Protecting Viewer Privacy in the 21st Century, 112th Cong. (2012) (statement of David Hyman), www.judiciary.senate.gov/pdf/12-1-31HymanTestimony.pdf.

68 *Lane v. Facebook, Inc.*, 2010 U.S. Dist. LEXIS 24762 (N.D. Cal. 2010).

CHAPTER EIGHT

Privacy Statutes About Online Activities

As discussed in Chapter 2, much of the regulation of Internet privacy has occurred through enforcement of federal and state statutes that prohibit unfair and deceptive practices, notably under Section 5 of the Federal Trade Commission Act. This chapter turns to two significant statutes that also apply to privacy on the Internet. First, the Children's Online Privacy Protection Act of 1998 (COPPA) is a federal law that applies to companies that collect personal information from children under the age of 13.

The California Online Privacy Protection Act is the state law of California, but is relevant to commercial practice nationally. The California law by its terms applies only to websites that collect personal information from state residents; however, the large population and reach of that state means that the statute covers many U.S. businesses. The statute *requires* the organization to post an online privacy notice. That requirement, combined with the laws about unfair and deceptive trade practices, increases the enforceability of Internet privacy—organizations are required to post privacy notices, and violations of those notices are typically considered deceptive practices.

1. The Children's Online Privacy Protection Act of 1998

COPPA regulates the collection and use of children's information by commercial website operators.[1] COPPA was passed soon after the FTC's 1998 *Privacy Online: A Report to Congress*, written in response to growing concern about the privacy of children using the Internet.[2] Specifically, the report discussed rapid growth in the number of interactive services directed at children, and detailed how children were actively engaging in discussion groups, online games, research surveys and contests. During this activity, a large amount of personally identifiable information about children and their families was being collected by websites without parent and guardian knowledge or consent.

COPPA applies to (1) the operators of commercial websites and online services directed to children under the age of 13, including mobile application developers[3] and (2) the general-audience websites and online services that know that they are collecting personal information from children under the age of 13.[4]

To determine whether a website or online service is targeted to children, the FTC looks at the subject matter, age of models and the visual and audio content used. Other factors the FTC considers include the language used, whether the site uses animated characters and children's activities and incentives.[5]

The act requires website operators to:

- Post a privacy notice on the homepage of the website and a link to the privacy notice on every page where personal information is collected
- Provide notice about the site's information collection practices to parents
- Obtain verifiable parental consent before collecting personal information from children
- Give parents a choice as to whether their children's personal information will be disclosed to third parties
- Provide parents access and the opportunity to delete the children's personal information and opt out of future collection or use of the information
- Not condition a child's participation in a game, contest or other activity on the child's disclosing more personal information than is reasonably necessary to participate in that activity
- Maintain the confidentiality, security and integrity of personal information collected from children

1.1 Privacy Notices Under COPPA

The COPPA privacy notice must be available via links on the website home page and any other page where personal information is disclosed. The link must be clearly labeled and placed in a prominent spot on each page that it appears. The privacy notice must include:

- Contact information for the website operators collecting/maintaining information
- The type of information collected
- How the information will be used
- Whether the information will be disclosed to third parties and, if so, the general purpose of the third party, as well as a description of its business and acknowledgment of confidentiality
- A disclaimer providing an option to consent to collection but not disclosure
- A statement that no condition may be placed on the disclosure of information
- A statement that it is the parent's final right to forfeit a child's disclosure of information, and the procedures to do so

Reasonable efforts must be taken to ensure that parents receive notice that information is being collected from their child, and that their consent is required for this collection.

As noted above, COPPA generally requires website operators to obtain verifiable parental consent before collecting personal information from a child. A variety of mechanisms have been developed to facilitate parental consent. According to the FTC's published guidance:[6]

If you are going to use the information only for internal purposes, that is, you will not be giving the information to third parties or making it publicly available through such activities as chat rooms or bulletin boards, then you can use what is being called the "email plus" method of obtaining consent. You may send an email to the parent containing the required notice, and request that the parent provide consent by responding in an email—as long as you take some additional, confirmatory step after receiving the parent's email. For example, after a reasonable time delay, you can send another email to the parent to confirm consent and let the parent know that he or she can revoke the consent if they wish. You may also request in your initial email that the parent include a phone number or mailing address in his or her reply so that you can follow up to confirm via telephone or postal mail.

If you are going to disclose children's information to third parties or make it publicly available through such activities as a chat room, message board, personal home page, pen pal service, or email service, then you must use the most reliable methods available to obtain parental consent. You can: provide a form for the parent to sign and mail or fax back to you; ask a parent to use a credit card in connection with a transaction (perhaps a fee just to cover the cost of processing the credit card); maintain a toll-free telephone number staffed by trained personnel for parents to call in their consent, or you can accept emails from parents where those emails contain a digital signature or other digital certificate that uses public key technology.

There are several exceptions to the consent requirement that allow an operator to collect a child's name and e-mail address:[7]

- If it is being collected along with the parent's e-mail address for purposes of providing the required notice and obtaining consent.
- To respond once to a specific request from a child, as long as the e-mail address is deleted immediately after responding.
- To respond more than once to a specific request of a child (for example, one who is requesting a subscription to an online newsletter or requesting site updates), as long as, after the first communication with the child, the operator sends notice to the parent's e-mail address to provide an opportunity for the parent to opt out of the information collection and order the operator to delete the e-mail address and stop contacting the child. With this multiple-contact exception, the parent needs only to contact the operator to discontinue the communication; affirmative consent is not required, so a lack of response will be presumed to be parental consent. Of course, at any time, the parent may contact the operator and request that the information be deleted and the contact halted.
- To collect a child's name and e-mail address where necessary to protect the safety of a child participating on the site or online service. The operator must give notice to the parent, use it only for such safety purpose and not disclose it on the site or service.

- To collect a child's name and e-mail address for the sole purpose of protecting the security or integrity of the site, take precautions against liability, respond to judicial process or for law enforcement on a matter related to public safety.

COPPA regulations contain a few additional requirements. For example, a child's participation in an online activity cannot be conditional on the disclosure of detailed personal information. Additionally, upon request, parents must be provided with access to the specific information collected from their child, and the opportunity to terminate the use and collection of the information.

Children's online privacy is also addressed through marketplace initiatives among industry groups such as the Better Business Bureau's Children's Advertising Review Unit (CARU). The CARU Guidelines for Children's Advertising are a self-regulatory framework. If a company violates one or more of the guidelines and does not correct the violation upon request from CARU, CARU will provide information on the violation directly to the FTC for enforcement.

1.2 Safe Harbor Program

Under COPPA, if an operator of a website or online service engages in and adheres to a self-regulatory program issued by an industry group approved by the FTC, then those services are considered to be compliant with COPPA requirements. To meet COPPA "Safe Harbor" requirements, the self-regulatory program must:

- Provide equal or greater protection for children,
- Implement mandatory mechanisms for assessing a participant's compliance, and
- Offer incentives for compliance.

As of mid-2012 there are five such COPPA Safe Harbor programs approved by the FTC: (1) CARU, (2) the Entertainment Software Rating Board (ESRB), (3) TRUSTe, (4) Privo, Inc. and (5) Aristotle International, Inc.[8]

1.3 Enforcement

Violations of COPPA may result in FTC enforcement actions and monetary fines. There is no private right of action under COPPA. States may bring civil actions for violations of COPPA; however, COPPA preempts state law. The FTC has regularly brought enforcement actions under COPPA, with penalties for four 2011 and 2012 consent decrees ranging from $50,000 to $3 million.[9]

In August 2011, the FTC brought its first case against a mobile application developer for violating COPPA requirements.[10] The FTC alleged that W3 Innovations collected children's information without parental consent, among other violations. The mobile application developer was required to pay a $50,000 penalty for violation of these rules, and was required to delete all private information collected in disregard of COPPA requirements. The case made it clear that the FTC expects both application developers and website operators to adhere to COPPA requirements, regardless of whether operating in the online or mobile environment.

1.4 2011 Proposed Rules

In September 2011, the FTC released proposed amendments to COPPA.[11] According to the FTC, the revisions are to "ensure that the Rule continues to protect children's privacy, as mandated by Congress, as online technologies evolve."[12] The proposed rules include revisions in five areas: parental notice, parental consent mechanisms, children's information security, safe harbor programs and definitions.

The proposed changes would expand the definition of "personal information" to include geolocation, tracking cookies, and other persistent identifiers common in mobile devices, which are typically used to track users across websites and applications for targeted marketing purposes. As a result, application developers would be required to obtain parental consent even when their applications are passively collecting data about children as they move across sites, creating potentially significant new compliance obligations on the providers of these services.

The proposed rule also would permit compliance with the statute with new methods to obtain verifiable parental consent, including electronic scans of signed parental consent forms, video conferencing, and use of government-issued identification checked against a database, provided that the parent's ID is deleted promptly after the verification is done. The proposed rule would also eliminate the "e-mail plus" method of parental consent.

2. California's Online Privacy Protection Act

The California Online Privacy Protection Act of 2003 was the first state law to require owners and operators of websites and online services to conspicuously post a privacy notice on their website.[13] Specifically, the act requires all such website operators that collect personally identifiable information from California citizens to post and comply with a privacy policy (notice) on their website. "Personally identifiable information," for this statute, refers to information collected about consumers, including name, address, e-mail address, telephone number, Social Security number and any other similar, identifying information.

The effect of this law extends beyond businesses located in California. Because of the state's large population, a great majority of online businesses in the United States collect PI from California citizens and fall under the purview of the law. The act's privacy policy requirements, however, do not apply to third parties that operate, host or manage websites and online services on behalf of the first party, such as Internet service providers.

California's Online Privacy Protection Act requires website operators and service providers to "conspicuously post" a privacy notice on their website. "Conspicuous" in this context means: (1) the privacy notice is on the homepage of the website, or the first significant page after entering the website, or (2) the privacy notice is hyperlinked to the homepage by an icon or text link that contains the word *privacy* and is in a color different from the background color of the homepage.[14]

The privacy notice itself must:

- Identify the categories of personally identifiable information the operator collects

- Identify the categories of third parties with whom the operator may share personally identifiable information
- Describe the process by which consumers review and request changes to their personally identifiable information, if such a process exists
- Describe the process by which the operator notifies consumers of material changes made to the privacy policy
- Identify its effective date

After receiving notification of noncompliance with the act, the website or online service operator has 30 days to post an appropriate privacy notice. If the operator fails to post the privacy notice within that timeframe, or if the operator fails to adhere to the terms in the notice, it will be found either (1) negligent and material or (2) knowingly and willfully noncompliant.

The California Online Privacy Protection Act does not include specific enforcement provisions. Instead, the law may be enforced through California's general consumer protection statute that prohibits unlawful, unfair or fraudulent business acts and practices.[15] Actions may be brought by state government officials or by private parties. However, there are no judicial decisions as of early 2012 for violations of the California Online Privacy Protection Act.

In 2012 the California attorney general announced that the California Online Privacy Protection Act privacy notice requirements extend to mobile application developers who collect personal information through their applications and services.[16] Under an agreement with six major application platforms, mobile application developers are now required to conspicuously post privacy notices in their applications or online services.

3. Conclusion

This chapter has highlighted important statutes that govern privacy on the Internet. Because almost all significant consumer-facing websites post enforceable privacy policies under the California Online Privacy Protection Act, the U.S. approach to Internet privacy today is less about "self-regulation" than some observers have believed.

Endnotes

1 Children's Online Privacy Protection Act of 1998, 15 U.S.C. § 6501-6506.

2 FTC, *Privacy Online: A Report to Congress*, 1998, www.ftc.gov/reports/privacy3/index.htm.

3 *Consent Decree and Order, U.S. v. W3 Innovations, LLC, also d/b/a Broken Thumbs Apps, and Justin Maples*, FTC File No. 102 3251 (Sept. 8, 2011), http://ftc.gov/os/caselist/1023251/110908w3order.pdf.

4 15 U.S.C. § 6502(a)(l).

5 16 C.F.R. § 312.2 (definition of "website or online service directed to children").

6 Federal Trade Commission, "Frequently Asked Questions about the Children's Online Privacy Protection Rule," under "Verifiable Parental Consent," www.ftc.gov/privacy/coppafaqs.htm#consent.

7 *Id.*

8 See Federal Trade Commission, "Frequently Asked Questions about the Children's Online Privacy Protection Rule," under "Safe Harbors," http://www.ftc.gov/privacy/coppafaqs.shtm#safe. Also see "FTC Approves Safe Harbor Program for Aristotle International, Inc." (Feb 24, 2012), http://ftc.gov/opa/2012/02/aristotle.shtm.

9 Federal Trade Commission, "Legal Resources," http://business.ftc.gov/legal-resources/30/35.

10 *Consent Decree and Order, U.S. v. W3 Innovations, LLC, also d/b/a Broken Thumbs Apps, and Justin Maples,* FTC File No. 102 3251 (Sept. 8, 2011) http://ftc.gov/os/caselist/1023251/110908w3order.pdf.

11 16 CFR Part 312, http://ftc.gov/os/2011/09/110915coppa.pdf.

12 FTC Seeks Comment on Proposed Revisions to Children's Online Privacy Protection Rule, Sept. 15, 2011, http:*//ftc.gov/opa/2011/09/coppa.shtm.*

13 California Business and Professions Code §§ 22575–22579 (2006).

14 California Business and Professions Code § 22577(b).

15 California Business and Professions Code § 17200 *et seq.*

16 State of California Office of the Attorney General, "Attorney General Kamala D. Harris Secures Global Agreement to Strengthen Privacy Protections for Users of Mobile Applications," (Feb. 22, 2012), http://oag.ca.gov/news/press_release?id=2630.

CHAPTER NINE

Information Security and Data Breach Notification Laws

- Reuters, April 26, 2011: "Sony suffered a massive breach in its video game online network that led to the theft of names, addresses and possibly credit card data belonging to 77 million user accounts."[1]
- The *New York Times*, June 10, 2012: "[H]ackers breached the [LinkedIn] site and stole more than six million of its customers' passwords, which had been only lightly encrypted. They were posted to a Russian hacker forum for all to see.[2]
- BankInfoSecurity, 2008: "News of the Hannaford Brothers breach broke on March 17, and subsequent investigation revealed that malware was surreptitiously placed on the servers at 300 of the store locations."[3]
- The *Wall Street Journal*, April 2, 2012: "Global Payments Inc., the credit-card processor that reported a significant security breach Friday, said that hackers stole account numbers and other key information from up to 1.5 million accounts in North America."[4]

Such massive, high-profile data breaches make the front pages, but according to a 2012 Ponemon Institute study, "Small and midsize businesses . . . are at a greater risk of their employees mishandling data than enterprises."[5] The United States does not have a comprehensive information security or data breach law, although Congress has repeatedly considered various data breach bills in recent years. Some states have enacted general information security statutes. Most states have passed data breach notification laws, which create important incentives for companies to develop good information security practices. As of June 2012, only Alabama, Kentucky, New Mexico and South Dakota lack some form of legislation. Even if a breach occurs in one of those states, consumers residing in other states may be entitled to notice of the breach.

1. Information Security

As discussed earlier, there are federally imposed information security provisions in the healthcare and financial sectors based on HIPAA (Chapter 4) and GLBA (Chapter 5), respectively. In addition, the FTC uses its Section 5 power (under the FTC Act) to bring actions against companies misrepresenting their information security practices (as a deceptive trade practice) or failing to provide "reasonable procedures" to protect personal information (as an unfair trade practice). Yet, no federal legislation directly imposes minimum information security standards across all industries. In the absence of such requirements, state legislatures have passed laws to ensure that companies protect their citizens' sensitive information.

In 2004, as consumers started receiving breach notifications pursuant to its existing state security breach notification law, California enacted Assembly Bill 1950 (AB 1950) to "encourage businesses that own or license personal information about Californians to provide reasonable security."[6] Specifically, the law requires a business "that owns or licenses personal information about a California resident" to "implement and maintain reasonable security procedures and practices appropriate to the nature of the information, to protect the personal information from unauthorized access, destruction, use, modification, or disclosure."[7] Furthermore, the bill required businesses using unaffiliated third-party data processors to contractually mandate similar security procedures.

In the case of AB 1950, "personal information" is defined as an individual's first name or initial and last name combined with Social Security number, driver's license number, financial account numbers or medical information. Personal information that is publicly available or encrypted is excluded from the law. This definition generally follows the definition of "personal information" that triggers the state's breach notification law.

Companies already subject to greater information security requirements (e.g., GLBA or HIPAA) are exempt from the law. Because AB 1950 provides no guidance as to what constitutes "reasonable security procedures and practices," some information security experts have suggested using the financial and healthcare sector framework as models. Similar legislation has since passed in other states, including Massachusetts, Minnesota, Nevada and Washington.

The Massachusetts state security law, Mass. 201 CMR 17, is generally considered the most prescriptive in the nation.[8] It establishes detailed minimum standards to "safeguard . . . personal information contained in both paper and electronic records." The law requires businesses holding "personal information" (defined as a Massachusetts resident's name plus a sensitive data element, such as a Social Security number) to:

1. Designate an individual who is responsible for information security
2. Anticipate risks to personal information and take appropriate steps to mitigate such risks
3. Develop security program rules
4. Impose penalties for violations of the program rules
5. Prevent access to personal information by former employees
6. Contractually obligate third-party service providers to maintain similar procedures

7. Restrict physical access to records containing personal information
8. Monitor the effectiveness of the security program
9. Review the program at least once a year, and whenever business changes could impact security
10. Document responses to incidents

From a technical perspective, Mass. 201 CMR 17 mandates user authentication, access controls, encryption, monitoring, portable devices, firewall protection, updates and training. The law came into effect in 2010.

The Washington state security law, HB 1149, also took effect in 2010.[9] This law is part of a growing trend to incorporate the Payment Card Industry Data Security Standard (PCI DSS) into statute to ensure the security of credit card transactions and related personal information. Minnesota and Nevada enacted similar laws earlier. HB 1149 permits financial institutions to recover the costs associated with reissuance of credit and debit cards from large processors whose negligence in the handling of credit card data is the proximate cause of the breach. Processors are not liable if the data was encrypted at the time of the breach or had been certified as PCI-compliant within one year of the breach.

A majority of states have laws limiting businesses' right to use Social Security numbers.[10] California law, for example, prohibits states from using Social Security numbers for a variety of purposes including public posting, printing on mailings (unless mandated by federal law) and printing on ID or membership cards.[11] Additionally, this law prohibits businesses from requiring that customers transmit their Social Security number over an unencrypted Internet connection.

2. Data Breach Notification

Laws that impose security requirements on businesses that process personal information, such as those discussed above, provide some protection of personal information. But even in organizations with extensive security controls, data breaches can occur.

In chronicling data breaches since 2005, the Privacy Rights Clearinghouse lists eight types of incidents:

1. Unintended disclosure—sensitive information posted publicly on a website, mishandled or sent to the wrong party via e-mail, fax or mail
2. Hacking or malware—electronic entry by an outside party, malware and spyware
3. Payment card fraud—fraud involving debit and credit cards that is not accomplished via hacking; for example, skimming devices at point-of-service terminals
4. Insider—someone with legitimate access, such as an employee or contractor, intentionally breaches information
5. Physical loss—lost, discarded or stolen nonelectronic records, such as paper documents
6. Portable device—lost, discarded or stolen laptop, PDA, smartphone, portable memory device, CD, hard drive, data tape, etc.

7. Stationary device—lost, discarded or stolen stationary electronic device such as a computer or server not designed for mobility
8. Unknown or other[12]

Regardless of the incident, the privacy professional must be prepared to support company efforts to detect, contain, report and prevent breaches of personal information. Accordingly, the privacy professional must also be familiar with the specific data breach notification requirements of the states in which his or her organization does business or in which it has customers.

3. Fundamentals of Incident Management

The first step in incident management is determining whether a breach has actually occurred. This may be fairly obvious for certain types of breaches, such as a lost laptop containing personal information or a misdirected file. For other breaches, which may be made by attackers testing a system or gaining entry for later use, the existence of a breach can be harder to detect. Evidence of a possible breach could be multiple failed login attempts, the sudden use of long-dormant access accounts, or the use of information systems during off-hours. IT managers should be alert for the presence of unknown programs, files, devices or users. Unfortunately, some of the largest breaches can occur as a result of advanced persistent threats that compromise the entire corporate network but are difficult to detect and to evaluate in terms of the personal information that may have been taken.

Once a breach is discovered, *the second step is containment and analysis of the incident.* The steps that need to be taken vary greatly with the nature of the breach. For example, if media or devices are lost, the organization should take whatever steps it can to recover the items. If a file is misdirected, the company should reach out to the actual recipient to confirm that the information has been deleted without use or further disclosure. For a network intrusion, the organization should shut down the infiltrated system(s), and revoke physical access to the area, if applicable. Forensic support may be needed to determine what files were accessed or acquired by the intruder. A full system audit should be performed to ensure that vulnerabilities are not reinstated when the system is back and running. After containment, organizations should engage in careful analysis and documentation of the incident, which can help in later stages of incident management, such as negotiations and litigation.

The third step in incident management is to notify affected parties—consumers and/or regulators as required, depending on the type of information, by the jurisdiction(s) in which the organization operates. A number of states have specific requirements for notification letter contents. Additionally, all letters should include information on the risks (if any) posed to the individual as a result of the breach along with steps that can be taken to mitigate the harm.

Finally, for organizational learning and prevention, *organizations should implement effective follow-up methods*, such as additional training, internal self-assessments and third-party audits where needed. These assessments should analyze the breach itself as well as the response plan and should identify deficiencies. Monitoring or "data loss prevention" systems can also be implemented to help prevent and mitigate future data breaches.

4. State Breach Notification Laws

Legislation such as Massachusetts 201 CMR 17 directly requires businesses to implement information security controls. Data breach notification laws create similar incentives to implement effective controls, because they expose companies to the financial and reputational harm associated with the public disclosure of their failure to adequately protect their sensitive personal information. As of June 2012, 46 of the 50 states, the District of Columbia, Puerto Rico and the U.S. Virgin Islands enacted such legislation, beginning with California in 2003 (California Civil Code § 1798.80-1798.84).[13]

While key differences do exist between state laws, there are far more similarities. State data breach notification laws generally contain the same basic provisions:

- The definition of personal information, meaning the specific data elements that trigger reporting requirements
- The definition of what entities are covered
- The definition of a "security breach" or "breach of the security of a system"
- The level of harm requiring notification
- Whom to notify
- When to notify
- What to include in the notification letter
- How to notify
- Exceptions that may exist to the obligation to notify (or when notification may be delayed)
- Penalties and rights of action

We will examine each of these elements, with special reference to the Connecticut law (Conn. Gen. Stat. § 36a-701b) as an example.

4.1 Definition of Personal Information

Connecticut defines personal information as "an individual's first name or first initial and last name in combination with any one, or more, of the following data: (1) Social Security number [although Nevada specifically excludes the last four digits as PI]; (2) driver's license number or state identification card number; or (3) account number, credit or debit card number, in combination with any required security code, access code or password that would permit access to an individual's financial account."[14]

These data are part of the definition of personal information in all state data breach notification laws, although many states contain additional elements. For example, Arkansas, California, Missouri, Texas and Virginia include medical and healthcare information. The laws in Oregon and Wyoming apply to any federal or state identification number, which serves as a catchall for passport numbers, DEA numbers and other tax identification numbers. Iowa,

Nebraska, North Carolina and Wisconsin include unique biometric data ("i.e., such as a fingerprint, retina or iris image, or other unique physical representation or digital representation of biometric data"[15]). Wisconsin specifically lists a DNA profile;[16] Puerto Rico includes tax information and work-related evaluations[17] and North Dakota adds mother's maiden name (often used as a security question), employee number and digital signature. Illinois specifically lists both computerized records and written material,[18] though laws in most states, such as California, apply only to computerized data.

Almost all states exclude "publicly available information that is lawfully made available to the general public from federal, state or local government records or widely distributed media" (from the Connecticut law), although Idaho, Louisiana and Michigan do not include such an exception in their laws. Ohio specifically expands its exclusion of publicly available information to include "any news, editorial, or advertising statement published in any bona fide newspaper, journal, or magazine, or broadcast over radio or television, or any type of media similar in nature; any gathering or furnishing of information or news by any bona fide reporter, correspondent, or news bureau to any bona fide newspaper, journal, magazine, radio or television news media, or any type of media similar in nature; or any publication designed for and distributed to members of any bona fide association or charitable or fraternal nonprofit corporation, or any type of media similar in nature."[19]

4.2 Definition of Covered Entities

Connecticut describes the covered entities as "Any person who conducts business in this state, and who, in the ordinary course of such person's business, owns, licenses or maintains computerized data that includes personal information."[20] Some states limit the definition of "covered entities" to those that conduct business in that state.[21] Note, however, that some state laws are narrower, such as the Georgia law applying only to "information brokers."[22] Texas law specifically requires notification to be sent to residents of other states that do not have a similar law requiring notification.[23]

4.3 Harm and Definition of Security Breach

Connecticut defines a breach of security as "unauthorized access to or acquisition of electronic files, media, databases or computerized data containing personal information when access to the personal information has not been secured by encryption or by any other method or technology that renders the personal information unreadable or unusable."[24] In California, a "breach of the security of a system" occurs when there is unauthorized acquisition of the personal information that "compromises the confidentiality, security or integrity" of the information. Virtually every state contains similar language, although some laws require "material compromise" (e.g., in Florida), and several states define "breach" to be an event that causes (or is likely to cause) identity theft or other material harm (Kansas and South Carolina, for example). Connecticut, California and other states do not have any similar requirement of harm for a defined breach to occur.

4.4 Whom to Notify

The primary recipients of a breach notification are those state residents who are at risk because their personal information has (potentially) been exposed based on the level of unauthorized access or harm. The Texas law requires Texas companies that experience a data breach to notify not only Texas residents, but also residents of states lacking a data protection notification law. In addition, some states, under specified circumstances, require notification to the state attorney general (AG), one or more state regulatory agencies and/or nationwide consumer reporting agencies (CRAs).

At least 14 states require entities who detected a data breach to notify the state attorney general and/or other state agencies:

- In Idaho, state agencies suffering a data breach must notify the AG within 24 hours of incident detection.
- In Illinois, state agencies must file a written report to the General Assembly within five business days.
- California entities must notify the AG if more than 500 California residents are affected.
- Louisiana entities must notify the AG within 10 days and include a list of all the affected individuals.
- Entities in Puerto Rico must notify the territorial Department of Consumer Affairs within 10 days of detection, and the department will make the breach public within 24 hours of receipt.
- In Hawaii, Missouri, South Carolina and Virginia, entities must notify the AG if more than 1,000 state residents are affected.
- Maryland, New Jersey and New York require AG notification *prior* to sending notices to affected data subjects.
- Entities in Maine, Massachusetts, New Hampshire and North Carolina must also report to the state AG.

At least 27 states require that entities notify nationwide CRAs of a data breach, but there are different provisions:

- Minnesota requires notification if more than 500 Minnesota residents are affected.
- Alaska, Colorado, the District of Columbia, Florida, Hawaii, Indiana, Kansas, Maine, Maryland, Michigan, Missouri, Nevada, New Jersey, Ohio, Oregon, Pennsylvania, South Carolina, Tennessee, Vermont, Virginia, West Virginia and Wisconsin require AG notification if more than 1,000 state residents are affected.
- In New York, entities must notify CRAs if more than 5,000 New York residents are affected.

- In Georgia, information brokers must notify CRAs if more than 10,000 Georgia residents are affected.
- In Texas, entities must notify CRAs if more than 10,000 individuals (Texas residents or residents of states without data breach notification laws) are affected.
- Montana requires entities to coordinate notification with CRAs.

In addition, all data breach state laws require third-party notification. The Connecticut law, for example, states: "Any person that maintains computerized data that includes personal information that the person does not own shall notify the owner or licensee of the information of any breach of the security of the data immediately following its discovery, if the personal information was, or is reasonably believed to have been accessed by an unauthorized person."[25]

4.5 When to Notify

All states with data breach notification laws use virtually identical language to describe the required timing of notifications. The most common phrase used in conjunction with timing is *the most expeditious time possible and without unreasonable delay*. Legislators, however, recognize the need for the affected entity to conduct a "reasonable investigation in order to determine the scope of the breach and to restore the reasonable integrity of the data system."[26] Only Florida and Ohio specify a limit (45 days) to "expeditious time."

When a data breach is suspected to be the result of criminal activity, most states also allow delays "for a reasonable period of time if a law enforcement agency determines that the notification will impede a criminal investigation and such law enforcement agency has made a request that the notification be delayed."[27] The entity is, however, expected to issue the notification as soon as possible after such an investigation is complete or the law enforcement agency decides that notification will not compromise the criminal investigation.

As noted above, Puerto Rico requires notification of the Department of Consumer Affairs within 10 days, and within 24 hours the department makes the breach public, making Puerto Rico arguably the most stringent (at least in terms of public exposure) data breach notification law in the country.

4.6 What to Include

Most states do not specify the contents of the notification to the data subject, but California, Iowa, Michigan, New Hampshire, New York, North Carolina, Oregon, Vermont, Virginia and West Virginia do. North Carolina's requirements, for example, are among the most extensive, including:

- A description of the incident in general terms
- A description of the type of personal information that was subject to the unauthorized access and acquisition
- A description of the general acts of the business to protect the personal information from further unauthorized access

- A telephone number for the business that the person may call for further information and assistance, if one exists
- Advice that directs the person to remain vigilant by reviewing account statements and monitoring free credit reports
- The toll-free numbers and addresses for the major consumer reporting agencies
- The toll-free numbers, addresses and website addresses for the Federal Trade Commission and the North Carolina attorney general's office, along with a statement that the individual can obtain information from these sources about preventing identity theft[28]

Oregon's requirements include "advice to the individual to report suspected identity theft to law enforcement,"[29] while West Virginia and Massachusetts requires the notification to specify how an individual can obtain a police report and request a credit freeze. Massachusetts law also prohibits including a description of the nature of the breach in the notification or the number of residents affected by the breach, while laws in other states require the notification to include a general description of the incident.[30] Privacy professionals residing in states that do not specify notification contents can use the requirements of those that do as guidance.

4.7 How to Notify

States generally provide notification options, but a written notice to the data subject is always required first. Telephonic and electronic messages are typical alternatives, but usually only if the data subject has previously explicitly chosen one of those as the preferred communication method.

Most legislation recognizes that data breach notifications involving thousands of impacted data subjects could place an undue financial burden on the organization and therefore allow substitute notification methods. In Connecticut, for example, "Substitute notice shall consist of the following: (A) Electronic mail notice when the person, business or agency has an electronic mail address for the affected persons; (B) conspicuous posting of the notice on the web site of the person, business or agency if the person maintains one; and (C) notification to major state-wide media, including newspapers, radio and television."[31]

Notification to attorneys general and regulators may be sent via letter or e-mail. Some states (notably NY and NC) have specific online forms that must be used for this reporting. The CRAs have established e-mail addresses to receive breach notification reports.

4.8 Exceptions to Notification

There are three basic exceptions for providing data breach notification. The first and most common exception allowed by states is for entities subject to other, more stringent data breach notification laws. This includes HIPAA- and GLBA-covered entities and financial institutions subject to and in compliance with the GLBA Safeguards Rule, discussed in Chapter 5.

Second, most states allow exceptions for entities that already follow breach notification procedures as part of their own information security policies as long as these are compatible with the requirements of the state law. Connecticut's relevant language is:

> *Any person that maintains such person's own security breach procedures as part of an information security policy for the treatment of personal information and otherwise complies with the timing requirements of this section, shall be deemed to be in compliance with the security breach notification requirements of this section, provided such person notifies subject persons in accordance with such person's policies in the event of a breach of security. Any person that maintains such a security breach procedure pursuant to the rules, regulations, procedures or guidelines established by the primary or functional regulator, as defined in 15 USC 6809(2), shall be deemed to be in compliance with the security breach notification requirements of this section, provided such person notifies subject persons in accordance with the policies or the rules, regulations, procedures or guidelines established by the primary or functional regulator in the event of a breach of security of the system.*[32]

Ohio similarly allows exceptions for preexisting contracts.

Third, many states also have an exception for data protected by encrypted and other technical controls. Typically, an incident is not considered a breach if the data was encrypted or redacted and the key remains secure, although the District of Columbia, Hawaii, Illinois, Iowa, Louisiana, Nevada and Ohio do not make such a distinction. Some states (like California) exclude encrypted data from the definition of breach. In other states, you avoid notification if the data is encrypted because there hasn't been a compromise (or, more pointedly, there is no risk of harm).

Encryption is the process of encoding information so that only the sender and intended recipients can access it. Encryption systems often use a public key, available to the public, and a private key, which allows only the intended recipient to decode the message. Most states exempt individuals and businesses from data breach notification and disclosure requirements if the data was encrypted when lost. Together, these laws help motivate many organizations to use encryption to protect data, and thus avoid the burden of providing notice of breaches, as well as the embarrassment and potential brand damage of a public data breach. However, the encryption exception typically applies only when the key remains secure. Most states make this explicit by stating that the exception does not apply when the decryption key is breached along with the encrypted data.

In 2010, Massachusetts adopted a more prescriptive encryption rule that may become a model for other states. The Massachusetts Personal Information Security Regulation (210 CMR 17) states that all parties that "own or license" personal information pertaining to Massachusetts residents must encrypt all personal information stored on laptops or other portable devices, as well as wireless transmissions and transmissions sent over public networks. As with the California data breach law, the level and type of encryption required is not specified.

While some state data breach statutes, such as in Massachusetts, mention encryption specifically, others contain more technology-neutral language. These states may stipulate that notification requirements do not apply when there is no "reasonable likelihood of harm to customers" after reasonable investigation, or similar language.

More importantly, if the data is encrypted, we conclude that the breach did not "compromise the confidentiality, security and integrity" of the information—therefore it is not a breach under any of the laws with that "compromise" standard. Connecticut is the only state that doesn't have this "compromise" language. Many other statutes only require notice in a smaller range of situations, but if the data is encrypted, there is no risk of harm, and the "compromise" requirement thus does not exist.

4.9 Penalties and Right of Action

The Connecticut law reserves enforcement, as many states do, to the state attorney general,[33] and some states specify penalties. In Missouri, for example, "The attorney general shall have exclusive authority to bring an action to obtain actual damages for a willful and knowing violation of this section and may seek a civil penalty not to exceed one hundred fifty thousand dollars per breach of the security of the system or series of breaches of a similar nature that are discovered in a single investigation."[34] Louisiana, Michigan, Rhode Island, Texas and Virginia also specify civil penalties.

The data breach notification laws of Alaska, California, the District of Columbia, Louisiana, Maryland, Minnesota, New Hampshire, North Carolina, South Carolina, Tennessee and Washington also grant a private right of action to individuals harmed by disclosure of their personal information in order to recover damages.

5. State Data Destruction Laws

As of July 2012, at least 26 states have data destruction laws[35] (sometimes incorporated in data breach laws), most with common elements describing to whom the law applies (government and/or private businesses), the required notice, exemptions (e.g., GLBA, HIPAA, FCRA), the covered media (electronic and/or paper), and penalties.

North Carolina's Law[36] (§ 7564), for example, applies to "any business that conducts business in North Carolina and any business that maintains or otherwise possesses personal information of a resident of North Carolina." It requires such entities to take "reasonable measures" to safeguard against unauthorized access to personal information "in connection with or after its disposal."

North Carolina provides a three-fold description of required "reasonable measures:"

> (1) *Implementing and monitoring compliance with policies and procedures that require the burning, pulverizing, or shredding of papers containing personal information so that information cannot be practicably read or reconstructed.*
>
> (2) *Implementing and monitoring compliance with policies and procedures that require the destruction or erasure of electronic media and other nonpaper media containing personal information so that the information cannot practicably be read or reconstructed.*
>
> (3) *Describing procedures relating to the adequate destruction or proper disposal of personal records as official policy in the writings of the business entity.*

The law allows businesses to subcontract with record destruction businesses "after due diligence", which requires reviewing an independent audit of the business' operations, reviewing references and requiring independent certification of the business and/or personally evaluating "the competency and integrity of the disposal business."

North Carolina exempts financial institutions subject to the GLBA, health insurers or healthcare facilities subject to HIPAA, and consumer reporting agencies subject the FCRA. The law does not specify damages but denies a public right of action in the absence of personal injury.

Most other state laws are essentially the same as North Carolina's although, for example, the Arizona law applies only to paper records, Alaska specifically authorizes a right to private action, California requires destruction such that records are "unreadable or undecipherable through *any* means," (emphasis added) Illinois and Utah apply only to government entities, New York applies only to for-profit businesses, and Massachusetts stipulates steep penalties ("not more than $100 per data subject affected, provided said fine shall not exceed $50,000 for each instance of improper disposal.") [7]

6. Conclusion

The spread of state data breach laws in the past decade has had a major impact on private-sector information security practices. When breaches occur, top management often focuses intensively on information management practices; in many instances, the budget and visibility increases for information security activities in the wake of a breach. Similarly, concerns about the possibility of data breaches, with the resulting negative publicity, financial penalties and other effects, provides an important incentive for companies to develop strong information security practices. While significant differences remain among the state laws, the end result today is that entities processing personal data in the United States are compelled to disclose data breaches in an expeditious manner.

Data breach laws, combined with information security laws in Massachusetts and other jurisdictions, have thus become an important component of protection of personal data in the United States. The United States lacks comprehensive private-sector information security and data breach notification statutes, leading some observers to suggest the nation is less stringent about protection of personal data than other jurisdictions, notably Europe. The draft EU Data Protection Regulation is proposing the introduction of data breach requirements to the member states. In practice to date, the intensive attention to data breaches in the United States has quite often led to more rigorous information security programs than has existed in other jurisdictions.

Endnotes

1 www.reuters.com/article/2011/04/26/us-sony-stoldendata-idUSTRE73P6WB20110426.

2 www.nytimes.com/2012/06/11/technology/linkedin-breach-exposes-light-security-even-at-data-companies.html?pagewanted=all.

3 www.bankinfosecurity.com/hannaford-data-breach-may-be-tip-iceberg-a-810/op-1.

4 http://online.wsj.com/article/SB10001424052702304750404577318083097652936.html.

5 www.eweek.com/c/a/Security/Data-Breach-Risk-Higher-Among-Small-Businesses-Ponemon-805511/.

6 http://info.sen.ca.gov/pub/03-04/bill/asm/ab_1901-1950/ab_1950_bill_20040929_chaptered.pdf.

7 *Id.*

8 www.mass.gov/ocabr/docs/idtheft/201cmr1700reg.pdf.

9 http://apps.leg.wa.gov/documents/WSLdocs/2009-10/Pdf/Bills/Session%20Law%202010/1149-S2.SL.pdf.

10 Federal Trade Commission, "State Laws: Social Security Numbers," www.ftc.gov/bcp/edu/microsites/idtheft/law-enforcement/state-laws-social-security.html.

11 Cal. Civ. Code § 1798.85.

12 www.privacyrights.org/data-breach.

13 www.leginfo.ca.gov/cgi-bin/displaycode?section=civ&group=01001-02000&file=1798.80-1798.84.

14 www.cga.ct.gov/2011/pub/chap669.htm#Sec36a-701b.htm.

15 http://search.legis.state.ia.us/nxt/gateway.dll/ic/1/13/25831/25832/26269/26270?f=templates$fn=document-frameset.htm$q=[field%20folio-destination-name:%27715C.1%27]$x=Advanced#0-0-0-341361.

16 www.legis.state.wi.us/statutes/Stat0134.pdf.

17 www.schwartzandballen.com/ImportedDocs/Puerto%20Rico%20security%20breach.pdf.

18 www.ilga.gov/legislation/ilcs/ilcs3.asp?ActID=2702&ChapAct=815%26nbsp%3BILCS%26nbsp%3B530%2F&ChapterID=67&ChapterName=BUSINESS+TRANSACTIONS&ActName=Personal+information+Protection+Act.

19 http://codes.ohio.gov/orc/1347.12.

20 www.cga.ct.gov/2011/pub/chap669.htm#Sec36a-701b.htm.

21 To view a sampling, see Ariz. Rev. Stat. tit. 44, Ch. 32, § 44-7501; Conn. Gen Stat. 36a-701(b); Del. C., Tit. 6, Ch. § 12B-102; and Fl. Stat. Tit. XLVI, Ch. 817, § 5681. The majority of state data breach notification laws contain this requirement.

22 Ga. Code Ann., Tit. 10, Ch. 1, § 910-912.

23 Texas H.B. 300 (effective Sept. 2012), www.legis.state.tx.us/tlodocs/82R/billtext/pdf/HB00300F.pdf.

24 www.cga.ct.gov/2011/pub/chap669.htm#Sec36a-701b.htm.

25 *Id.*

26 www.cga.ct.gov/2011/pub/chap669.htm#Sec36a-701b.htm.

27 *Id.*

28 www.ncleg.net/EnactedLegislation/Statutes/HTML/BySection/Chapter_75/GS_75-65.html.

29 www.leg.state.or.us/ors/646a.html.

30 Compare Mass. Gen. Laws § 93H-3(b) with California's new notification requirements, Cal. Civil Code § 1798.29 and § 1798.82.

31 www.cga.ct.gov/2011/pub/chap669.htm#Sec36a-701b.htm.

32 *Id.*

33 *Id.*

34 www.moga.mo.gov/statutes/C400-499/4070001500.HTM.

35 *See* National Conference of State Legislatures, Data Disposal Laws, http://www.ncsl.org/issues-research/telecom/data-disposal-laws.aspx.

36 N.C. Gen. Stat. § 75-64, www.ncleg.net/EnactedLegislation/Statutes/HTML/BySection/Chapter_75/GS_75-64.html.

37 Mass. Gen. Laws Ch. 93I, § 2, www.malegislature.gov/Laws/GeneralLaws/PartI/TitleXV/Chapter93i/Section2.

CHAPTER TEN

Privacy Issues in Investigations and Litigation

This chapter examines privacy issues that arise when a company is responding to investigations and litigation. Before trial, a company may receive civil discovery requests, or face requests or orders to produce information in the course of a law enforcement or national security investigation. At a civil or criminal trial, the tradition of public records and open courtrooms in the United States means that additional personal information may be revealed.

Historically, outside counsel and in-house lawyers often played the predominant role in determining what personal information would be disclosed in the course of investigations or litigation. Disclosures in litigation were often done manually, after lawyers, paralegals, or other individuals read through document files to determine what had to be produced.

Today, disclosures in investigations and litigation are more likely to be made through cooperative efforts of lawyers with a company's privacy and information technology (IT) professionals. Companies that hold large amounts of personal information often have information management plans that set policies for how and when disclosures will occur. Those plans are created through collaborative efforts that include experts on relevant privacy requirements and implementation through automated IT systems. To avoid data breaches, authorization may be required by specific, responsible people in the organization. To ensure implementation of company policies, audit trails are often in place concerning disclosures of sensitive information to third parties, including for investigation and litigation purposes. With this convergence of professionals for privacy, law and IT, organizations thus often need a more systematic approach to responding to investigations and litigation.

This chapter begins with an outline of how disclosures may be required, permitted or forbidden by law. Organizations sometimes are required by law either to disclose or not to disclose personal information. In other situations, the organization faces a choice about whether and how to make such disclosures. The chapter next turns to civil litigation. The U.S. tradition of public records in litigation is paired today with 2007 revisions to the Federal Rules of Civil Procedure, under which lawyers are required to redact certain sensitive personal information before it goes into court files. Since 2006, federal civil litigation has operated under the "e-discovery" rules, which require automated and large-scale production of e-mails and other corporate documents during the discovery process prior to trial. These large volumes of disclosure raise important privacy issues, illustrating the need for privacy professionals to work closely with lawyers and IT professionals.

The chapter next turns to privacy issues in law enforcement investigations. Protecting privacy is a major theme of the Fourth Amendment to the U.S. Constitution, which prohibits the government from making unreasonable searches and seizures. The Fourth Amendment sets limits on both physical searches and searches for personal information through wiretaps and access to company records. Fourth Amendment principles have also informed a number of statutes, including wiretap laws, the Electronic Communications Privacy Act, the Right to Financial Privacy Act (applying to financial institutions), and the Privacy Protection Act (applying to reporters and media companies). Privacy professionals need to be aware of these statutes as a company can face legal consequences, depending on the context, for turning over either too much or too little information.

The chapter concludes with an examination of privacy issues and national security investigations. Under the Foreign Intelligence Surveillance Act (FISA), telephone companies and e-mail services can face especially complex rules about when and in what way they are permitted or required to provide information to the government. For both the law enforcement and national security discussions in this chapter, the goal is not to provide enough detail to answer the questions of these specialized practitioners. The goal instead is to set forth the basic principles and specific provisions that apply to a wide range of organizations. For instance, FISA, as amended by the USA Patriot Act of 2001, authorizes Section 215 orders, which can require any company to provide any "tangible record" (including e-mails and other computer files) to the government for national security purposes. Section 215 orders include strict provisions about who can even know that such an order has been issued, so privacy professionals far outside of the telecommunications sector can potentially need to know some basics about national security rules.

1. Disclosures Required, Permitted or Forbidden by Law

For investigations and litigation, the law can be complex about when information must be disclosed, when the organization has a choice about whether to disclose, and when the organization is prohibited from disclosing it. Sometimes the same statute requires production of information in some circumstances, such as when a judge issues a court order, but prohibits production of the same information in other circumstances, such as when no court order exists.

1.1 Disclosures Required by Law

Certain U.S. laws require disclosure of personal information held by an organization. Chapter 5, "Financial Privacy," discussed the Bank Secrecy Act and related reporting requirements designed to reduce money laundering. Other examples of required disclosure:

- The U.S. Food and Drug Administration (FDA) requires health professionals and drug manufacturers to report serious adverse events, product problems or medication errors suspected to be associated with the use of an FDA-regulated drug, biologic, device or dietary supplement under the Food, Drug and Cosmetic Act.[1]

- The U.S. Department of Labor's Occupational Health and Safety Administration requires compilation and reporting of information about certain workplace injuries and illnesses.[2]
- Many states require reporting of certain types of injuries and medical conditions, such as gunshot wounds, immunization records or specific contagious diseases. HIPAA permits disclosure of protected health information (PHI) where disclosure is required by law.[3]

Outside of these regulatory systems, records sometimes must be disclosed during an investigation or in the course of litigation. The discussion in this chapter of e-discovery will describe how parties to civil litigation in the United States are routinely required to produce e-mails, documents and other company records containing substantial personal information. "Discovery" in litigation, which essentially means information disclosed to another party in a lawsuit before trial, is governed by the rules of civil and criminal procedure, as overseen by state and federal judges.

Companies with information relevant to a government investigation or in civil litigation may receive a subpoena, which is an instruction to produce a witness or records. For instance, Federal Rule of Civil Procedure 45 says that a subpoena must:

1. State the court from which it is issued
2. State the title of the action, the court in which it is pending and its civil-action number
3. Command each person to whom it is directed to do the following at a specific time and place: attend and testify; produce designated documents, electronically stored information or tangible things in that person's possession, custody or control; or permit the inspection of premises
4. Set out the text of the rules describing a person's right to challenge or modify the subpoena

The party seeking information must "serve" the subpoena, to put that person on notice of the obligation to respond and of the recipient's right to seek to quash or modify the subpoena. The rule states: "The issuing court may hold in contempt a person who, having been served, fails without adequate excuse to obey the subpoena."[4] Contempt of court can result in fines or imprisonment.

Differing legal standards may of course apply to government investigations and civil (private) litigation, and standards also vary depending on the types of records sought. For instance, as discussed further below, law enforcement can get phone numbers called and similar information under a pen register order. A judge issues that type of order under the relatively easy-to-meet standard that the information "is relevant to an ongoing investigation."[5] Many stored e-mails are accessed under court orders defined by 18 U.S.C. § 2703(d), which require the government to provide a judge with "specific and articulable facts showing that there are reasonable grounds" to believe communications are relevant to a criminal investigation.[6] One step stricter is the traditional search warrant issued by a judge or magistrate under the Fourth Amendment to the U.S. Constitution, which requires showing that there is probable cause that a crime has been, is or will be committed. Even stricter is the standard for a telephone wiretap, which has the requirements of a probable cause warrant as well as other requirements, such as that alternative means of getting the evidence have been exhausted.[7] This range of standards is intended to provide more protection for more sensitive information—a list of phone numbers called is easier to get than permission to listen to an entire telephone conversation.

1.2 Disclosures Permitted by Law

For some categories of information, an organization is permitted, but not required, to disclose personal information. HIPAA itself, for instance, requires very few disclosures. The Privacy Rule requires covered entities to disclose PHI only to the individual to whom it pertains[8] and to HHS in the course of an enforcement action.[9] It permits (but does not require) companies to disclose PHI when required to do so by another applicable law, such as the state laws that require reporting of medical information. HIPAA also permits covered entities to disclose PHI for defined public health, law enforcement and national security reasons.

Another example is the "computer trespasser" exception (sometimes called the "hacker trespasser" exception) created by Section 217 of the USA Patriot Act.[10] In general, a law enforcement officer needs to have a court order or some other lawful basis to intercept wire or electronic communications. As discussed later in the chapter, the owner or operator of a computer system can face penalties under the Electronic Communications Privacy Act for providing access to law enforcement. Section 217 of the USA Patriot Act permits, but does not require, the owner or operator of a computer system to provide such access in defined circumstances. For computer trespassers, law enforcement can now perform interceptions if:

1. The owner or operator of the protected computer authorizes the interception of the computer trespasser's communications on the protected computer
2. The person acting under color of law (in an official capacity) is lawfully engaged in an investigation
3. The person acting under color of law has reasonable grounds to believe that the contents of the computer trespasser's communications will be relevant to the investigation
4. Such interception does not acquire communications other than those transmitted

1.3 Disclosures Forbidden by Law

Many of the privacy laws discussed in this book forbid disclosures of categories of personal information to categories of recipients. For instance, HIPAA and COPPA forbid disclosures of covered information to third parties, unless there is opt-in consent or a different exception applies. The Gramm-Leach-Bliley Act (GLBA) forbids disclosures to third parties, unless the individual has not opted out or a different exception applies. Many websites similarly provide an opt-out, and disclosures in violation of such promises can trigger Section 5 enforcement under the FTC Act.

In the context of investigations and litigation, evidentiary "privileges" can also prohibit disclosure. These privileges are generally defined under state law.[11] One example is the attorney-client privilege, which means that an attorney cannot be compelled to testify or produce records about a client concerning matters within the scope of the representation. As with other privacy rules, there can be exceptions to the attorney-client privilege, such as client consent or to prevent imminent physical harm to another person. Other common evidentiary privileges include doctor-patient, priest-penitent and spousal privilege. Where these apply, a doctor, member of the clergy or spouse cannot be compelled to testify about the other party, absent consent or some other exception. Nationally, a person accused of a crime in state or federal court can assert the privilege against self-incrimination under the Fifth Amendment to the U.S. Constitution.

2. Privacy and Civil Litigation

A large amount of personal information may be disclosed to parties in the course of civil litigation. Although the United States has a strong tradition of public access to court records, privacy concerns are also recognized. Courts can mandate protective orders to prohibit disclosure of personal information revealed in litigation, and attorneys increasingly are required to redact Social Security numbers and other sensitive information when filing documents with the courts. The systematic management of personal information has also become more prominent since the 2006 adoption of the "e-discovery" rules, which often require civil litigants to turn over large volumes of a company's electronic records in litigation.

2.1 Public Access to Court Records, Protective Orders and Required Redaction

The United States has a strong tradition of public access to government records, including under the federal Freedom of Information Act and state open records laws. States and localities often provide access to a wide range of public records, including birth and death records, professional and business licenses, real estate ownership and appraisal records, voter registration records and many more. The activities of courts historically have also been public records. Criminal and civil trials in the United States are almost always open for the public to attend. Historically, people could also go to the local courthouse and read the materials submitted to the court, including documents and other exhibits introduced at trial. With the growth of the Internet, court systems began to consider putting their records online for beneficial reasons such as providing transparency in government and reducing the cost of storing and accessing records.

Placing court records on the Internet, however, also raised privacy issues. Paper records stored in local courthouses provided practical obscurity for most of the information, because of the expense and difficulty of searching the records. Online searchable public records greatly reduced this obscurity. In 2000, the federal bankruptcy courts proposed to place their records online, including Social Security numbers and the details of the person's financial status, including bank account numbers and the amount in each account. Internet publication of these details raised the risk that these accounts would be the target of identity fraud. The federal government issued a report on the privacy issues,[12] and the bankruptcy court rules were amended to protect Social Security numbers and privacy.[13] In recent years, the Administrative Office of U.S. Courts and the Center for Legal and Court Technology have held an annual conference in Williamsburg, Virginia, with extensive documentation of how state and federal courts address the issues of privacy and public access to court records.[14] Certain categories of records often receive the greatest protection, including juvenile, financial and medical records.

One response to public access to court records has been for litigants to seek **protective orders** for personal information. With a protective order, a judge determines what information should not be made public, and what conditions apply to who may access the protected information. Rule 26(c) of the Federal Rules of Civil Procedure states that a party may seek a protective order providing that confidential information may not be revealed or must be revealed in a particular way—such as attorney's eyes only—during litigation. The moving party must demonstrate good cause, and a court will apply a three-part test in deciding whether to grant the request. First, the resisting party must show the information to be confidential. Second, the requesting party must show that the information is relevant and necessary to the case. Third, the court must weigh the harm of disclosure against the need for the information.[15]

The HIPAA Privacy Rule, for instance, discusses the standards for a "qualified protective order" (QPO), which applies in state courts that are not covered by the Federal Rules of Civil Procedure. A QPO prohibits the parties from using or disclosing the protected health information for any purpose other than the litigation or proceeding for which such information was requested. It also requires the return to the covered entity or destruction of the protected health information (including copies) at the end of the litigation.[16] If a QPO is in place, a covered entity complies with privacy requirements for disclosure in litigation or administrative proceedings.

More generally, court rules today require redaction of certain personal information by the litigants themselves. **Redaction** is the practice of identifying and removing or blocking information from documents being produced pursuant to a discovery request or as evidence in a court proceeding. One important example is the 2007 adoption of Rule 5.2 of the Federal Rules of Civil Procedure, "Privacy Protection for Filings Made with the Court." The rule applies to both paper and electronic filings and to both parties and nonparties filing documents. Specifically, attorneys are required to redact documents so that no more than the following information is included in court filings:

1. The last four digits of the Social Security number and taxpayer-identification number
2. The year of the individual's birth
3. If the individual is a minor, only the minor's initials
4. The last four digits of the financial account number[17]

Certain exemptions may apply and parties may request that filings be made under seal without redaction when appropriate. In cases where additional protection may be necessary, parties can seek protective orders. If granted, the protective order may require additional redaction or may restrict electronic access to the court filings.[18] Enforcement and penalties apply as for other violations of court rules.[19]

Rule 49.1 of the Federal Criminal Rules of Procedure and Rule 9037 of the Federal Rules of Bankruptcy Procedure contain similar redaction requirements. In criminal proceedings, city and state of the home address are a fifth category requiring redaction, so that the precise home address is not revealed.[20]

Federal district courts often have supplementary redaction or privacy requirements that apply in their court proceedings. Similarly, state and local courts have increasingly adopted redaction requirements. Attorneys and privacy professionals thus should be mindful of the privacy procedure rules that may apply depending on where the litigation actually takes place.

2.2 Electronic Discovery

Prior to trial, the parties usually engage in "discovery," or the exchange of information relevant to the litigation. In discovery, the information typically is exchanged with the other party or parties and their attorneys. In doing so, as just discussed, there may be confidentiality protections such as protective orders and redaction requirements. Information exchanged in discovery also raises at least the possibility that it will be disclosed more broadly, such as in a trial or public court filing, or because those who receive the information in discovery may disclose it to others.

Since the 2006 revisions to the Federal Rules of Civil Procedure, electronically stored information (ESI) has become an increasingly large focus of pretrial discovery in U.S. litigation.[21] The discovery of ESI has become a subdiscipline, known as e-discovery. E-discovery implicates both domestic privacy concerns and issues arising in trans-border data flows.

Managing e-discovery and privacy begins with a well-managed **data retention program.** In designing a retention policy it should be remembered that ESI takes not only obvious forms such as e-mail or word processing documents, but can also manifest itself as server logs, instant messaging transcripts, voicemail systems, social networking records, thumb drives or even the microSD cards found in smartphones. An important source of standards and best practices for managing electronic discovery compliance through data retention policies is the Sedona Conference.[22] Regarding e-mail retention, the Sedona Conference offers four key guidelines:

1. E-mail retention policies should be administered by interdisciplinary teams composed of participants across a diverse array of business units.
2. Such teams should continually develop their understanding of the policies and practices in place and identify the gaps between policy and practice.
3. Interdisciplinary teams should reach consensus as to policies, while looking to industry standards.
4. Technical solutions should meet and parallel the functional requirements of the organization.

Database design should also be considered when addressing a company's retention policies. When done in good faith, data that is "transitory in nature, not routinely created or maintained by [d]efendants for their business purposes, and requiring of additional steps to retrieve and store," may be considered outside the duty of preservation.[23] Retention policies should also consider employee hard drives. While it may be an accepted practice to wipe and reimage personal computers after an employee is terminated so that the computer can be provided to a new employee, "in order to take advantage of the good faith exception [to discovery obligations], a party needs to act affirmatively to prevent the system from destroying or altering information, even if such destruction would occur in the regular course of business."[24] One solution to this problem is to collect forensic images of such devices prior to reassignment.

Initial problems with invasion of privacy concerns related to such retention can be countered by clearly articulating a usage policy for employees. For example, by discouraging employees from using their company e-mail account for personal communications, a company can reduce the future risk of handing over sensitive or embarrassing information when complying with a discovery request. Similarly, placing limits on the permitted uses of company computers may aid in preventing later forensic discovery of hard drives from revealing private information about employees. Conversely, employees should be discouraged from conducting company business on personal devices to prevent the subsequent risk of an invasion of privacy if an employer needs to examine such devices.[25]

While these best practices are widely accepted, it should be noted that where discovery obligations are in direct conflict with business practices, the discovery obligations will likely prevail. When a court finds conflict between a corporate retention policy and a discovery request, the court will likely apply a three-factor test: (1) A retention policy should be reasonable considering the facts of the situation, (2) courts may consider similar complaints against the organization and (3) courts may evaluate whether the organization instituted the policy in bad faith.[26] Finally, in regard to retention policies, it must be remembered that even a reasonable policy may need to be suspended in the face of a litigation hold, which exists when the company is on notice of discovery because litigation is already under way.[27]

U.S. sectoral laws such as HIPAA and GLBA create some tension between broad pretrial discovery powers and privacy protections. Generally, however, these laws exist in harmony with discovery obligations. For example, the HIPAA Privacy Regulation specifically addresses when protected health information may be disclosed during discovery. First, a covered entity may disclose PHI if the subject of those records authorizes their release.[28] Second, absent a release, a covered entity may release PHI subject to a court order.[29] Third, a covered entity may disclose PHI subject to a discovery request if satisfactory assurances are provided. An assurance is satisfactory under HIPAA if the parties seeking the request for information have agreed to a qualified protective order and have submitted it to the court, or if the party seeking the information has requested a qualified protective order from the court.[30] A qualified protective order requires both that the parties are prohibited from using or disclosing the PHI for any purpose other than the litigation and that the PHI will be returned or destroyed at the end of the litigation.[31]

Similarly, under GLBA, a financial institution may disclose otherwise protected information "to comply with federal, state, or local laws, rules, and other applicable legal requirements; to comply with a properly authorized civil, criminal, or regulatory investigation or subpoena or summons by federal, state, or local authorities; or to respond to judicial process or government regulatory authorities having jurisdiction over the financial institution for examination, compliance, or other purposes as authorized by law."[32] Federal courts have been willing to read this clause to encompass civil discovery requests, although protective orders should still be obtained by those disclosing the information.[33]

The issue of **trans-border data flows** creates a more complicated situation. When engaged in pretrial discovery in U.S. courts, parties can be caught between conflicting demands. On one hand, they must comply with U.S. discovery rules that expressly recognize the importance of broad preservation, collection and production. At the same time, however, they must comply with foreign laws that place an emphasis of the protection of personal data and recognize privacy as a fundamental right. In addition to the broad language of the EU Data Protection Directive, several states have "blocking statutes" that limit the trans-border production of data. Consequently, when a foreign company litigates an issue in the U.S. but has computers in its home country or involves data relating to non-U.S. employees, clients or customers, a conflict of law issue arises.[34]

Courts have taken different approaches to resolving this conflict. Some courts have sought to resolve this tension by looking to whether the side claiming a need for data protection compliance has sought to take advantage of U.S. jurisdiction. For example, in *Spain v. American Bureau of Shipping*, a federal district court found that privacy laws were not a barrier to production because Spain sought out the benefits of the U.S. court system, and in doing so should not also be able to claim the benefits of their domestic laws.[35] Other courts, however, have extended exceptions to data production rules to parties that did not seek the benefit of U.S. courts. For example, in *Columbia Pictures v. Bunnell,* Dutch defendants—sued in U.S. district court for copyright infringement resulting from the operation of file sharing servers in the Netherlands—asserted that a Dutch blocking statute prohibited preservation or production of the server log data.[36] There, the court rejected the defendant's assertions on the grounds that "[i]t is well settled that [foreign] statutes do not deprive an American court of the power to order a party subject to its jurisdiction to produce evidence even though the act of production may violate that statute."[37]

The production of trans-border data may also be avoided by invoking the Hague Convention on the Taking of Evidence.[38] Under the treaty, the party seeking to displace the Federal Rules of Civil Procedure bears the burden of demonstrating that it is more appropriate to use the Hague Convention and must establish that the foreign law prohibits the discovery sought. Such prohibitions may be established by expert testimony. *Aerospaciale v. S.D. of Iowa* outlines the factors that an American court will use to reconcile the conflict.[39] These factors include: [40]

1. The importance of the documents or data to the litigation at hand
2. The specificity of the request
3. Whether the information originated in the United States
4. The availability of alternative means of securing the information

5. The extent to which the important interests of the United States and the foreign state would be undermined by an adverse ruling

The fifth factor is often referred to as being the most important. For example, when victims of a terrorist attack sued a British bank for aiding and abetting a terrorist organization, British bank secrecy laws did not preempt the discovery request because the information was central to the case and the disclosure would advance both American and British interests in combating terrorism.[41] Courts have also been willing to look to additional factors, such as the good faith of the party resisting compliance, in applying such a test.

The Fourth Amendment to the Constitution provides: "The right of the people to be secure in their persons, houses, papers, and effects, against unreasonable searches and seizures, shall not be violated, and no warrants shall issue, but upon probable cause, supported by oath or affirmation, and particularly describing the place to be searched."

An alternative source of guidance is the Article 29 Working Party, which has produced a working paper that explores the relationship between the Data Protection Directive and pretrial discovery in trans-border lawsuits.[42] Essentially, the processing of data for discovery purposes must be done pursuant to a legitimate purpose under Article 7 or subject to contractual clauses under Article 26. The use of Safe Harbor provisions is cautioned against because such transfers are permitted only to listed recipients and may not extend to the use of the data in court.

Once data has been culled for e-discovery, preservation and transport present final considerations. Data may either be "preserved in place" by maintaining it in its native repository,[43] or it may be preserved in a separate form. For transfer, data should be encrypted and the key transferred by a secure second method of transport. If shipped as physical media (such as a hard drive or optical media), it should be transported in a manner that preserves an audit trail. Alternatively, data may be transferred by using a secure connection, such as FTP.

3. Law Enforcement and the Role of Privacy Professionals

Along with civil litigation, a company can face requests to provide personal information in connection with criminal investigations and litigation. The discussion here begins with an introduction to Fourth Amendment limits on law enforcement searches. Fourth Amendment cases have articulated some of the most fundamental concepts used by privacy lawyers and other privacy experts in the United States, including the "reasonable expectation of privacy" test developed in the context of government wiretaps. The discussion then moves to other statutes that can apply to criminal investigations, including HIPAA, the Electronic Communications Privacy Act (ECPA), the Stored Communications Act (SCA), the Right to Financial Privacy Act and the Privacy Protection Act.

This chapter does not attempt to provide the many details that prosecutors and criminal defense lawyers need to know about the handling of personal information in criminal litigation. Nor does it go into the complex details of ECPA and the SCA as those laws apply to communications providers such as telephone companies and e-mail services. Instead, the focus is on general principles and issues that can arise in a wide range of companies.

3.1 Fourth Amendment Limits on Law Enforcement Searches

The Fourth Amendment's limits on government power stem in part from objections to "general warrants" used by the British king's customs inspectors before the American Revolution. Officers of the Crown could get one general warrant and search all of the houses in a neighborhood or town when looking for contraband goods. At the most basic level, the Fourth Amendment authorizes reasonable government searches while setting limits on their scope and how they are issued. The Supreme Court has stated: "The overriding function of the Fourth Amendment is to protect personal privacy and dignity against unwarranted intrusion by the State."[44]

The Fourth Amendment provides a ban against "unreasonable searches and seizures" by the government. For search warrants, the government must show "probable cause" that a crime has been, is or is likely to be committed. Search warrants must be supported by specific testimony, often provided by a police officer. A neutral magistrate (judge) approves the search warrant. They cannot be general warrants, but instead must describe the place to be searched with particularity.

Evidence gathered by the government in violation of the Fourth Amendment is generally subject to what is called the "exclusionary rule," meaning that the evidence can be excluded from the criminal trial. The exclusionary rule creates a powerful incentive for criminal defendants to seek to show that the government has violated the Fourth Amendment. Consequently, state and federal courts have issued an enormous number of judicial decisions interpreting the Fourth Amendment, and the case law is notably complex.

Company privacy professionals are not likely to encounter the type of search warrant that provides the police physical entry to a house, auto or other private space. The legal rules are likely to be more important when the government seeks to conduct surveillance in connection with a company's facilities. For instance, the government might conduct wiretaps using the facilities of a telephone company or e-mail service. In addition, and increasingly over time, the government may seek to gain access to company databases containing personal information about customers, employees, and others.

Telephone wiretap law has been important to the last century of Fourth Amendment jurisprudence. In the 1928 case of *Olmstead v. United States*, a majority of the Supreme Court held that no warrant was required for wiretaps conducted on telephone company wires outside of the suspect's building.[45] The majority emphasized that the purpose of the Fourth Amendment was to protect the home and other private spaces. In one of the most famous statements about privacy, Justice Louis Brandeis argued in dissent that new technologies meant that the Fourth Amendment must have a "capacity of adaptation to a changing world." He said: "The makers of our Constitution . . . conferred, as against the government, the right to be let alone—the most comprehensive of rights and the right most valued by civilized men. To protect that right, every unjustifiable intrusion by the government upon the privacy of the individual, whatever the means employed, must be deemed a violation of the Fourth Amendment."

The Supreme Court essentially overruled *Olmstead* in the 1967 case of *Katz v. United States.*[46] The majority stated: "What a person knowingly exposes to the public, even in his own home or office, is not a subject of Fourth Amendment protection. But what he seeks to preserve as private, even in an area accessible to the public, may be constitutionally protected." The court found that a warrant was needed for a police bug in a restaurant, placed to hear the calls behind the closed doors of a phone booth.

Katz is best remembered today for the widely cited "reasonable expectation of privacy" test. In a concurring opinion, Justice John Marshall Harlan stated: "There is a twofold requirement, first that a person have exhibited an actual (subjective) expectation of privacy and, second, that the expectation be one that society is prepared to recognize as 'reasonable.'"

In practice, important exceptions exist to the requirement of a warrant where a reasonable expectation of privacy exists. The "in public" and "third party" exceptions are especially important to privacy professionals. *Katz* itself said that what a person knowingly exposes to the public is not protected by the Fourth Amendment. Police thus have broad discretion to follow a suspect down the street or take advantage of other information that is in plain view. The Supreme Court has also held that information that a person puts into the hand of someone else—a "third party"—is not protected by the Fourth Amendment. For instance, the court has held that the Fourth Amendment does not require a warrant for the police to get a person's checking account records or the list of phone numbers a person has called.[47] The court has stated that the individual consented to letting the bank or phone company have that information, so the companies can lawfully turn the information over to the government without a search warrant. The third-party doctrine has been especially important in connection with company privacy practices—companies are generally permitted under the Constitution to turn over customer and employee records to the government (although statutory and other legal limits may apply).

In the 2012 case of *United States v. Jones,* the Supreme Court may have signaled important changes to the "in public" and third-party exceptions. The court held unanimously that a warrant was needed when the police placed a global positioning system (GPS) device on a car and tracked its location for over a month. The majority decision emphasized that the police had trespassed onto the car when they physically attached the GPS device. Four of the nine justices, however, would have held that a search occurred even without they physical attachment, and even for movements that took place entirely in public. A fifth justice seemed to indicate sympathy for this constitutional limit on "in public" activities, and also stated that the time had come to reexamine the third-party doctrine. It is too soon to tell where *Jones* will fall on the spectrum between a narrow decision about GPS devices and a broad decision that could lead to new constitutional rules limiting surveillance in public as well as access to records held by third parties.

3.2 Statutes That Go Beyond Fourth Amendment Protections

A number of federal statutes affect law enforcement access to personal information. Some of the statutes placed additional requirements on law enforcement after the Supreme Court held that search warrants were not needed. For instance, the Right to Financial Privacy Act of 1978 was passed after the Supreme Court held that the Fourth Amendment did not apply to checking accounts, and the Electronic Communications Privacy Act of 1986 was passed after the court held that it did not apply to telephone numbers called. In these instances, Congress has required some legal process for law enforcement to access the records, but the requirements are not as strict as a probable cause warrant approved by a neutral magistrate. These two statutes are examples where disclosure to law enforcement agents is prohibited by law, unless the statutory requirements are met.

Some law enforcement provisions permit but do not require companies to release personal information to law enforcement. HIPAA illustrates the sometimes-complex trade-offs between protecting confidentiality and providing information for law enforcement purposes. The general rule in HIPAA is that protected health information may be disclosed to third parties, including law enforcement, only with opt-in consent from the patient. Unauthorized disclosures can lead to enforcement by HHS. Section 512(f), however, goes into considerable detail about precisely when disclosure to law enforcement is permitted.[48] Disclosure is permitted pursuant to a court order or grand jury subpoena, or through an administrative request if three criteria are met:

1. The information sought is relevant and material to a legitimate law enforcement inquiry.
2. The request is specific and limited in scope to the extent reasonably practicable in light of the purpose for which the information is sought.
3. De-identified information could not reasonably be used.

Disclosure is also permitted in other specific instances, such as about a crime on the premises, about decedents in connection with a suspected crime, in emergencies, and about victims of a crime even in the absence of patient consent if a multifactor test is met. Limited information may in some instances also be released for identification and location purposes.

As discussed at the beginning of the chapter, other statutes require the release of personal information to law enforcement. Companies thus can face multiple, potentially conflicting laws about when and how to disclose to law enforcement. HIPAA addresses this problem by saying that disclosure is permitted when it is "required by law," even if a disclosure does not otherwise fit within the law enforcement or other exception.[49]

The discussion now turns to federal statutes that govern law enforcement access to personal information from telephone and electronic communications, financial institution records and media records.

3.3 The Wiretap Act, Electronic Communications Privacy Act and Stored Communications Act

From strictest to most permissive, federal law has different rules for (1) telephone monitoring and other tracking of oral communications; (2) privacy of electronic communications; and (3) video surveillance, for which there is little applicable law. Federal law is also generally stricter for "interception" of a communication, as contrasted with retrieval of a stored record. In each area, states may have statutes that apply stricter rules. Furthermore, monitoring that is offensive to a reasonable person can give rise to claims under state invasion of privacy or other common-law claims.

3.3.1 Intercepting Communications

Federal law is generally strict in prohibiting wiretaps of telephone calls. The law today derives from Title III of a 1968 anticrime law, and its rules are thus often called Title III requirements.[50] The law applies to "wire communications," which includes a phone call or other aural communication made through a network. The law also applies to "oral communications," such as hidden bugs or microphones, and defined as "any oral communication uttered by a person exhibiting an expectation that such communication is not subject to interception under circumstances justifying such expectation."[51] The Electronic Communications Privacy Act of 1986 (ECPA) extended the ban on interception to "electronic communications," which essentially are communications, including e-mails, that are not wire or oral communications.[52] The exact rules for wire, oral and electronic communications vary. Unless an exception applies, however, interception of these communications is a criminal offense and provides a private right of action.

The prohibition on interception has a number of exceptions, each of which may have its own nuances requiring an expert to analyze. Under federal law, interception is permitted if a person is the party to the call or if one of the parties has given consent.[53] A number of states, however, have the stricter rule that all of the parties to the call must consent.[54] This all-party consent requirement is why customers often hear a message giving notice that a call is being recorded for quality assurance or other purposes.

A second exception relevant to many companies concerns interception done in the ordinary course of business.[55] This exception can apply where the device used for the interception is "furnished to the subscriber or user by a provider of wire or electronic communication service in the ordinary course of its business."[56] This language, for instance, supports the ability to intercept for an employer who provides the communication service, such as the company telephone or e-mail service. To qualify for the exception, the interception itself must also be in the normal course of the user's business.[57] Normal course of business here would apply to routine monitoring in a call center or scanning of company e-mails for viruses or other malware. By contrast, the employer listening to an employee's purely personal call would risk running afoul of the wiretap laws. Courts have split on how broadly to define "ordinary course of business,"[58] which is a reason that many employers rely instead on the consent exception for interception of telephone calls. Note that the federal law is not preemptive, so if you are monitoring or recording calls, you have to consider the "all-party consent" states mentioned above—you cannot rely on any of these exceptions outside the specific state.[59]

3.3.2 Stored Communications

The Stored Communications Act (SCA) was enacted as part of ECPA in 1986.[60] It creates a general prohibition against the unauthorized acquisition, alteration or blocking of electronic communications while in electronic storage in a facility through which an electronic communications service is provided. As for interceptions, violations can lead to criminal penalties or a civil lawsuit, so an expert in the SCA should generally be consulted before turning over such records in a law enforcement investigation. For monitoring within a company, the exceptions are simpler than for interceptions. The SCA has an exception for conduct authorized "by the person or entity providing a wire or electronic communications service," which will often be the company.[61] It also has an exception for conduct authorized "by a user of that service with respect to a communication of or intended for that use."[62] In general, legal limits on interceptions are stricter than for access to stored records.

It should also be noted that ECPA does not preempt stricter state privacy protections, and that state laws may protect e-mail communications. For example, Delaware law prohibits employers from "monitor[ing] or otherwise intercept[ing] any telephone conversation or transmission, electronic mail or transmission, or Internet access or usage" without prior written notice and daily electronic notice.[63] Similarly, Connecticut law requires that "each employer who engages in any type of electronic monitoring shall give prior written notice to all employees who may be affected, informing them of the types of monitoring which may occur. Each employer shall post, in a conspicuous place which is readily available for viewing by its employees, a notice concerning the types of electronic monitoring which the employer may engage in."[64]

3.3.3 Preservation Orders

The SCA states that a provider of wire or electronic communication services or a remote computing service, upon the request of a governmental entity, shall take all necessary steps to preserve records and other evidence in its possession pending the issuance of a court order or other process.[65]

3.3.4 Pen Register and Trap and Trace Orders

Traditionally, a pen register recorded the telephone numbers of outgoing calls, and a trap and trace device recorded the telephone numbers that called into a particular number. ECPA provided for pen register and trap and trace orders from a judge under the relatively lenient legal standard of "relevant to an ongoing investigation."[66] The USA Patriot Act expanded the definitions beyond telephone numbers to include "dialing, routing, addressing, or signaling information" transmitted to or from a device or process.

3.4 The Communications Assistance to Law Enforcement Act

The U.S. Communications Assistance to Law Enforcement Act of 1994 (CALEA)[67] (sometimes referred to as the "Digital Telephony Bill") lays out the duties of defined actors in the telecommunications industry to cooperate in the interception of communications for law enforcement and other needs relating to the security and safety of the public. It notably requires telecommunications carriers to design their products and services to ensure that they can carry out a lawful order to provide government access to communications. The Federal Communications Commission (FCC) has implemented CALEA through various rule-making processes.[68]

CALEA applies to "telecommunications carriers," but not to other "information services." As enacted, therefore, the law was interpreted not to apply to Internet services. In 2004, however, the Department of Justice, Federal Bureau of Investigation, and Drug Enforcement Administration petitioned to expand the interpretation of the scope of the legislation. In 2005, the FCC issued an order that providers of broadband Internet access and VoIP services were "telecommunications services," and so they now operate under CALEA requirements.[69]

3.5 Right to Financial Privacy Act

The special requirements of the Right to Financial Privacy Act (RFPA) of 1978 apply to disclosures by a variety of financial institutions, including banks, credit card companies and consumer finance companies.[70] The RFPA states that "no Government authority may have access to or obtain copies of, or the information contained in the financial records of any customer from a financial institution unless the financial records are reasonably described" and meet at least one of these conditions:

1. The customer authorizes access.
2. There is an appropriate administrative subpoena or summons.
3. There is a qualified search warrant.
4. There is an appropriate judicial subpoena.
5. There is an appropriate formal written request from an authorized government authority.[71]

By its terms, the RFPA applies only to requests from federal agencies, although over a dozen states have similar requirements.[72] It applies to the financial records of individuals and partnerships of fewer than five people. With limited exceptions, customers must receive notice in advance of the government request for the records, and they have the right to challenge disclosure of such records. As with other privacy statutes, a number of important exceptions exist. Financial institutions that produce records under the RFPA are eligible for reimbursements for reasonably necessary costs. Penalties for violation can include actual damages to the customer, punitive damages and attorney's fees.

3.6 Media Records and the Privacy Protection Act

The Privacy Protection Act (PPA) of 1980 provides an extra layer of protection for members of the media and media organizations from government searches or seizures in the course of a criminal investigation.[73] The PPA was passed in the wake of the 1978 Supreme Court case of *Zurcher v. Stanford Daily*.[74] In that case, police used a search warrant to look through a newspaper's unpublished photographs of a demonstration. Lower courts found the search unlawful, saying that the government should have used less invasive methods than a full search of the newspaper's premises. The Supreme Court, however, found that valid search warrants "may be used to search any property" where there is probable cause to believe that evidence of a crime will be found.

Under the PPA, government officials engaged in criminal investigations are not permitted to search or seize media work products or documentary materials "reasonably believed to have a purpose to disseminate to the public a newspaper, book, broadcast or other similar form of public communication." In practice, rather than physically searching a newsroom, "the PPA effectively forces law enforcement to use subpoenas or voluntary cooperation to obtain evidence from those engaged in First Amendment activities."[75]

The PPA applies to government officers or employees at all levels of government. It applies only to criminal investigations, and not to civil litigation. Several states provide additional protections.[76] Violation can lead to penalties of a minimum of $1,000, actual damages and attorney's fees.

One important exception is if there is probable cause to believe that a reporter has committed or is in the process of committing a crime. This PPA exception does not apply if the member of the media's only crime is possession, receipt or communication of the work product itself. Other exceptions exist, such as to prevent death or serious injury or where there is reason to believe documents will be destroyed or concealed if the materials were requested through a subpoena.[77]

The PPA was drafted to respond to police physical searches of traditional newspaper facilities. Going forward, courts may face claims that the PPA is significantly broader, because disseminating "a public communication" may apply to blogs, other web publishing and perhaps even social media.

4. National Security and the Role of Privacy Professionals

Compared with the law enforcement issues discussed in the previous section, somewhat different rules and issues arise when the government seeks personal information for national security purposes. This section briefly explains the key differences. It then provides an overview of the Foreign Intelligence Surveillance Act of 1978 (FISA),[78] as amended by the USA Patriot Act in 2001 and more recently. As with the discussion above of ECPA, the discussion here does not delve into as many details of the law as would be needed by attorneys who work for the government or communications providers. Instead, the focus is on issues that can arise in a wide range of companies. Notably, any company can be faced with a request for records under Section 215 of the Patriot Act, and a significant range of companies can receive a National Security Letter.

4.1 Introduction to Debates About National Security Surveillance

National security wiretaps and other national security searches create a fundamental constitutional question. Under Article II of the Constitution, defining executive powers, the president is commander-in-chief of the armed forces, and the Supreme Court has stated the president has "plenary" powers in foreign affairs.[79] On the other hand, Article III of the Constitution grants judicial power to the Supreme Court and lower courts. In 1967, in *Katz v. United States*, the Supreme Court underscored the importance of judges under the Fourth Amendment—wiretaps require a warrant signed by a neutral magistrate.[80]

The ongoing and difficult question is where the president's inherent authority leaves off, and judicial and legal limits on that authority apply. The decision in *Katz* stated that its warrant rules applied for ordinary wiretaps, used for domestic law enforcement rather than national security. A few years later, the court expressed skepticism about a general exception for "national security" cases, in part out of concerns that the term *national security* was too vague and could extend too far. In the *Keith* case, the court specifically left undecided the extent of the president's power to conduct wiretaps without warrants "with respect to the activities of foreign powers, within or without this country."[81]

In passing FISA in 1978, both supporters and critics of broad surveillance powers achieved important goals. Supporters of surveillance gained a statutory system that expressly authorized foreign intelligence wiretaps, lending the weight of congressional approval to surveillance that did not meet all the requirements of ordinary Fourth Amendment searches. Critics of surveillance institutionalized a series of checks and balances on the previously unfettered discretion of the president and the attorney general to conduct surveillance in the name of national security.

The attacks of September 11, 2001, led to important changes to FISA, from the USA Patriot Act passed in the wake of attacks to later statutes. Supporters of the changes emphasized the new types of national security threat posed by Al Qaeda and international terrorism. The original FISA statute was passed during the Cold War, when a major target of national security efforts was to track the activities of agents of the Soviet Union and its allied foreign nation states. For instance, foreign intelligence wiretaps could be used in connection with communications of the Soviet Embassy or people who worked there. By contrast, the war on terrorism after 2001 involved threats from hard-to-detect individuals who had few or no links to foreign governments. Supporters of broader surveillance argued that foreign intelligence wiretaps should be used more often and with more flexible legal limits. The USA Patriot Act provided more of that flexibility.

Over time, however, national security surveillance received a major new round of criticism. The *New York Times* and other newspapers published detailed stories that showed large numbers of national security wiretaps and access to stored communications records without judicial authorization.[82] Among other lawsuits, the largest telephone companies were sued for tens of billions of dollars under the Stored Communications Act for their role in providing records to the government.[83] Other reports revealed that the number of national security letters (NSLs) for communications and other records was orders of magnitude higher than previously stated by the government.[84]

In the wake of these disclosures, Congress updated FISA once again, notably in the FISA Amendments Act of 2008.[85] This statute gave legal authorization to some of the new surveillance practices, especially where one party to the communication is reasonably believed to be outside of the United States. It also granted immunity to the telephone companies, so they would not be liable for the records they had provided to the government in the wake of September 11. On the other hand, the new rules required more reporting from the government to Congress, and put limits on some of the secrecy about NSLs and other government requests for records in the national security realm.

For privacy professionals, this recent history illustrates the competing values that come into play when the government makes a national security request for personal information. Company employees, including privacy professionals, generally have a strong desire to help where possible with national security requests. On the other hand, as illustrated by the lawsuits against the telephone companies, providing personal information too broadly can lead to legal, public relations and civil liberties objections.

Responding to national security requests is more complicated because U.S. privacy laws have varying scope and differing definitions for national security exceptions. For instance, HIPAA permits disclosure of protected health information "to authorized federal officials for the conduct of lawful intelligence, counter-intelligence, and other national security" under the National Security Act.[86] GLBA has a privacy exception that is more vaguely worded, "for an investigation on a matter related to public safety."[87] By contrast, the Children's Online Privacy Protection Act and implementing regulation make no mention of a national security exception.[88] Privacy professionals, IT professionals who provide access to records, and attorneys thus may need to do research in particular settings to determine what sorts of national security disclosures are permitted, for what sorts of records and to which agencies.

At the time of writing in mid-2012, debates about cybersecurity legislation are providing another illustration of the tension between national security on the one hand, and civil liberties concerns and limits on lawful sharing of personal information on the other. A bill passed in the House of Representatives authorized broad information sharing for cybersecurity purposes, beyond that allowed by existing privacy laws. Supporters of this approach underscore the severity of cybersecurity threats and the complexity of existing law about whether and when a company can share personal information with the government or other companies. Critics of the bill, however, argue that the exemptions were too broad. They have said that the definition of what counts as a cybersecurity threat is so loose that it could cover an enormous range of personal information, and they argue against a blanket exemption from all existing privacy laws.[89]

4.2 Overview of FISA

FISA establishes standards and procedures for use of electronic surveillance to collect "foreign intelligence" within the United States.[90] FISA orders can issue where foreign intelligence gathering is "a significant purpose" of the investigation. FISA orders issue from a special court of federal district court judges, with the Department of Justice making the applications for court orders and no lawyer appearing for the target of investigation or the party who holds records. For law enforcement cases, court orders issue based on probable cause of a crime; FISA orders issue on probable cause that the party to be monitored is a "foreign power" or an "agent of a foreign power." Parties that receive a FISA order to produce records cannot disclose the fact of the order to the targets of investigation; unlike for law enforcement wiretaps, there is generally no disclosure after the fact to the target of a FISA wiretap. In addition to wiretap orders, FISA authorizes pen register/trap and trace orders (for phone numbers, e-mail addresses, and other addressing and routing information) and orders for video surveillance.

Over time, FISA orders have grown so that they outnumber traditional law enforcement wiretap orders.[91] The legal details of FISA can be important for communication providers, such as telephone companies and e-mail services, but such issues arise much less often for most other companies.

4.3 Section 215 Orders for Tangible Records

Section 215 of the USA Patriot Act provides that a federal court order can require the production of "any tangible thing" for defined foreign intelligence and antiterrorism investigations.[92] Privacy professionals in a broad range of organizations should be aware of the possibility of such an order, because the definition of "tangible thing" is broad, including "books, records, papers, documents, and other items." FBI agents above a certain rank can apply for such an order, with a more senior official required for certain categories such as records of library use, book sales, firearms sales, tax returns, educational records and medical records.

Recipients of such an order receive notice that they are forbidden from disclosing the existence or contents of the order.[93] Disclosure is permitted, however, to the persons necessary to comply with the order (such as employees who gather the records), and to an attorney for purposes of receiving legal advice. Production of the records in good faith provides immunity for such production.

4.4 National Security Letters

A national security letter is a category of subpoena that prior to the Patriot Act in 2001 was used narrowly, only for certain financial and communication records of an agent of a foreign power, and only with approval of FBI headquarters.[94] The Patriot Act expanded use of NSLs. The number of NSLs rose to tens of thousands per year, most involving the records of U.S. citizens. Separate and sometimes differing statutory provisions now govern access, without a court order, to communication providers, financial institutions, consumer credit agencies and travel agencies.[95] A series of reports by the inspector general of the Department of Justice has criticized the lack of effective procedures for implementing rules governing NSLs and related investigatory tools.[96]

As amended in 2006, NSLs can be issued by authorized officials, often the special agent in charge of an FBI field office. The precise language in the statutes varies, but NSLs generally can seek records relevant to protect against international terrorism or clandestine intelligence activities. NSLs can issue without any judicial involvement. Under the 2006 amendments, however, recipients can petition to a federal court to modify or set aside an NSL if compliance would be unreasonable or oppressive.[97]

The Patriot Act included strict rules against disclosing that an organization had received an NSL. After court decisions questioned this ban on disclosure on First and Fourth Amendment grounds,[98] the 2006 amendments said that recipients are bound to confidentiality only if there is a finding by the requesting agency of interference with a criminal or counterterrorism investigation or for other listed purposes. Recipients may disclose the request to those necessary to comply with the request and to an attorney for legal assistance. Recipients can also petition a court to modify or end the secrecy requirement. Breach of the confidentiality requirements, however, is treated as a serious offense, punishable by up to five years' imprisonment and fines of up to $250,000 for an individual.[99]

5. Conclusion

Many privacy issues can arise in the course of investigations and litigation. Companies can face complex legal rules about when they are required to or forbidden from disclosing personal information, and when they have a choice about whether to do so. As the volume of records involved in investigations and litigation has mounted, the earlier case-by-case approach led by lawyers has evolved into a greater role for organization policies and procedures under more comprehensive information management plans. Lawyers, privacy professionals, and IT experts increasingly must work together to meet the organization's goals while still complying with privacy and disclosure requirements.

Endnotes

1 U.S.C. Title 21, Chapter 9.

2 See www.osha.gov/pls/oshaweb/owadisp.show_document?p_id=16312&p_table=FEDERAL_REGISTER.

3 45 C.F.R. § 164.512(k)(1).

4 Fed. R. Civ. Pro. 45(e).

5 18 U.S.C. § 3123(a).

6 18 U.S.C. § 2703(d).

7 18 U.S.C. §§ 2510-2522.

8 45 C.F.R. § 164.524 and § 164.528.

9 45 C.F.R. § 164.502(a)(2).

10 18 U.S.C. §§ 2510-2511.

11 The scope of evidentiary privileges in the federal courts is defined by the courts and generally is similar to state law. For civil cases, the evidentiary privileges are governed by Federal Rules of Evidence 501.

12 www.peterswire.net/privarchives/Study%20of%20Financial%20Privacy%20and%20Bankruptcy.mht.

13 www.justice.gov/ust/eo/public_affairs/articles/docs/walton_ssn3-04.htm.

14 www.legaltechcenter.net/education/conferences/8th-conference-on-privacy-public-access-to-court-records/.

15 *See Madanes v. Madanes*, 186 F.R.D. 279, 288 (S.D.N.Y. 1999).

16 45 C.F.R. § 164.512(e).

17 Fed. R. Civ. Pro. 5.2.

18 Fed. R. Crim. Pro. 49.1(e).

19 11 U.S.C. § 105(a).

20 Fed. R. Crim. Pro. 49.1(a)(5).

21 *See generally* Federal Rules of Civil Procedure governing e-discovery, www.fiosinc.com/case-law-rules/e-discovery-federal-rules-civil-procedure-frcp.aspx (last visited April 17, 2012).

22 https://thesedonaconference.org/system/files/sites/sedona.civicactions.net/files/private/drupal/filesys/publications/Best_Practices_Retrieval_Methods___revised_cover_and_preface.pdf.

23 *Arista Records LLC v. Usenet.com, Inc.*, 608 F. Supp. 2d 409, 413 (S.D.N.Y. 2009).

24 *Doe v. Norwalk Cmty. College*, 248 F.R.D. 372, 378 (D. Conn. 2007).

25 *Cf. Wal-Mart Stores v. Lee*, 348 Ark. 707 (Ark. 2002).

26 *Lewy v. Remington Arms Co.*, 836 F.2d 1104, 1111 (8th Cir. Mo. 1988).

27 *Zubulake v. UBS Warburg LLC*, 220 F.R.D. 212, 218 (S.D.N.Y. 2003). ("Once a party reasonably anticipates litigation, it must suspend its routine document retention/destruction policy and put in place a 'litigation hold' to ensure the preservation of relevant documents.")

28 45 C.F.R. § 164.502(a)(1)(iv) (2011).

29 45 C.F.R. § 164.512(e)(1)(I).

30 45 C.F.R. § 164.512(e)(iv)(A & B).

31 45 C.F.R.. § 164.512(e)(v).

32 15 U.S.C. 6802(e)(8).

33 *Marks v. Global Mortg. Group, Inc.*, 218 F.R.D. 492 (S.D.W.Va. 2003).

34 See Fred H. Cate and Margaret P. Eisenhauer, "Between a Rock and a Hard Place: The Conflict Between European Data Protection Laws and U.S. Civil Litigation Document Production Requirements," *BNA Privacy and Security Law Report* 7 (2007): 229.

35 *Spain v. American Bureau of Shipping*, 2006 WL 3208579 (S.D.N.Y. 2006).

36 *Columbia Pictures, Inc. v. Bunnell*, 245 F.R.D. 443 (C.D. Cal. 2007).

37 *Id.* at 453.

38 www.hcch.net/index_en.php?act=conventions.text&cid=82.

39 *Societe Nationale Industrielle Aerospatiale v. United States Dist. Court for S. Dist. IA*, 482 U.S. 522 (U.S. 1987).

40 *Id.* at 568.

41 *Weiss v. Nat'l Westminster Bank, PLC*, 242 F.R.D. 33 (E.D.N.Y. 2007).

42 Working Paper 1/2009 (00339/09/EN WP 158).

43 *See generally* Mikki Tomlinson, "Is Preservation 'In Place' Technology the Panacea to the Preservation Headache? *eDiscovery Journal*, http://ediscoveryjournal.com/2011/12/preservation-%E2%80%9Cin-place%E2%80%9D-technology-the-panacea-to-the-preservation-headache; Barry Murphy, "In-Place Preservation—A Workable Solution?" *eDiscovery Journal*, http://ediscoveryjournal.com/2010/11/in-place-preservation-a-workable-solution.

44 *Schmerber v. California*, 384 U.S. 757 (1966).

45 *Olmstead v. United States*, 277 U.S. 438 (1928).

46 *Katz v. United States*, 389 U.S. 347 (1967).

47 *United States v. Miller*, 425 U.S. 435 (1976) (checking account records); *Smith v. Maryland*, 442 U.S. 735 (1979) (phone calling records).

48 45 C.F.R. § 164.512(f).

49 45 C.F.R. § 164.512(a).

50 Omnibus Crime Control and Safe Streets Act of 1968, Pub. L. No. 90-351.

51 18 U.S.C. § 2510.

52 *Id.*

53 18 U.S.C. § 2511(2)(D).

54 Charles Kennedy and Peter Swire, "State Wiretaps and Electronic Surveillance After September 11," *Hastings L.J.* 54: 971 (2003) (Appendix A listing state wiretap laws).

55 8 U.S.C. § 2511(2)(a)(i).

56 8 U.S.C. § 2510(5).

57 Martha W. Barnett & Scott D. Makar, " 'In the Ordinary Court of Business': The Legal Limits of Workplace Wiretapping," *Comm. & Ent. L.J.* 10 (1988): 715.

58 Matthew W. Finkin, *Privacy in Employment Law*, 3d edition (Arlington, VA: BNA Books, 2009), at 365–369.

59 For instance, for a call from a state with one-party telephone recording notification to California, the latter's two-party notification law outweighs the one-party notification law—that is, both or all parties must consent to the telephone call recording. *Kearney v. Salomon Smith Barney Inc.*, 39 Cal. 4th 95 (2006).

60 18 U.S.C. §§ 2701-2712.

61 18 U.S.C. § 2701(c)(1).

62 18 U.S.C. § 2701(c)(2).

63 19 Del. C. § 705.

64 Conn. Gen. Laws. Chap. 557, § 31-48d.

65 18 U.S.C. § 2703(f).

66 18 U.S.C. § 3123.

67 Communications Assistance to Law Enforcement Act of 1994, 47 U.S.C. §§ 1001-1021 (1994).

68 See www.askcalea.net/.

69 American Council on Education v. FCC, 451 F.3d 226 (D.C. Cir. 2006).

70 12 U.S.C. §§ 3401-3422.

71 12 U.S.C. § 3402.

72 http://epic.org/privacy/rfpa/.

73 42 U.S.C. §§2000aa to 2000aa-7.

74 *Zurcher v. Stanford Daily*, 436 U.S. 547 (1978).

75 https://www.cdt.org/privacy/guide/protect/laws.php#ppa.

76 Nine states are listed at http://epic.org/privacy/ppa/.

77 42 U.S.C. § 2000aa(b)(3).

78 The Foreign Intelligence Surveillance Act of 1978, Pub. L. No. 95-511, 92 Stat. 1783 (1978).

79 *United States v. Curtiss-Wright Export Corp.*, 299 U.S. 304 (1936).

80 389 U.S. 347 (1967).

81 *United States v. United States District Court (Keith)*, 407 U.S. 297 (1972).

82 James Risen and Eric Lichtblau, "Bush Lets U.S. Spy on Callers Without Courts," *New York Times*, Dec. 16, 2005, A1.

83 Peter Swire and Judd Legum, "Telcos Could Be Liable for Tens of Bilions of Dollars for Illegally Turning Over Phone Records," *ThinkProgress*, May 11, 2006, http://thinkprogress.org/politics/2006/05/11/5300/telcos-liable/.

84 Testimony of Peter Swire before the U.S. Senate Judiciary Committee, "Responding to the Inspector General's Findings of Improper Use of National Security Letters by the FBI" (2007), www.americanprogress.org/issues/2007/04/swire_testimony.html.

85 Foreign Intelligence Surveillance Act Amendments Act of 2008, Pub. L. 110-261, 2008.

86 45 C.F.R. § 164.512(k)(2).

87 15 U.S.C. § 6803(e).

88 15 U.S.C. § 6501.

89 Leslie Harris, "In Cybersecurity Bill CISPA Passage, Voices of the Internet Community Were Heard," *Daily Beast*, Apr. 30, 2012, http://www.thedailybeast.com/articles/2012/04/30/house-passage-of-cybersecurity-bill-cispa-wasn-t-a-complete-loss.html.

90 FISA is codified at 50 U.S.C. §§ 1801-1811. The description here is how FISA operates as of 2012.

91 Wiretap reports, http://www.uscourts.gov/Statistics/WiretapReports.aspx.

92 50 U.S.C. § 1861(a).

93 50 U.S.C. § 1861(d).

94 Testimony of Peter Swire before the U.S. Senate Judiciary Committee, "Responding to the Inspector General's Findings of Improper Use of National Security Letters by the FBI" (2007), http://www.americanprogress.org/issues/2007/04/swire_testimony.html.

95 Charles Doyle, *National Security Letters in Foreign Intelligence Investigations: Legal Background and Recent Amendments*, Congressional Research Service (2009), http://www.fas.org/sgp/crs/intel/RL33320.pdf.

96 The most recent is Office of the Inspector General, U.S. Department of Justice, *A Review of the Federal Bureau of Investigation's Use of Exigent Letters and Other Informal Requests for Telephone Records* (2010), www.justice.gov/oig/special/s1001r.pdf.

97 28 U.S.C. § 3511.

98 *Doe v. Ashcroft*, 334 F.Supp. 2d 471 (S.D.N.Y. 2004); *Doe v. Gonzales*, 386 F.Supp.2d 66 (D.Conn. 2005).

99 18 U.S.C. § 1510.

CHAPTER ELEVEN

Workplace Privacy

This chapter provides an introduction to workplace privacy, with a focus on the sources of law that apply to private-sector employment in the United States. It examines privacy issues before, during and after employment.

1. Legal Overview

There is no overarching or organized law for employment privacy in the United States. Federal laws apply in specific areas, such as to prohibit discrimination and regulate certain workplace practices, including employment screening and the use of polygraphs and credit reports. State contract and tort law in some instances provides protections for employees, but usually the employee must show fairly egregious practices to succeed. State legislatures have enacted numerous employment privacy laws, providing protections to employees in a bewildering range of specific situations, which often vary state by state. Taken together, there is considerable local variation and complexity on employment privacy issues.

Along with laws protecting privacy, many labor laws in the United States mandate employee data collection and management practices, such as to conduct background checks and to ensure and document a safe workplace environment. Companies also have incentives to gather information about employees and monitor the workplace to reduce the risk of being sued for negligent hiring or supervision of employees.

The regulation of employment privacy in the United States stands in contrast to nations with comprehensive data protection laws. The EU, for example, includes employee privacy within its general rules applying to the protection of individuals. Monitoring is permitted only with specific legal justification, and background checks are limited in scope. Generally, employees have broad workplace privacy expectations and rights. Companies with employees in the United States and other countries thus must be alert to the possibility that different workplace rules apply in connection with employment privacy.

1.1 Constitutional Law

The U.S. Constitution has significant workplace privacy provisions that apply to the federal and state governments, but it does not affect private-sector employment. Notably, the Fourth Amendment prohibits unreasonable searches and seizures by state actors. Courts have interpreted this amendment to place limits on the ability of government employers to search employees' private spaces, such as lockers and desks.[1]

Some states, including California, have extended their constitutional rights to privacy to private-sector employees.[2] In general for private-sector actors, however, there is no state action and no constitutional law governs employment privacy.

1.2 State Contract, Tort and Statutory Law

U.S. law looks at the relationship between the employer and employee as fundamentally a matter of contract law. The general rule in the United States is employment at will, which means that the employer has broad discretion to fire an employee. That discretion, in turn, has been understood to grant the employer broad latitude in defining other aspects of the employment relationship, such as issues about the employer's knowledge about an employee.

A contract, however, can alter the rules between employer and employee. An individual employee, for instance, might negotiate a contract that says that certain private activities are outside the scope of the employment relationship. More generally, negotiation of a contract can create binding obligations on the employer. If the employer makes promises in a contract to honor employee privacy, then violations of those promises can constitute an enforceable breach of contract.

The most important contracts concerning employee privacy are collective bargaining agreements. Unions have often negotiated provisions that protect employee privacy, including, for instance, limits on drug testing and monitoring of the workplace by the employer.

Turning to tort law, at least three common-law torts can be relevant to employee privacy, although U.S. law generally requires a fairly egregious fact pattern before imposing liability on the employer. First is the tort of "**intrusion upon seclusion**," which states: "One who intentionally intrudes, physically or otherwise, upon the solitude or seclusion of another or his private affairs or concerns, is subject to liability to the other for invasion of his privacy, if the intrusion would be highly offensive to a reasonable person."[3] A classic example of such intrusion is if the employer puts a camera or peephole in a bathroom or employee changing room—a jury may well find that such surveillance is highly offensive to a reasonable person. Another example could be secret wiretaps or other intrusive surveillance of an employee. Although such an employee tort claim may succeed, this chapter will later discuss some of the ways that employers can actually defeat that sort of wiretap claim, such as by an announced policy that the company's computers are owned by the employer and subject to monitoring.

A second tort claim can be "**publicity given to private life**," which states: "One who gives publicity to a matter concerning the private life of another is subject to liability to the other for invasion of his privacy, if the matter publicized is of a kind that (a) would be highly offensive to a reasonable person, and (b) is not of legitimate concern to the public."[4] A plaintiff would need to show a relatively broad dissemination of the facts involved and also that the facts disseminated would be highly offensive to a reasonable person. Courts have been cautious in finding such offensiveness, even for dissemination of a person's salary or other information the employee considers private. Free speech principles under the First Amendment also often provide a defense against such a tort claim.

A third tort claim is for **defamation**, which focuses on a false or defamatory statement, defined as a communication tending "so to harm the reputation of another as to lower him in the estimation of the community or to deter third persons from associating or dealing with him."[5] For employment law, defamation torts can arise if, for instance, a false drug testing report is issued or if a former employer provides a factually incorrect reference to a possible future employer.

Although the common law thus supplies some possible protections for employees, according to Matthew W. Finkin in *Privacy in Employment Law*, they have a narrow scope: "If privacy is to be protected by law, the task falls largely to the legislatures" rather than to the common-law courts.[6] State legislatures have indeed passed a large number of statutes that affect employee privacy. Finkin cites some striking examples, such as a California law guaranteeing a woman's right to wear pants at work or the Florida right for employees to shop where they will, free of an employer's dictate. Other state statutes prohibit marital status discrimination,[7] and categories of inquiries regarding prospective employees, such as asking whether a worker has ever filed a claim for worker's compensation benefits.[8] Statutes vary enormously state by state, leading to "a patchwork of near bewildering complexity and large lacunae," or gaps.[9]

To summarize on state law and employment privacy, employees tend to have narrow protections under contract, tort and statutory law. The free market approach of U.S. law applies broadly, except where a discrete problem has arisen and prompted a response by the legal and political system. Against this general backdrop of employer discretion, however, there may be significant state and local laws that apply in a particular setting.

1.3 Federal Laws on Employment Privacy

Given this context of relatively limited constitutional or state law protections, a number of federal statutes have been enacted that bear on employment privacy.

1.3.1 U.S. Laws Protecting Employee Privacy

The United States has a number of federal laws that prohibit **discrimination**. Antidiscrimination laws provide employees with some privacy protection—for example, by limiting questioning with respect to what is being protected, such as age, national origin or disability. The following laws protect different aspects of employee privacy:

- The **Civil Rights Act of 1964** bars discrimination due to race, color, religion, sex, and national origin.[10]
- The **Pregnancy Discrimination Act** bars discrimination due to pregnancy, childbirth and related medical conditions.[11]

- The **Americans with Disabilities Act** bars discrimination against qualified individuals with disabilities.[12]
- The **Age Discrimination Act** bars discrimination against individuals over 40 years of age.[13]
- The **Equal Pay Act of 1963** bars gender-based wage discrimination.[14]
- The **Genetic Information Nondiscrimination Act of 2008** bars using genetic information to discriminate in the hiring, termination and determination of benefits processes.

The United States also has federal laws that regulate **employee benefits management**. These laws offer certain privacy and security protections for benefits-related information. They also often mandate collection of employee medical information. These laws include the following protections:

- The **Health Insurance Portability and Accountability Act of 1996 (HIPAA)** contains privacy and security rules that regulate "protected health information" for health insurers, including self-funded health plans.[15]
- The **Consolidated Omnibus Budget Reconciliation Act (COBRA)** requires qualified health plans to provide continuous coverage after termination to certain beneficiaries.[16]
- The **Employee Retirement Income Security Act (ERISA)** ensures that employee benefits programs are created fairly and administered properly.[17]
- The **Family and Medical Leave Act (FMLA)** entitles certain employees to leave in the event of birth or illness of self or a family member.[18]

Other federal laws with employment privacy implications **regulate data collection and record keeping**:

- The **Fair Credit Reporting Act (FCRA)** regulates the use of "consumer reports" obtained from "consumer reporting agencies" (CRAs) in reference checking and background checks of employees.[19]
- The **Fair Labor Standards Act (FLSA)** establishes the minimum wage and sets standards for fair pay.[20]
- The **Occupational Safety and Health Act (OSHA)** regulates workplace safety.[21]
- The **Whistleblower Protection Act** protects federal employees and applicants for employment who claim to have been subjected to personnel actions because of whistleblowing activities.[22]
- The **National Labor Relations Act (NLRA)** sets standards for collective bargaining.[23]
- The **Immigration Reform and Control Act (IRCA)** requires employment eligibility verification.[24]

- The **Securities and Exchange Act of 1934** requires disclosures about payment and other information about senior executives of publicly traded companies, as well as registration requirements for market participants such as broker-dealers and transfer agents.[25]

Later in this chapter we will also discuss two statutory regimes that govern **specific monitoring practices** by employers:

- The **Employee Polygraph Protection Act of 1988**, which limits employer use of lie detectors.[26]
- **Electronic surveillance laws**, including the Wiretap Act,[27] the Electronic Communications Privacy Act,[28] and the Stored Communications Act.[29]

1.3.2 U.S. Regulatory Bodies That Protect Employee Privacy

Employee privacy is protected by several federal agencies, including the Department of Labor, the Equal Employment Opportunity Commission (EEOC), the Federal Trade Commission (FTC), the Consumer Financial Privacy Board (CFPB) and the National Labor Relations Board (NLRB).

The U.S. Department of Labor oversees "the welfare of the job seekers, wage earners, and retirees of the United States by improving their working conditions, advancing their opportunities for profitable employment, protecting their retirement and health care benefits, helping employers find workers, strengthening free collective bargaining, and tracking changes in employment, prices, and other national economic measurements."[30]

To achieve this mission, the department administers a variety of federal laws, including the Fair Labor Standards Act (FLSA), the Occupational Safety and Health Act (OSHA) and the Employee Retirement Income Security Act (ERISA).

The **Equal Employment Opportunity Commission (EEOC)** works to prevent discrimination in the workplace. The EEOC oversees many laws, including Title VII of the Civil Rights Act, the Age Discrimination in Employment Act of 1967 (ADEA) and Titles I and V of the Americans with Disabilities Act of 1990 (ADA).

The **Federal Trade Commission** regulates unfair and deceptive commercial practices and enforces a variety of laws, including the Fair Credit Reporting Act, which limits employers' ability to receive an employee's or applicant's credit report, driving records, criminal records and other "consumer reports" obtained from a "consumer reporting agency."[31]

The **National Labor Relations Board** administers the National Labor Relations Act. The board conducts elections to determine if employees want union representation and investigates and remedies unfair labor practices by employers and unions.

In addition, each state has an agency, often called the Department of Labor, that oversees the state labor laws. These laws include state minimum wage laws and laws limiting work by minors. The same department in most states may administer state unemployment insurance programs and employee rehabilitation programs. Some departments also conduct safety inspections of worker conditions.

2. Privacy Issues Before, During and After Employment

Workplace privacy issues exist in all stages of the employment life cycle—before, during and after employment. Before employment, employers should consider rules and best practices about background screening, including rules for accessing employee information under the Fair Credit Reporting Act. During employment, major topics include polygraphs and psychological testing; substance testing; employee monitoring, including of phone calls and e-mails; and emerging issues such as social network monitoring and "bring your own device." After employment, the main issues are terminating access to physical and informational assets, and proper human resources practices postemployment.

For privacy professionals whose role encompasses human resources, multiple legal issues can arise in the employment life cycle. In addition to consulting with the legal and information technology (IT) departments, a privacy professional should keep in close contact with the human resources experts in the organization. Human resources (HR) professionals developed good practices for handling confidential information even before the IT revolution put personnel records on computers. HR records are often physically segregated from other organization records or handled within IT systems with strict access controls. Because HR records apply to every person in an organization, including the most senior management, HR professionals have special responsibility to respect the confidentiality of employee information.

Employment laws in the United States often provide employers with more discretion than laws in the EU and other countries in the handling of personal information. U.S. laws also often vary by state. Organizations thus have to consider what jurisdiction's rules apply to personal information about particular employees.

2.1 Privacy Issues Before Employment

Employers today can have access to a wealth of information about applicants, gathered both directly from the candidate and through searches of public records and private databases. In the United States, the Fair Credit Reporting Act and antidiscrimination laws create national rules that structure how information is gathered and used preemployment. As in other areas of workplace privacy, states often have additional laws, and egregious practices can create tort suits under the common law. Collective bargaining agreements may also apply. As discussed in other chapters of this book, the privacy professional thus must be aware of the many beneficial uses of personal information, but also the legal and other risks that can arise from improper handling of personal information.

2.1.1 Common Reasons for Employee Background Screening

Before employees are hired—or even brought in for an interview—they are often subject to background screening. The type and extent of screening varies depending on the work environment. There are many reasons and motivations for employers to conduct background screening. Some important recent trends have stimulated an increase in applicant screening. For example:

- The terrorist attacks of September 11, 2001, resulted in heightened attention to security issues and support for more stringent identity-verification requirements.
- Greater attention to child abuse and abductions has led to laws in almost every state requiring criminal background checks for people who work with children.
- Business governance scandals, such as at Enron and WorldCom, spurred passage of the Sarbanes-Oxley Act in 2002, which has increased the incentives for corporate leaders to scrutinize practices in the areas they manage.
- The rapid increase of information about candidates from online search and social media sites has made background checks easier.[32]

Certain professions are subject to background screening by law. Typically, anyone who works with the elderly, children or the disabled must now undergo background screening. The federal National Child Protection Act authorizes state officials to access the FBI's National Crime Information Center database for some positions that involve contact with children. Many state and federal government jobs require rigorous background checks to obtain a security clearance.[33] Other groups that are targeted in background checks, depending on the state, include emergency medical service personnel, county coroners, humane society investigators, euthanasia technicians in animal shelters, bus and truck drivers, athletic trainers, in-home repair services, firefighters, gaming industry employees, real estate brokers and information technology workers.

Employers use background screening to ensure they are hiring the "best" candidate for the job. Screenings can help determine whether the applicant will fit in the organization's culture and make positive contributions to its growth. Screening can counter false or inflated information provided by job applicants, and helps identify candidates who may damage the organization's brand and reputation. In addition, employers seek to mitigate the risk of liability. Careful background screening can help defeat a later claim for negligent hiring, such as if a person later causes harm when there was prior evidence the employee was dangerous.

Changing information technology has led to changes in screening. An unprecedented amount of candidate data is now available to employers. The sophistication of today's Internet search, coupled with the ever-greater amount of information publicly accessible about many people, has enormously expanded the ability of employers to use "do it yourself" screening on the Internet. Searches of publicly available information have generally been considered reasonable practice in the United States. Significant privacy issues can accompany such practices, however, as discussed later in this chapter. For instance, Internet searches should not be a basis for making impermissible, discriminatory hiring decisions, and there are emerging laws to prohibit more invasive practices, such as requiring candidates to provide their Facebook or other social network passwords so that prospective employers can see information that the candidate has taken steps to keep private.

2.1.2 Antidiscrimination Laws as Limits on Background Screening

The United States has a number of federal laws that prohibit discrimination in employment and have sometimes been used to limit background checks, notably:

- Title VII of the **Civil Rights Act of 1964** bars discrimination in employment due to race, color, religion, sex and national origin.[34]
- The **Age Discrimination Act** bars discrimination against individuals over 40.[35]
- The **Pregnancy Discrimination Act** bars discrimination due to pregnancy, childbirth and related medical conditions.[36]
- The **Americans with Disabilities Act of 1990** bars discrimination against qualified individuals with disabilities.[37]
- The **Genetic Information Nondiscrimination Act of 2008** bars discrimination based on individuals' genetic information.[38]
- The **Bankruptcy Act** provision 11 U.S.C. § 525(b) prohibits employment discrimination against persons who have filed for bankruptcy. However, there is some ambiguity as to whether the statute applies to discrimination prior to the extension of an offer of employment, and courts have read the statute both ways.[39]

The primary purpose of these laws is to prohibit discrimination in hiring and other employment decisions. A secondary effect, however, is that they often affect how interviews and other background screen activities are conducted. For instance, an employer risks possible discrimination claims for interview questions about national origin or race under Title VII, about current or intended pregnancy under the Pregnancy Discrimination Act, about age under the Age Discrimination Act or about disability under the Americans with Disabilities Act. Along with these federal laws, many states have their own antidiscrimination laws. Some of these have the same protected classes as the federal laws, and some include additional protected classes. Almost half the states currently prohibit sexual preference discrimination in both public- and private-sector jobs, while other states prohibit such discrimination in public workplaces only.[40] Roughly half the states prohibit discrimination based on marital status.[41]

The complexities of antidiscrimination law are beyond the scope of this book. Extensive case law has grown up under each of these statutes, so that legal research beyond the text of each statute may be needed to assess current good practice. The risk for employers is that their interview questions and other background screening activities may provide evidence of discrimination. On the other hand, information that a candidate is a member of a protected class may be required by statute (such as when age is revealed in the course of verifying eligibility for employment), may be a bona fide occupational qualification or may become known to the employer for some other nondiscriminatory reason.

In practice, human resources professionals often receive detailed training about how to collect information relevant to employment decisions while avoiding practices that increase the risk of an antidiscrimination claim. Many companies have established policies that prohibit discrimination and provide more detailed guidance about what interview and background screening practices are permitted. One strategy to reduce risk is to avoid asking questions that elicit information about membership in a protected class. For instance, avoid asking about membership in organizations that reflect religion or national origin. Another strategy is to be consistent and ask the same questions of all candidates. For instance, the company faces a greater risk of pregnancy or sex discrimination claims if only women are asked about how long they expect to stay on the job, and not men.

2.1.3 The Americans with Disabilities Act and Medical Screenings

The Americans with Disabilities Act of 1990 created important restrictions on medical screening of candidates before employment. The law forbids employers with 15 or more employees from discriminating against a "qualified individual with a disability because of the disability of such individual," and specifically covers "medical examinations and inquiries" as grounds for discrimination.[42] Before an offer of employment is made, the ADA permits such examinations and inquiries only where "job related and consistent with business necessity."[43]

A company may require a medical examination after the offer of employment has been made, and may condition the offer of employment on the results of such an examination. Such an examination is permitted only if: (1) all entering employees are subjected to such an examination regardless of disability, (2) confidentiality rules are followed for the results of the examination and (3) the results are used only in accordance with the statutory prohibitions against discrimination on the basis of disability.[44]

The ADA requires an employer to provide reasonable accommodation to qualified individuals who are employees or applicants for employment, unless to do so would cause undue hardship.[45] During the hiring process and before a conditional offer is made, an employer generally may not ask applicants whether they need a reasonable accommodation for the job, except when the employer knows that an applicant has a disability. After a conditional offer of employment is extended, an employer may inquire whether applicants will need reasonable accommodations so long as all entering employees in the same job category are asked this question.

The ADA restrictions on medical examinations and inquiries significantly affect a range of prehiring practices that previously were widespread.[46] Employers can no longer routinely ask questions about prior injuries and illnesses, including prior worker compensation claims. Psychological tests, previously used to predict conditions such as depression or paranoia, may well qualify as medical examinations. The ADA does not cover the use of drugs or alcohol, although it does cover questions about recovered drug addicts and alcoholics. In general, before hiring employers should use caution about inquiring into the likelihood that a candidate has a covered disability or will seek a reasonable accommodation.

Policies regarding preemployment inquiries should be updated to reflect changes to the ADA by the ADA Amendments Act of 2008 (ADAAA).[47] Most importantly, the ADAAA legislatively overturned two U.S. Supreme Court cases under which ADA claims were frequently rejected: *Sutton v. United Air Lines*[48] and *Toyota v. Williams.*[49]

In *Sutton,* the court held that pilots with severe myopia—but correctable with glasses—did not have a disability under the ADA because a "'disability' exists only where an impairment 'substantially limits' a major life activity, not where it 'might,' 'could,' or 'would' be substantially limiting if mitigating measures were not taken."[50]

Toyota further limited the scope of the ADA, rejecting a claim that carpal tunnel syndrome limited a worker's ability to work with power tools, holding that "an individual must have an impairment that prevents or severely restricts the individual from doing activities that are of central importance to most people's daily lives. The impairment's impact must also be permanent or long-term." The ADAAA significantly expanded the scope of ADA protections by broadly defining disabilities to include conditions that are mitigated, in remission or episodic if they would substantially limit a major life activity of an employee when active or absent mitigation.[51] Pursuant to the ADAAA, the EEOC released new regulations addressing the scope of the ADA in 2011.[52]

2.1.4 FCRA Restrictions on Background Checks

The Fair Credit Reporting Act, discussed in more detail in Chapter 5 on financial privacy, regulates how employers perform background checks on job applicants. This law is not limited to background credit checks; it also covers any other type of background check, such as criminal records or driving records, obtained from a "consumer reporting agency." A "consumer reporting agency" includes any organization that regularly engages in the assembling or evaluating of consumer information for the purpose of furnishing consumer reports to third parties for a fee.[53]

Under the FCRA, the term "consumer report" includes all written, oral or other communications bearing on the consumer's creditworthiness, credit standing, credit capacity, character, general reputation, personal characteristics or mode of living. Examples of inquiries covered by FCRA include a credit report obtained from a credit bureau and a driving history report obtained from an information aggregator.

FCRA prohibits obtaining a consumer report unless a "permissible purpose" exists. However, permissible purposes include "employment purposes" which in turn include (1) preemployment screening for the purpose of evaluating the candidate for employment and (2) determining if an existing employee qualifies for promotion, reassignment or retention.

The FCRA also permits employers to obtain an "investigative consumer report" on the applicant if a permissible purpose exists. An investigative consumer report is one in which some of the information is acquired through interviews with neighbors, friends, associates or acquaintances of the employee, such as reference checks.

To obtain any consumer report under FCRA, an employer must meet the following standards:

- Provide written notice to the applicant that it is obtaining a consumer report for employment purposes and indicate if an investigative consumer report will be obtained
- Obtain written consent from the applicant
- Obtain data only from a qualified consumer reporting agency, an entity that has taken steps to assure the accuracy and currency of the data
- Certify to the consumer reporting agency that the employer has a permissible purpose and has obtained consent from the employee
- Before taking an adverse action, such as denial of employment, provide a pre-adverse action notice to the applicant with a copy of the consumer report, in order to give the applicant an opportunity to dispute the report
- After taking adverse action, provide an adverse action notice

If employers do not comply with these requirements, they may face civil and criminal penalties, including a private right of action.

In 2003 the Fair and Accurate Credit Transactions Act (FACTA) amended FCRA. The amendments preempted a wide range of state laws on credit reporting, identity theft and other areas within the FCRA.[54] FACTA, however, specifically left some existing state laws in effect, notably the California Investigative Consumer Reporting Agencies Act (ICRAA).[55] Under the ICRAA, employers must notify applicants and employees of their intention to obtain and use a consumer report. Once disclosure is made, the employer must obtain the applicant or employee's written authorization prior to requesting the report. On the notice and authorization form, employers must enable applicants and employees to check a box to receive a copy of their consumer report anytime a background check is conducted. If employers wish to take adverse employment action, they must provide the employee with a copy of the report, regardless of whether the employee waived the right to receive a copy. This exception does not apply to employees suspected of wrongdoing or misconduct.

Disclosure requirements under the ICRAA are more stringent than under the FCRA. Under the ICRAA, any person who acquires an investigative consumer report for employment purposes must provide separate written disclosure to the applicant or employee before the report is obtained. The written disclosure must state:

- The fact that a report may be obtained
- The permissible purpose of the report
- The fact that the disclosure may include information on the consumer's character, general reputation, personal characteristics and mode of living
- The name, address and telephone number of the investigative consumer reporting agency

As of 2012, the disclosure must also include the web address where the applicant or employee "may find information about the investigative consumer reporting agency's privacy practices, including whether the consumer's personal information will be sent outside the United States or its territories."[56] If the CRA does not have a website, then the employer must provide the consumer with a telephone number where the applicant or employee can obtain the same information.

The FCRA and ICRAA also differ with regard to consent requirements. The FCRA allows employers to use the original written consent to get updates to the employee's credit report as needed. However, under the ICRAA, the employer must obtain written consent every time a background check is requested. Also, the FCRA requires that an employer get written consent only if the employer obtains data from a consumer reporting agency. If the employer does the background check itself (such as by directly accessing public records from the government records keeper and calling references), it does not need to obtain written consent under the FCRA. The ICRAA, on the other hand, requires employers to give the employee or applicant any public records resulting from an in-house background check unless the employee waives that right. If the investigation results in an adverse action, then the employer must give the employee or applicant a copy of the public records whether he or she waived that right or not. If the employer conducts an in-house reference check, it does not have to give that information to the applicant or employee.[57] Note that if the employer obtains records from any third-party data aggregators, such as online criminal records suppliers, those entities will be deemed to be CRAs under the FCRA.[58]

The FCRA does not preempt states from creating stronger legislation in the area of employment credit history checks, such as the California ICRAA just discussed. Six other states—Connecticut, Hawaii, Illinois, Maryland, Oregon and Washington—currently limit the use of credit information in employment.[59] These states require that credit history information be used only as related to the position applied for. The requisite degree of relation differs among states. While most states require a "substantial" relationship,[60] Hawaii requires the applicant's credit history to "directly" relate to an occupational qualification.[61] Additionally, some states allow credit history checks to be performed if the position applied for fits within predefined occupational categories, generally involving financial or managerial responsibility or exposure to confidential information.[62]

2.2 Privacy Issues During Employment

A range of workplace privacy issues can arise once an applicant is hired. The discussion here addresses polygraphs and psychological testing; substance testing; employee monitoring, including of phone calls and e-mails; and emerging issues such as social network monitoring and "bring your own device."

2.2.1 Polygraphs and Psychological Testing

The **Employee Polygraph Protection Act of 1988 (EPPA)** is a prominent example of federal protection of privacy in the workplace.[63] Under the act and its regulations, issued by the Department of Labor, employers are prohibited from using "lie detectors" on incumbent workers or to screen applicants. A "lie detector" is defined to include polygraphs, voice stress analyzers, psychological stress evaluators or any similar device used for the purpose of rendering a diagnostic opinion regarding an individual's honesty.[64] The act prohibits employers from requiring or requesting that a prospective or current employee take a lie detector test. Employers cannot use, accept, refer to or inquire about lie detector test results. The act also prohibits employers from taking adverse action against an employee who refuses to take a test.[65]

EPPA has exceptions for certain occupations, including for government employees, employees in certain security services, those engaged in the manufacture of controlled substances, certain defense contractors and those in certain national security functions. Tests are allowed, however, in connection with "an ongoing investigation involving economic loss or injury to the employer's business," such as theft, embezzlement or industrial espionage. Even for such investigations, there must be reasonable suspicion to test an employee, and other protections for the employee apply. An employee cannot be discharged because of the results of a polygraph or for refusing to submit to a polygraph, unless additional supporting evidence also exists.

EPPA requires employers to post the act's essential provisions in a conspicuous location so that employees are aware of its existence. If the act is violated, employers may be subject to a $10,000 fine from the Department of Labor, as well as to private lawsuits. Also, state laws are not preempted, and a large number of states have enacted laws further restricting the use of lie detectors in private employment.[66]

EPPA and the Americans with Disabilities Act together place significant national limits on psychological testing in the workplace. Employers must comply with the rules limiting lie detectors as well as the ADA prohibitions on the use of medical tests, including those designed to test an impairment of mental health. Employers continue to use psychological tests measuring personality traits such as honesty, preferences and habits in hiring and employment, although one expert reports that such tests may be concentrated in specific positions such as management and sales.[67]

2.2.2 Substance Testing

Employers test for substance use for varied reasons: (1) to reduce costs resulting from lowered productivity, accidents and absenteeism caused by drug use; (2) to reduce medical care costs related to drug use; (3) to reduce theft or other illegal activity in the workplace associated with drug trafficking; (4) to bolster corporate image; and (5) to comply with external legal rules that impose or support a drug testing policy.[68]

There is no federal privacy statute that directly governs employer testing of employees for substances such as illegal drugs, alcohol or tobacco. For public-sector employees, there is considerable case law under the Fourth Amendment about when such testing is reasonable. As previously mentioned, the Americans with Disabilities Act prohibits discrimination based on disability, although the application of the ADA varies for illegal drugs and alcohol, for current and past use. The ADA specifically excludes current illegal drug use from its protections, and a test for drug use is not considered a medical examination.[69] By contrast, the responsible federal agencies have stated that "an alcoholic is a person with a disability and is protected by the ADA if s/he is qualified to perform the essential functions of the job."[70] Concerning a history of illegal drug use, the U.S. Department of Justice states that "policies that screen out applicants because of a history of addiction or treatment for addiction must be carefully scrutinized to ensure that the policies are job-related and consistent with business necessity."[71]

Federal law mandates drug testing for certain positions within the federal sector, including employees of the U.S. Customs and Border Protection. Federal law also creates regulation for drug testing for employees in the aviation, railroading and trucking industries.[72] The rules preempt state laws that would otherwise limit drug testing.

Drug testing can be used in a variety of settings:

- Preemployment—generally allowed if not designed to identify legal use of drugs or addiction to illegal drugs
- Reasonable suspicion—generally allowed as a condition of continued employment if there is "reasonable suspicion" of drug or alcohol use based on specific facts as well as rational inferences from those facts (e.g., appearance, behavior, speech, odors)

- Routine testing—generally allowed if the employees are notified at the time of hire, unless state or local law prohibits it
- Post-accident testing—generally allowed to test as a condition of continued employment if there is "reasonable suspicion" that the employee involved in the accident was under the influence of drugs or alcohol
- Random testing—sometimes required by law, prohibited in certain jurisdictions, but acceptable where used on existing employees in specific, narrowly defined jobs, such as those in highly regulated industries where the employee has a severely diminished expectation of privacy, or where testing is critical to public safety or national security

A majority of states have passed one or more statutes governing the testing of employees for drugs and/or alcohol.[73] States such as Connecticut, Iowa and Minnesota have laws that generally prohibit employee drug tests unless there is reasonable suspicion to test a particular employee,[74] although state law varies on whether employer violation of the statute prevents discharge of an employee who tests positive. There has also been extensive litigation over time under the common law of the various states, on theories including defamation (if the test was inaccurate), negligent testing, invasion of privacy, and violation of contract and collective bargaining agreements.

Generalizing in the face of this state-by-state variation is risky. Cases upholding random drug testing usually involve occupational roles in highly regulated industries or positions that are critical to the protection of life, property or national security. More invasive tests, such as collecting a blood sample, are more prone to scrutiny than less invasive tests, such as a breathalyzer. Testing has generally been permitted in settings where (1) there is a reasonable suspicion of drug or alcohol use based upon specific, objective facts; (2) there has been an accident, with a reasonable suspicion of drug or alcohol use; and (3) as part of rehabilitation, as a condition of continued employment.

Finally, approximately half the states have passed legislation limiting employers from prohibiting employees to smoke tobacco or drink outside of work.[75] The details of the legislation vary. Some states permit employees to smoke or drink outside of work, but allow employers to differentiate with respect to employee-contributed insurance premiums attributable to the use of the substances.[76]

2.2.3 Monitoring in the Workplace

Strong policies both favor and limit monitoring of employees in the workplace. A few reasons for monitoring are to:

- Follow workplace safety and other laws that require or encourage monitoring
- Protect physical security (such as video cameras near entrances) and cybersecurity (such as activity on computer systems)
- Protect trade secrets
- Limit liability for unlicensed transmission of copyrighted material and other confidential company information

- Improve work quality, such as by monitoring service calls with customers
- Try to keep employees on task rather than spending time on personal business, such as surfing the web

In the United States, private-sector employees in general have limited expectations of privacy at the workplace. The physical facilities belong to the employer, and employers in the private sector thus generally have broad legal authority to do monitoring and searches at work.[77] Computers and other IT equipment are similarly understood to be the property of the employer, with consequent broad employer rights about how the equipment is used. These employer rights are frequently more limited in Europe and other countries, where employees often have a broader set of protections against monitoring under data protection, collective bargaining and other employment laws.

On the other hand, workplace monitoring can intrude on the privacy of employees. Although monitoring is justified in some settings, there can be serious privacy concerns from excessive video monitoring (such as in changing rooms), monitoring of workplace conversations (such as bugs secretly placed by a supervisor to listen to employees) or e-mail and other computer monitoring (such as when e-mails that an employee believes are personal are reviewed by the employer). Employers often choose not to monitor even where they may have legal ability to do so, for reasons including ethics, cost and morale. Monitoring costs include the legal obligations to detect and act on misconduct revealed by the monitoring program.

Collective bargaining agreements can be an additional limiting factor on an employer's ability to monitor the workplace. Many such agreements contain provisions designed to limit workplace monitoring, or require that a union representative be informed of an employer's monitoring activities.

Technological trends have increased the range of ways that employers can monitor employees. The cost of video cameras and other sensors has fallen over time. The increasing portion of work conducted with computers and phones means that a greater portion of the workday, for many employees, is conducted on systems that are subject to monitoring. For instance, many conversations around the old water cooler, which were hard to monitor, have shifted to texts and e-mails, which leave a record in the employer's IT system. The increase of telecommuting and work from home also means that lines have blurred between the workday, traditionally under the supervision of the employer, and time at home, which traditionally was considered more private and not usually the business of the boss.

Organizations should consider establishing formal policies about workplace monitoring and accompanying documents, such as acceptable use policies for IT equipment. These policies may also be required by state law in order for such monitoring to be lawful.[78] Such policies often include when monitoring can or will occur, purposes of data use, to whom data may be disclosed and the consequences to employees for violations. In special circumstances where additional monitoring is conducted, the employer may be required to describe the approval process and document when it is implemented. Providing employees with notices of these policies helps establish their knowledge and reasonable expectations about workplace activities. Such policies have proven broadly effective in addressing employee claims for improper monitoring.[79]

2.2.3.1 Legal Obligations or Incentives to Monitor

Employers sometimes have strong legal reasons to monitor in the workplace. For example, OSHA requires employers to provide a safe workplace that complies with occupational health and safety standards. These standards require employees to perform tasks in a safe manner, to avoid injury. Thus, ensuring compliance with OSHA is one legal reason to monitor employees.[80]

Call centers and firms that do financial transactions over the phone often record telephone conversations for reasons including agent training, quality assurance and security/liability. If a dispute arises with a customer after the fact, the recording can often resolve what was said or agreed upon. However, such recordings must comply with the rules about phone call recording discussed below. As noted in Chapter 7, certain activities that may result in charges placed using preacquired account numbers, such as telemarketing, must be recorded.[81]

Employers also monitor the workplace as a way to defend against a possible tort claim for negligent supervision, especially where the employer is on notice of a specific risk from one employee to other employees or third parties. The claim of negligent supervision is similar to the claim, discussed above, of negligent hiring. In both instances, there is uncertainty about what a jury will find to have been negligent, and so employers have an incentive to err on the side of caution, to reduce the risk of a successful claim.

Some business lawyers have counseled companies to monitor e-mail and other employee computer usage to reduce the risk that the employer will be held liable for creating a hostile work environment, such as if sexually explicit or racially derogatory material is viewed at work.[82] An authority on employment law, Professor Matthew Finkin, has disagreed, saying: "The bald fact is that employers have no more a duty to monitor their employees' e-mail, to assure that untoward messages are not being communicated, than they have a duty to place hidden microphones or cameras at the water coolers to detect sexually offensive remarks or leering glances."[83] Courts that have addressed the issue have stressed that the speech involved must be so pervasive as to alter working conditions,[84] and so the risk of such claims may well be lower than business lawyers believed when Internet usage was first becoming common.

2.2.3.2 Laws Applying to Types of Monitoring

Federal laws governing wiretaps and access to stored communications are notoriously complex, and electronic monitoring of employees thus should often be done in consultation with a lawyer knowledgeable about the area. Chapter 10 discusses key aspects of these laws. The discussion here focuses on monitoring in the workplace.

Federal and state laws regulate and restrict workplace surveillance activities, including video surveillance, monitoring of telephone calls and electronic surveillance, such as accessing e-mails and monitoring Internet activities.

Video surveillance. Cameras and video recordings that do not have sound recordings are outside the scope of the federal wiretap and stored-record statutes. Many U.S. employers use closed-circuit television (CCTV) or other video surveillance in the workplace. Security cameras are often used at the perimeter of a business to deter and detect burglary or other unauthorized intrusion.

They are used within a business establishment to deter crimes such as shoplifting and armed robbery, and outside to detect drive-aways from gas stations or other businesses. They are used within warehouses and other parts of a business to reduce the incidence of stealing by employees, and insurance companies may give companies a discount for installing CCTV systems.[85]

Although federal law generally does not limit use of either photography or video cameras, state statutes and common law create limits in some settings. California is similar to other states in forbidding video recording in areas such as restrooms, locker rooms and places where employees change clothes.[86] Michigan's statute is broader, forbidding installation of a device for observing or photographing a "private place" as defined by the statute.[87] Even in the absence of a statute, employees may be able to bring a common-law tort claim for invasion of privacy, especially where a jury would find the use of the camera to be offensive. In addition, as with other areas of workplace monitoring, collective bargaining agreements may apply.

Intercepting communications. As discussed in Chapter 10, the Wiretap Act and the Electronic Communications Privacy Act (ECPA) are generally strict in prohibiting the interception of wire communications, such as telephone calls or sound recordings from video cameras; oral communications, such as hidden bugs or microphones; and electronic communications, such as e-mails. The exact rules for wire, oral and electronic communications vary, and unless an exception applies, interception of these communications is a criminal offense and provides a private right of action.

Two exceptions to the prohibition on interception often apply in the workplace. Under federal law interception is permitted:

1. If a person is a party to a call or where one of the parties has given consent[88]
2. The interception is done in the ordinary course of business[89]

An employer who provides communication services, such as a company telephone or e-mail service, has the ability to intercept provided the interception occurs in the normal course of the user's business.[90] However, the employer who listens to an employee's purely personal call risks violation of the wiretap laws. As courts have split on how broadly to define the "ordinary course of business," many employers rely on the consent exception for interception of telephone calls.[91]

Stored communications. As previously discussed, the Stored Communications Act (SCA) creates a general prohibition against the unauthorized acquisition, alteration or blocking of electronic communications while in electronic storage in a facility through which an electronic communications service is provided. Violations for interceptions can lead to criminal penalties or a civil lawsuit. The law provides for exceptions. Two exceptions which may apply to the employer are for conduct authorized:

1. "by the person or entity providing a wire or electronic communications service," (often the employer)[92]
2. "by a user of that service with respect to a communication of or intended for that use"[93]

ECPA does not appear to preempt stricter state privacy protections, and some state laws may protect e-mail communications.

Postal mail monitoring. U.S. federal law generally prohibits interference with mail delivery. Mail is considered "delivered," however, when it reaches a business. As a result, the opening of business letters and packages by a representative of the business does not violate that statute, even if that representative is not the intended recipient. However, there is always some risk involved with monitoring postal mail under state common law. Employers can mitigate this risk by advising employees not to receive personal mail at work, declining to read mail once it is clear that it is personal in nature, and maintaining confidentiality for any personal information obtained in the course of monitoring.

Location-based services. Mobile phones, GPS devices and some tablet computers provide geolocation data, which enables tracking of the user's physical location and movements. This creates a category of personal information that typically did not exist before the prevalence of these mobile devices. Employers interested in monitoring the location of company vehicles equipped with GPS may generally do so without legal hindrance, provided that the monitoring occurs for business purposes during work hours and employees have been informed beforehand.

A company wishing to monitor the location of its employees themselves, however, may face greater legal barriers. Some state laws limit monitoring of employee geolocation data to an extent. Connecticut, for example, prohibits any type of electronic employee monitoring without written notice, and provides a civil penalty of $500 for a first offense.[94] California has increased protection for its employees by outlawing the use of "an electronic tracking device to determine the location or movement of a person" as a misdemeanor criminal offense.[95] In addition, the utilization of location-based services to monitor employees runs the risk of incurring invasion of privacy claims in situations where the employee has a reasonable expectation of privacy.

2.2.3.3 Emerging Technologies to Monitor Employees

Companies today often already have in place a variety of systems to monitor electronic communications. Companies routinely run antispam and antivirus software on e-mails. The computer security activities of the IT department include a range of intrusion detection and other measures. Depending on the company and job description, there may also be limits on acceptable use of work computers, including bans on accessing websites that are inappropriate for the workplace.

Two emerging areas are how companies are using social media to monitor prospective and current employees, and how the IT department copes with what is called "the consumerization of information technology" or "bring your own device."

Using social media to monitor prospective and current employees. Social media sites such as Facebook, Twitter and LinkedIn facilitate easy and immediate sharing, collaboration and interaction. Employers can use social media to their advantage—for example, a strong social media presence helps increase visibility in the marketplace. Social media can be used by employers to stay in touch with customer needs, and its effective use conveys a level of technological sophistication to its followers. It is also a helpful platform for receiving immediate feedback from consumers, clients and employees, at a very low cost.

In recent years, social media has increasingly been used to screen prospective hires. Companies now exist dedicated entirely to tracking an individual's online presence and screening candidates for predesignated elements selected by the employer. These may include potential drug use, criminal activity or unsafe behavior. Social media monitoring is also used to keep track of current employees to mitigate brand or reputation damage.

Despite the advantages of using social media, employers should be aware of potential risks that come with using these mechanisms to monitor employees. Though employers are generally legally permitted to use social media in informing their decisions, they must not violate existing antidiscrimination and privacy laws. Invasive monitoring practices may provide the basis for discrimination lawsuits if the employer accesses and appears to use information that is legally protected. This includes protected classes such as religion, ethnicity, gender or sexual orientation, political affiliations and other sensitive information, all of which is commonly available on people's social media pages. Although reading publicly available information is clearly lawful, acting in a discriminatory way in the workplace is not. Employers should thus consider what policies and training should exist to avoid taking actions that could be considered discriminatory, including monitoring information about an employee on social media sites.

Employers face risks when engaging in social engineering—the use of manipulation to gain access to otherwise private information. This includes connecting with potential hires or employees through a false online profile, or requesting access to private networks that are not available to the general public. If employers engage in these practices, they may be confronted with invasion of privacy actions for violating the applicant's or employee's reasonable expectation of privacy.[96]

Finally, employers should not require prospective or current employees to divulge access information to private networks as a condition of employment. In 2012, Maryland was the first state to ban employers from asking employees or applicants for their social network login information and passwords.[97] Similar laws have been proposed in Congress and in other states. Employers have not traditionally had access to an employee's personal e-mail accounts, and a similar analysis applies to gaining access to the private parts of a person's social network activities.

Consumerization of information technology and bring your own device. Individuals today have more information technology options than ever before. Computing devices range from traditional desktop computers and laptops to powerful smartphones, tablet computers and netbooks. Social networks, webmail and applications can be accessed across devices. Marked improvement in device capability and widespread Internet access allow employees to connect to their online networks from almost any location.

Increasingly, individuals are also using their personal devices for work purposes, blurring the line between personal and professional environments. The consumerization of information technology (COIT) trend refers not only to the use of personal computing devices in the workplace, but also to online services, such as webmail, cloud storage and social networking. Traditionally, adoption of high-level information technology started with major public- and private-sector organizations, with consumer adoption later after the price became affordable. In recent years the trend has reversed. Today information technology often emerges in the consumer market and is driven by employees who use their personal devices, accounts and applications both in and outside of the office for work tasks.

Bring your own device (BYOD) is a manifestation of the COIT trend, in which employees use their personal computing devices for work purposes. BYOD offers significant advantages.

It allows employees to use the same technology at work as they use at home, which means more flexibility, efficiency and productivity in employee work schedules. Employers benefit from increased accessibility to their employees as well as reduced overhead and workplace device expenses. BYOD, however, presents significant security challenges that stem from the lack of employer control over employee devices. BYOD may expose organizations to security vulnerabilities and threats that they could otherwise protect against with work-issued devices.

Organizations adopting a BYOD strategy must move beyond traditional device management practices to ensure the security of company data. Before implementation, organizations should carefully evaluate their existing security policies to determine how they align with employees' use of personal devices for work purposes. Where there are discrepancies, employers should modify their policies accordingly. For example, if an organization's current policy requires specific security controls for company-owned devices, but not personal devices, the company puts itself at risk by allowing employee devices to be used in the workplace. However, security controls required for company-owned devices may not be suitable or necessary for personal devices, depending on how they are used. Lesser security may be adequate for personal devices that are not permitted to store sensitive employer data. One consideration is what information triggers breach notification laws—stricter policies are called for when loss of the device would require breach notices. Ultimately, policies should reflect organization requirements, and devices should be secured in a way that protects employers from liability and legal risk.

BYOD also presents new workplace privacy implications. The same devices that employees use to access personal e-mail accounts, social networking sites and surf the Internet will also be used for work purposes. Though it is generally acceptable for employers to monitor employees' activities on a work network and work-issued devices, it's less clear how employers should handle monitoring of personal devices. Employee expectations of privacy in a BYOD context are likely to be higher because a personal device is involved. As a result, the same surveillance and monitoring activities used for work-issued devices may not be appropriate for personal devices. Further privacy issues arise in event of an investigation or security breach. If an employee's personal device must be searched or analyzed, that employee's personal (nonwork) information is likely to be exposed. Employers can limit the scope of their searches but must be thorough enough to capture evidence of the breach.

In designing BYOD policies, employers should clearly address these issues and convey to employees the privacy limits and risks when using personal devices in the workplace. If the employer is engaged in device monitoring or surveillance, it should disclose that information and obtain employee consent. When monitoring and searching the device, exposure of private employee data should be minimized.

2.2.4 Investigation of Employee Misconduct

When employee misconduct occurs, the employer should be aware of issues such as the following:

- Be careful to avoid liability or loss due to failure to take the allegations seriously. Ignoring a problem may allow it to grow or otherwise become more difficult to resolve later.

- Treat the employee with fairness during the investigation to reduce possible employee resentment as well as the risk that later litigation will result in harsher penalties if the employer is seen to have been unfair.
- Follow laws and other corporate policies during the investigation. Particular attention should be given to collective bargaining agreements, which often contain provisions concerning investigations of employee misconduct.
- Document the alleged misconduct and investigation to minimize risks from subsequent claims by the employee.
- Consider the rights of people other than those being investigated, such as fellow employees who could be subject to retaliation or other problems.

Investigations are often conducted in cooperation with an organization's human resources office. HR policies often apply to investigations. Progressive and documented discipline for initial or minor infractions can provide a reasoned basis for more serious discipline or termination if necessary. The privacy professional should work with the compliance department to determine the appropriate level of documentation.

Frequently, employers use third parties to investigate employee misconduct. Formerly, this exposed corporations to liability under the FCRA. The FCRA generally requires notice and employee consent when the employer obtains a consumer report. According to an opinion letter issued for the FTC known as the "Vail Letter," if an employer hired an outside organization such as a private investigator or background research firm to conduct these investigations, the outside organization constituted a "consumer reporting agency" under the FCRA, and any report furnished to the employer by the outside organization was an "investigative consumer report."[98] Under this opinion, an employer that received these reports was required to comply with the FCRA by providing notice to the suspected employee and obtain consent. This destroyed the undercover aspect of investigations.[99]

The Fair and Accurate Credit Transactions Act of 2003 (FACTA) amended the FCRA to address the problems created by the Vail Letter.[100] Along with other FCRA and FACTA provisions discussed in Chapter 5 on financial privacy, FACTA provided that (if certain conditions were met) an employer is no longer required to notify an employee that it is obtaining an investigative consumer report on the employee from an outside organization in the context of an internal investigation. Specifically, FACTA changed the definition of "consumer report" under FCRA to exclude communications relating to employee investigations from the definition if three requirements are met:

- The communication is made to an employer in connection with the investigation of: (i) suspected misconduct related to employment, or (ii) compliance with federal, state, or local laws and/or regulations, the rules of a self-regulatory organization, or any pre-existing written employment policies;
- The communication is not made for the purpose of investigating a consumer's creditworthiness, credit standing, or credit capacity and does not include information pertaining to those factors; and,

- The communication is not provided to any person except: (i) the employer or agent of the employer, (ii) a federal or state officer, agency, or department, or an officer, agency, or department of a unit of general local government, (iii) a self-regulating organization with authority over the activities of the employer or employee, (iv) as otherwise required by law, or (v) pursuant to 15 U.S.C. § 1681f, which addresses disclosures to government agencies.[101]

If the employer takes adverse action on the basis of these reports, FACTA requires that the employer disclose a summary of the nature and substance of the communication or report to the employee. This report can be issued after the investigation has been conducted and allows employers to maintain the secrecy of the investigation.[102]

2.3 Privacy Issues After Employment

At the end of the employment relationship, an employer should restrict or terminate the former employee's access to physical and informational assets, follow the correct termination procedures, minimize risks of post-termination claims, help management to transition after the termination and address any privacy claims that arise.

2.3.1 Access to Physical and Informational Assets

When a person leaves a company or is no longer supposed to have access to specific facilities or information, there should be clear procedures for terminating such access. Basic steps include:

- Secure the return of badges, keys, smartcards and other methods of physical access.
- Disable access for computer accounts.
- Ensure the return of laptops, smartphones, storage drives and other devices that may store company information.
- Seek, where possible, to have the employee return any company data that is held by the employee outside of the company's systems.
- Remind employees of their obligations not to use company data for other purposes.
- Clearly marked personal mail, if any, should be forwarded to the former employee, but work-related mail should be reviewed to ensure that proprietary company information is not leaked.

Because the departure of employees is a predictable event, IT systems should be designed to minimize the disruption to the company and other employees when a person no longer has authorized access. Access may end not only for a firm employee, but also for contractors, interns and others who have temporary access to company facilities. To take a simple example, the same password should not be used by multiple people, because of the need to change the password when one employee leaves.

2.3.2 Human Resources Issues

The human resources office is often significantly involved in the period before an employee leaves, especially when employees are not leaving entirely of their own initiative. The human resources office often will have detailed and sensitive information about an employee's performance in the period before termination. This sort of information is gathered, for instance, to document the basis for the company's decisions, in case the former employee brings a wrongful termination or other claim against the employer.

A similar level of care is appropriate for post-termination contacts with the employee. External communications to the former employee should be crafted with care, especially if the termination resulted from misconduct. Communications with remaining employees, customers and others should meet company goals while refraining from disparaging the former employee.

When an employer is asked to provide references for the former employee, the human resources office, working with legal counsel, should have policies about what sorts of references to provide. Companies balance reasons to provide references with the risk of a suit for defamation. The law can vary significantly state by state.[103] The common law imposes no duty on a former employer to supply a reference for a former employee, but some modern state statutes do require references for specific occupations, such as airplane pilot and public school teacher. The common law provides what is known as a "qualified privilege" for employers to report their experience with and impressions of the employee, to help in defense against defamation suits. In recent years, publicity about winning defamation suits has made some employers reluctant to provide references. On the other hand, state legislatures have responded by passing laws that are designed to encourage accurate reports about former employees. A company also often has good reasons to provide references, including to retain goodwill with former employees, whose statements will affect the company's reputation and with whom the company may do business in the future.

3. Conclusion

This chapter introduced major themes relating to privacy in the workplace. In the United States, constitutional protections apply specifically to government employees. Contract and tort remedies can provide protections to employees, but they apply in a relatively narrow set of circumstances. States have enacted a considerable number of statutory protections, but the protections exist against a general backdrop of a free market approach to employment and workplace privacy.

Personal information is involved in virtually every phase of the employment relationship—from evaluation and hiring to employee management, monitoring and termination or departure. As organizations grow in size, expand to new geographies and involve larger numbers of outside partners and vendors, the employment privacy challenges become more acute. Global employers must navigate through a complex patchwork of applicable U.S., EU and international workplace privacy laws.

Effective legal compliance and thoughtful management of employee personal information can help reduce the risk of any potential legal claims as well as offer many benefits to both employer and employee. These benefits include minimizing the risk of information mishandling, disclosure or theft; increased employee morale; and an improved working relationship between employer and employee.

Endnotes

1 O'Connor v. Ortega, 480 U.S. 709 (1987).

2 California Constitution, Art. 1, § 1.

3 Restatement (Second) of Torts, § 652B.

4 Restatement (Second) of Torts, § 652D.

5 Restatement (Second) of Torts, §§ 558–559.

6 Matthew W. Finkin, *Privacy in Employment Law*, 3d edition (Arlington, VA: BNA Books, 2009), xlv.

7 See, e.g., Cal. Gov't Code 12940; N.Y. Exec. Law § 296; Del. Code Ann. Tit. 19, § 711.

8 See, e.g., Illinois Right to Privacy in the Workplace Act, 820 I.L.C.S. § 55.

9 *Id.*

10 Civil Rights Act of 1964, Title VII, 42 U.S.C. §§ 2000e-2000e-17 (2005).

11 Pregnancy Discrimination Act, Title VII, 42 U.S.C. §§200e-2000e-17 (2005).

12 Americans with Disabilities Act, 42 U.S.C. §§ 12101-12213 (2005).

13 Age Discrimination in Employment Act, 29 U.S.C. §§ 621-634 (2005).

14 Equal Pay Act of 1963, 29 U.S.C. §§ 206(d), 209, 211, 213, 215-219, 255, 256, 259, 260, 262 (2005).

15 Health Insurance Portability and Accountability Act, 42 U.S.C. §§ 300gg-300gg-2 (2005).

16 Consolidated Omnibus Budget Reconciliation Act of 1986, 42 U.S.C. §§ 300bb-1-300bb-8 (2005).

17 Employee Retirement Income Security Act of 1974, 29 U.S.C. §§ 1001-1461 (2005).

18 Family Medical Leave Act of 1993, 29 U.S.C. §§ 2601-2654 (2005).

19 Fair Credit Reporting Act, 15 U.S.C. §§1681-1681v (2005).

20 Fair Labor Standards Act of 1938, 29 U.S.C. §§ 201-219 (2005).

21 Occupational Safety and Health Act of 1970, 29 U.S.C. §§ 651-678 (2005).

22 Whistleblower Protection Act of 1989, Public Law No. 101-112, 5 U.S.C. §§ 1201 et seq.

23 National Labor Relations Act, 29 U.S.C. §§ 151-159 (2005).

24 Immigration Reform and Control Act of 1986, 8 U.S.C. §§ 1324a-b (2005).

25 15 U.S.C. § 78A.

26 29 U.S.C. §§ 2001-2009.

27 18 U.S.C. §§ 2510-2522.

28 18 U.S.C. §§ 2510-2511.

29 18 U.S.C. §§ 2701-2712.

30 Department of Labor, "Our Mission." www.dol.gov/opa/aboutdol/mission.htm.

31 See Fair Credit Reporting Act, 15 U.S.C. §§ 1681 *et seq.*, and FTC, "FCRA Guidance for Employers," http://business.ftc.gov/documents/bus08-using-consumer-reports-what-employers-need-know.

32 Privacy Rights Clearinghouse, Employment Background Checks: A Jobseeker's Guide, www.privacyrights.org/fs/fs16-bck.htm.

33 *Id.*

34 Civil Rights Act of 1964, Title VII, 42 U.S.C. §§ 2000e-2000e-17 (2005).

35 Age Discrimination in Employment Act of 1967, 29 U.S.C. § 621.

36 Pregnancy Discrimination Act, Title VII, 42 U.S.C. §§ 200e-2000e-17 (2005).

37 Americans with Disabilities Act, 42 U.S.C. §§ 12101-12213 (2005).

38 42 U.S.C. § 2000ff.

39 *Pastore v. Medford Sav. Bank*, 186 B.R. 553 (D. Mass. 1995) (applies only after an offer is extended); *In re Hopkins*, 81 B.R. 491 (same); *Leary v. Warnaco, Inc.*, 251 B.R. 656 (S.D.N.Y. 2000) (applies prior to extension of offer).

40 www.nolo.com/legal-encyclopedia/sexual-orientation-discrimination-rights-29541.html.

41 www.unmarriedamerica.org/ms-employment-laws.htm.

42 42 U.S.C. § 12112(a).

43 42 U.S.C. § 12112(b)(4).

44 42 U.S.C. § 12112(b)(3).

45 www.eeoc.gov/policy/docs/accommodation.html.

46 Paul F. Gerhart, "Employee Privacy Rights in the United States," *Comparative Labor Law Journal* 17 (1995): 195.

47 *Pub. L.* 110-325 (2008).

48 527 U.S. 471 (1999).

49 534 U.S. 184 (2002).

50 527 U.S. at 482-483.

51 *Pub. L.* 110-325, § 4.

52 See generally www.eeoc.gov/laws/regulations/adaaa_fact_sheet.cfm.

53 15 U.S.C. § 1581a.

54 15 U.S.C. § 1681t.

55 Investigative Consumer Reporting Agencies Act, 1.6A Cal. Civ. Code §§ 1786-1786.60 (2005).

56 Cal. Civ. Code §§ 1786.16, 1786.20.

57 Cal. Civ. Code § 1786.53.

58 www.ftc.gov/opa/2012/02/mobileapps.shtm.

59 National Conference of State Legislatures, "Use of Credit Information in Employment 2012 Legislation," www.ncsl.org/issues-research/banking/use-of-credit-info-in-employ-2012-legis.aspx.

60 See, e.g., Conn. Gen. Stat. § 31-51tt; Md. Code, Lab. & Empl. § 3-711; Wash. Rev. Code § 19.182.020.

61 Haw. Rev. Stat. § 378-2.7.

62 See, e.g., Cal. Lab. Code § 1024.5; 820 Ill. Comp. Stat. § 70/10.

63 Employee Polygraph Protection Act, 29 U.S.C. §§ 2001-2009.

64 29 U.S.C. § 2001(3).

65 Finkin, Privacy in Employment Law, 159–173.

66 *Id.* at 175.

67 *Id.* at 184.

68 *Id.* at 67.

69 www.ada.gov/employmt.htm.

70 *Id.*

71 www.ada.gov/copsq7a.htm.

72 49 U.S.C. § 1834 (App.) (aviation); 45 U.S.C. § 431 (App.) (railroading); and 49 U.S.C. § 277 (App.) (trucking).

73 Finkin, *Privacy in Employment Law*, xxxii to xxxiii (listing statutes).

74 *Id.* at 138–140.

75 *Id.* at xxxiii.

76 *Id.* at 154.

77 Frank J. Cavico, "Invasion of Privacy in the Private Employment Sector: Tortious and Ethical Aspects," *Houston Law Review* 30 (1993): 1304–1306.

78 For example, see Conn. Gen. Stat. § 31-48d; 19 Del. C. § 705.

79 David Bender, *Bender on Privacy and Data Protection* § 10.02 (Dayton, OH: LexisNexis, 2011).

80 OSHA, Occupational Injury and Illness Recording and Reporting Requirements, 29 C.F.R Parts 1904 and 1952 (January 19, 2001), www.osha.gov/pls/oshaweb/owadisp.show_document?p_id=16312&p_table=FEDERAL_REGISTER.

81 *See generally* 16 C.F.R. § 310.5(a).

82 National Institute of Business Management, "You & the Law: Quick, Easy-to-Use Advice on Employment Law 2" (2002).

83 Matthew Finkin, "Information Technology and Workers' Privacy: The United States Law," *Comparative Labor Law and Policy Journal* 23 (2002): 471.

84 E.g., *Custis v. DiMaio*, 46 F. Supp. 2d 206 (E.D.N.Y. 1999).

85 Risk Control, Inc., "Why Your Business Needs a CCTV System," www.rciutah.com/securitysystems.html.

86 Cal. Lab. Code § 435.

87 Mich. Comp. Laws § 750.539d.

88. 18 U.S.C. § 2511(2)(D).

89. 8 U.S.C. § 2511(2)(a)(i).

90. Martha W. Barnett and Scott D. Makar, "In the Ordinary Court of Business": The Legal Limits of Workplace Wiretapping, *Comm. & Ent. L.J.* 10 (1988): 715.

91. Finkin, *Privacy in Employment Law,* 365-369.

92. 18 U.S.C. § 2701(c)(1).

93. 18 U.S.C. § 2701(c)(2).

94 Conn. Gen. Stat. § 31-48d.

95 Cal. Pen. Code § 637.7.

96 In 2006, Hewlett Packard's chairman Patricia Dunn authorized the use of false pretenses to investigate press leaks originating from the board of directors, a practice termed "pretexting." The investigative tactics were widely condemned, triggering congressional hearings and both federal and state felony charges against Dunn and others. For a detailed overview of the case, see Miriam Hechler Baer, "Corporate Policing and Corporate Governance: What Can We Learn from Hewlett-Packard's Pretexting Scandal?" *U. Cin. L. Rev.* 77: 523 (2008).

97 Maryland SB 433 (HB 964), 2012.

98 www.ftc.gov/os/statutes/fcra/vail.shtm.

99 Patricia A. Kotze and Eric H. Joss, *Breathing Easier Over Workplace Misconduct*, May 18, 2005, www.diversifiedriskmanagement.com/articles/workplace-misconduct.html.

100 *Id.*

101 *Id.*

102 *Id.*

103 Finkin, *Privacy in Employment Law,* 267–295.

Index

D

E

F

G

M

N

O

P

T

U

V

About the Authors

Peter P. Swire, CIPP/US

Peter Swire is the C. William O'Neill Professor of Law at The Ohio State University, a senior fellow at the Future of Privacy Forum and the Center for American Progress, and policy fellow at the Center for Democracy and Technology.

Swire has been a leading scholar, government leader and privacy practitioner since the 1990s. Under President Clinton, Swire served in the White House as the chief counselor for privacy in the Office of Management and Budget, where he had U.S. government-wide responsibility for privacy policy. In that role, he was the White House coordinator for the proposed and final HIPAA medical privacy rules and chaired a White House task force on how to update wiretap laws for the Internet age. He also participated in the negotiation of the Safe Harbor agreement for trans-border data flows between the EU and the United States.

Swire returned to the White House in 2009 and 2010, serving as special assistant to President Obama for economic policy, working in the National Economic Council under Lawrence Summers.

He has written three books and numerous scholarly articles on privacy and cybersecurity (many of his writings and speeches are available at www.peterswire.net) and has served on privacy and security advisory boards for companies including Google, IBM, Intel and Microsoft. For eight years he was a consultant with the global law firm of Morrison & Foerster, LLP.

Swire graduated from Princeton University, summa cum laude, and the Yale Law School, where he was an editor of the *Yale Law Journal*.

Kenesa Ahmad, CIPP/US

Kenesa Ahmad is an information privacy attorney and co-author of *Foundations of Information Privacy and Data Protection: A Survey of Global Concepts, Laws and Practices*. Ahmad received her law degree from the Moritz College of Law of The Ohio State University, where she served as an articles editor of the *Ohio State Law Journal*. She also received her LLM from Northwestern University Law School. From 2011–2012 Ahmad completed a legal and policy fellowship with the Future of Privacy Forum. She is now an associate in the global privacy practice of Promontory Financial Group.